SAMS
Teach Yourself
Today

e-Travel

SAMS
Teach Yourself
Today

e-Travel

Mark Orwoll

A Division of Macmillan USA
201 West 103rd Street, Indianapolis, Indiana 46290

Sams Teach Yourself e-Travel Today

International Standard Book Number: 0-672-31822-9

Library of Congress Catalog Card Number: 99-067011

Printed in the United States of America

First Printing: **December, 1999**

01   00   99   4   3   2   1

Trademarks

Warning and Disclaimer

Acquisitions Editor
Jeff Schultz

Development Editor
Damon Jordan

Associate Publisher
Mark Taber

Managing Editor
Charlotte Clapp

Project Editor
George E. Nedeff

Copy Editor
Sean Medlock

Indexer
Greg Pearson

Proofreaders
Kim Cofer
Maryann Steinhart

Team Coordinator
Amy Patton

Interior Design
Gary Adair

Cover Design
Jay Corpus

Copy Writer
Eric Borgert

Production
Dan Harris
Staci Somers
Mark Walchle

Dedication

Hugs and kisses to the three most important people in my life who are less than five feet tall: Kiki, Gigi, and Moochie. Most importantly, eternal thanks and love to my wife, Kathleen F. Fox, whom I adore. No writer ever had a finer muse. This book's for you, Kat!

Table of Contents

Introduction   1

PART I   Getting Started in e-Travel

1   A Novice's Guide to the Net's Major Travel
Resources   9

2   Keeping Your Electronic Information in Order   21

3   Evaluating a Web Site's Accuracy and Validity   29

4   Guidebooks on the Web   39

5   Regional and Foreign Newspapers Online   51

6   Virtual Tourist Bureaus   63

PART II   Planning a Vacation on the Internet

7   Quiz: What's Your e-Travel Type?   83

8   Serendipitous Travels on the Hyperlink Trail   103

9   Using Web Sites for Specific Countries
and Cities   109

10   Internet Resources for Seasonal Vacation
Activities   119

11   When and How Long to Go   131

PART III Booking Your Trip Online

12	Online Travel Agents	145
13	Learning to Be Your Own Electronic Travel Agent	159
14	Making Hotel Reservations on the Web	171
15	Airline Schedules and Internet Ticketing	181
16	Electronic Booking for Train Travel, Foreign and Domestic	193
17	Rental Car Reservations by Modem	205
18	Cruisin' the Net	217

PART IV Preparing on the Web for Your Departure

19	Bringing a Laptop	229
20	Online Info about Passports, Visas, and Customs	241
21	Digital Photography Means Doing It with Your Fingers	253
22	Packing, Handling Money, and Staying Safe	261

PART V Appendix

| A | Web Sites | 277 |
| | Index | 291 |

Acknowledgements

A lot of people helped me with this book. Some of them don't even know they did, so please don't blame them for anything I wrote! I would like to thank Nancy Novogrod and Dan Brewster for their support; blood brother J. Michael Straczynski for his inspiring example (Joe, can I be an alien in the next B5 movie?); fellow scribblers Tamara Jones, Rob Golum, Howard Ruben, Dan Trigoboff, Jeannette De Wyze, Joe Applegate (here's to the days when we were young, hopeful, and living in San Diego); my cantankerous and betimes costive editors at Macmillan, Jeff Schultz and Damon Jordan; mentors Richard Busch, Jim Mullin, Maria Shaw, and Chris Hunt; *Travel & Leisure* Web czar Chris Haines and Web czarina Ann Shields for giving good upload; my colleagues past and present at *T&L*, especially Pamela Fiori, Ila Stanger, Barbara Peck, Andrew Forester, Mike Herson, Henry Weil, Bob Ciano, Joe Paschke, Liz Curtis, and Elisa Shevitz; Ivan Saperstein and Sara Camilli, who, my publisher assures me, have earned their 15 percent; the original Ghetto Lord Gary Jaycox, of the La Mirada Jaycoxes, and David "Quickdraw" Voss; Fred Justice and my mom, Pat Orwoll (who gave me life, a musical ear, and a love of words); John and Joan Hughes; Vicki Busch, Bob Orwoll, Matt Orwoll, and Chris Orwoll, and their families; and my late father, Pete Orwoll, who would have looked at this book and said, with understated Norwegian generosity, "Not too bad."

INTRODUCTION

Planning Ahead... And If You Know of Any Other Way to Plan, Let Me Know

Before we begin, please shut down your PC for a moment. Shortly, we'll be cutting a wide and somewhat roguish swath through the Internet, you and I. We'll be tripping along those T-1 connections, doing the modem mambo to a cyber-beat, and generally surfing our way across the Internet like Duke Kahanamoku on a 20-foot swell at Waimea Bay. But for now, cool your jets because we're just going to chat for a few pages, share some ideas, consider how best to organize things before you begin researching your next travel adventure. So draw near to the fire, friends.

Creative Chaos—Not!

There's a school of thought that creative chaos, 11th-hour deadlines, and enforced spontaneity are crucial components in making decisions—at least, the kind of decisions that are often regarded as inspired, revolutionary, and, well, just plain cool. To which I reply: "Yeah? Bull." I don't care whether we're discussing which college courses to take, how to invest your retirement savings, or where you want to go on vacation; nothing beats a well-organized plan.

To a great extent—whether it's due to nature or nurture—you're either a good planner or not a good planner. Face it, most people are pretty clueless. Maybe they make a few notes to themselves, stick the notes on their refrigerator door with a souvenir magnet, cover over the notes with the movie listings torn from the newspaper, and then forget where they put the notes until it's too late to use them. Most people look at planning the same way most teenagers look at shopping with their parents—something abhorrent to be avoided at all costs.

That's not to imply that the nonplanners of the world, those laissez-faire, devil-may-care, Type B personalities, are doomed to run around in circles, wasting their vacation time and money as payment for their lack of foresight. Unfortunately for people like you and me (and I include you as a planner; otherwise you wouldn't be reading this book), those career *imprompteurs* generally make out all right, no matter whether their lack of planning has to do with work or play. Not so with you and me. If a planner fails to plan, he's screwed.

Have you ever traveled with a nonplanner? I have. Several trips have found me somehow hooked up with daisy-sniffers and stargazers, people who have never owned a wristwatch, the sort who buy calendars only for the pretty pictures. Traveling with someone like that is a complete nightmare for me, mainly because I end up looking and feeling like some ramrod-stiff Prussian colonel trying to lead a corps of poets and math majors in military drills, a demon attempting to thwart the serendipitous inclinations of the free spirits sharing the trail with me.

On the, Like, Road, Brother

In the summer of 1972, I drove across this Great Land Of Ours in a Datsun pickup truck with my old pal Gary, doing the buddies-on-the-road thing. It was a sort of Jack Kerouac transcontinental spiritual quest, only with a better sound system. If you met Gary today, dressed in the threads of an Organization Man and using phrases like "team player" and "growing the business," you would never think of him as the hairy hipster sitting next to me in that Datsun. Ponytailed, sandaled, peace-sign-waving hippies turn into dutiful salarymen more often than you might care to think.

But back in the freewheeling summer of '72, Gary was the ultimate Mr. Cool Guy, not letting anything bug him, not buying into the corporate culture that the Establishment was trying to push down our throats, man. And that meant no schedules. That meant turning left because left looked more interesting than right. That meant never making a reservation for a night's lodging because "something always turns up."

I, too, had the sandals, the ponytail, the perpetual smug look of a cooler-than-thou would-be rock star, but beneath it all I was uptight. I got nervous if we didn't make enough mileage each day. I bit my nails when we had to miss some hoped-for roadside attraction because instead we'd taken an unplanned detour. Was I miserable? No, of course not. I was eighteen years old and had a full tank of gas, literally and figuratively. But I realized during the course of our several weeks on the road that I would never be a Gary. I would never be a nonplanner. I understood that not only was I a Type A personality, I was a Type A+.

Most people fall somewhere in-between. They understand the need for some basic planning when it comes to travel, yet they're loose enough to respond positively when serendipity gives them a come-hither look, eyelashes aflutter and wristwatches nowhere to be seen. May you be among them. More important, though, is to be honest with yourself. The worst thing you can do is overcompensate in the opposite direction for fear that your natural inclinations are somehow aberrant. They're not.

You Just Plan Too Much

I can vividly recall the first day of my first trip to Europe. I was a college student who had just received a sizeable student loan. Naturally, instead of enrolling for the spring semester, I decided I'd rather spend the dough on a four-month sojourn on the Continent. (Note to federal authorities with power to investigate abuses of the government's guaranteed student loan program: "Just kidding!")

My plan for that first day, after arriving at the airport in Frankfurt and taking a bus to my hotel, was to do nothing more than wander, meander, and stroll about aimlessly, simply taking the measure of Germany. So there I sat in my hotel room that glorious spring afternoon, trying to decide exactly where I should go on my unplanned walkabout. I pulled out a Frankfurt street map and more or less memorized it over the course of the next two hours. I read the Frankfurt section of my guidebook for about the 12th time. I went down to the lobby and asked the desk clerk, in my very best Berlitz German, for directions to the town's main plaza. To which he replied, as best I could translate, "Four o'clock, except on Sundays." I immediately retreated to my room to contemplate the Hegelian subtext of his answer, as well as to read once again the more utilitarian phrases in my Berlitz book.

Why didn't I just go out walking, come what may? If I got a little bit lost, so what? If I'd let whimsy be my guide, perhaps my ultimate destination would have been something grand and unexpected. Well, I confess that I spent the rest of the afternoon writing up a highly detailed itinerary to cover the next two days, at which point I planned to leave Frankfurt behind for my next destination. Make no mistake, I thoroughly enjoyed those next 48 hours. I managed to see the glorious Altes Rathaus (Old Town Hall), the Dom Cathedral (begun in the 13th century), and Sachsenhausen, the ancient neighborhood known for its many charming cafés serving *ebbelwei,* a potent apple cider. But I was increasingly aware of just what kind of traveler I was, what I wanted from my wanderings, and what I needed to do in the way of planning to ensure that I got the most from my travels.

Required of All Readers of This Book: A Sense of Awe

Back when Gary and I hit the road on our post-high-school bohemian road trip, and when I took my first trip to Europe, state-of-the-art travel information meant a guidebook. There was nothing else, except perhaps some dry history texts in the library. Fast-forward to the present. The array of travel resources now available to us is nearly incomprehensible. The technological development that's most germane here is the Internet, specifically the World Wide Web, where in the span of an hour you can learn more about the world than most of our grandparents ever learned about it in their entire lives. You can pack handheld computers with you on your trip. From the top of the loneliest mountain in the most remote corner of the world, you can flip open your cell phone and call for a pizza. Using a wireless modem on your laptop, you can send electronic images that you just took two minutes ago with your handy digital camera across continents.

If I told you fifteen years ago that all this would be possible one day, you might have scoffed. And yet, with each new hi-tech invention, our excitement wanes. We tend to take even the most amazing advances in stride. Someday we'll be saying things like, "What's that? A pill that turns you invisible and makes you rich? Yeah, so tell me something interesting for a change." We're living with the threat that no space-age innovation will ever thrill us again. We're slowly losing our sense of wonder.

And yet, if there's one thing in our lives that continues to make us marvel, it's travel. "Those people over there, they look different, they speak differently, they dress differently from me. That building! What's it made of? I've never seen anything like it. Did you see the color of the ocean? Why, this is simply the most magnificent tropical beach I've ever encountered in my life. What kind of bizarre animal is that? And that gorgeous canyon takes my breath away. Are we there yet? Where *are* we, anyway? Here's the greatest little shop on the cutest cobblestoned medieval street in the most out-of-the-way village in a land that I'd never heard of until three weeks ago. Let's go!"

Yes, travel still has the power to awaken our sometimes deadened sense of awe. In that spirit, let me offer one caveat as you begin this book: *Do not let either your fear of or your familiarity with computers and the Internet stand in the way of your natural sense of wonder.* Even though you'll be traveling on the Information superhighway, your ultimate goal is to travel in the real world, which is more wondrous, more delightful, more heart-stopping, and far, far more astonishing than the bits, bytes, and chips you may use to get there.

PART I

Getting Started in e-Travel

CHAPTER 1

A Novice's Guide to the Net's Major Travel Resources

"Astonish me!"

Jean Cocteau—auteur, poet, artist—once greeted a guest in that fashion, and so I say it to you.

Astonish me with your interest in travel and the places you've been. Astonish me with how well you pack your travel gear, with your extravagant collection of travel guides, and with the travel journals you've kept over the years. But if you really want to astonish me, tell me about your little bag of travel tricks, the resources you rely on for your vacation planning. You know the things I mean. That little store where you buy your maps. The phone number of that travel agent who can get you a decent air-fare no matter when or where you want to go. The name of that concierge in New York who always has tickets to the best Broadway shows.

When it comes to e-travel (by which I mean planning your travels via the Internet), you can develop similar resources. Every e-traveler has his own special tools that he uses again and again. True, a wimpy e-traveler might have a roster of resources that barely extends beyond the online reservations sites, like Travelocity and Expedia, but an expert's list of links might stretch to the far horizon. I don't expect you, the beginner, to have much background in e-travel, if any. All I ask is that you supply the toolbox. This book will help you select the tools to fill it and develop the skills to use those tools.

What You'll Learn in This Chapter

- ▶ Basic travel-related uses for the Web's most popular search engines.
- ▶ Finding and using online maps.
- ▶ Using distance calculators.
- ▶ The pros and cons of route planners.
- ▶ Making the most of currency and time converters.
- ▶ Airport codes.

I say "tools," but I mean Web sites. The ones that we'll investigate in this chapter are those I consider the fundamentals of e-travel, the building blocks of an e-traveler's repertoire. They may not be the sexiest sites on the Internet, but once you have them under your belt, there'll be no holding you back, tiger. (Grrr.) We'll cover search engines. (Yeeaahh!) We'll delve into online maps. (Yip yip yieeeee!) We'll have a look at distance calculators and route planners and all sorts of great things! (Rooooaaaarrr!!!)

Just don't get too carried away, all right?

Looking for Search Engines

Search engines—those cantankerous, can't-live-with-'em-can't-live-without-'em Web tools that, ideally, help you find whatever you're looking for—can lead you on the road to righteousness and glory or down a convoluted path with more forks than a restaurant supply warehouse. Search engines are plagued with more perils than a Michael Crichton thriller—not the least of which is their penchant for returning results that have nothing to do with your goal. Let's say you're doing a search of "scuba diving vacations." You might read through page after page of useless results until you grow so weary that you'd just as soon read a volume of Rod McKuen's poetry as click on any more worthless links… and that's what I call desperation. So you refine your search parameters. And just as you think you're making progress, you come up with a match like "Navy enlistment offices." Not exactly a vacation.

Now You Know

The name Yahoo! supposedly stands for Yet Another Hierarchical Officious Oracle, but the founders have admitted that they chose the name to describe…themselves.

Which search engines do you use? WebCrawler, Yahoo!, and Infoseek? How about HotBot, About.com, and Lycos? Or do you prefer the likes of Snap, GoTo.com, and AltaVista? Whichever one you use most, try to make it your friend. The best way to do that is to get to know it. As an example, let's use my favorite search engine—Yahoo! (*www.yahoo.com*).

Near the top of Yahoo!'s home page, you'll see a question mark icon. Click it for a quick lesson on how to use search engines and Internet directories. In Yahoo!, the search engine is where you type in the word or phrase you want to look for. The category listings lower down on the page represent the Internet directory.

Click the question mark icon on Yahoo!'s home page for a quick tutorial on using search engines.

As the Yahoo! tutorial explains, if the Internet were a book, you might think of an Internet directory as a table of contents. It starts out with the most general topics, and then gradually it becomes more specific. A directory is best used when you want to find links regarding a fairly broad subject. By the same token, you can think of a search engine as an index—best used when you want to find something more specific. For example, if you wanted to look up travel agents (a broad category, to be sure), you'd be wise to use the directory. But if you wanted to find a travel agent in Ohio who specializes in active vacations, you'd do better with a search engine.

▼ **Try It Yourself**

1. On the home page, locate and click the Travel link (which you'll find under Recreation & Sports).

2. The following window lists a number of travel-related topics. Go to Travel Agents and look at the results.

3. Return to the home page and type "Travel Agents" in the search box.

4. Compare your search results with the results you got from following the directory.

▲

Entire books could be written (and probably have been) about how to use search engines with maximum efficiency. It would be foolhardy to show you how to master those techniques in this beginner-level book. The key points to remember are that most search sites offer both a search engine and an Internet directory, and that a search engine is best for specific topics while a directory is best for general topics.

Also, every search engine that I know of has a user's guide—almost always found under Help on the search engine's home page. Read this advice for better searching techniques. Learn how your chosen search site works. You will end up hating it for not giving you the results you want. You will want to put your foot through your monitor when it lists endless pages from the same, useless Web site. But you will probably end up using your search site almost every day. Don't just live with it, though. Live in harmony with it. Talk to it. Give it presents on its birthday. Be at one with your search engine. Ommm.

Directions to the Best Maps

Search engines and Internet directories are the Doberman pinschers of the Web—nobody likes 'em, but who has the guts to grab 'em by the collar and drag 'em to the pound? Maps, however, are something everyone can love. There are geopolitical maps and geographical maps, maps of city streets and maps of entire nations. Maps for your every need. I must confess to being a map lover. At some point, everyone needs a map. And yet, if you're an American, I bet that you totally suck when it comes to geography. Am I right? From now on you'll have no excuse, because this section is a synopsis of some of the best map sites available.

Pop Quiz

How's your map knowledge? Quick, what's the capital of Burundi? Bujumbura! Which is farther west—Los Angeles or Las Vegas? Las Vegas! Which is farther east—the state of New York or the nation of Chile? Chile! Did you get *any* of those right?

The Perry-Castaneda Library Map Collection at the University of Texas can be found on the Web at *www.lib.utexas.edu/Libs/PCL/Map_collection/Map_collection.html*. The section called Online Maps of General Interest covers everything from the entire planet to specific countries. For maps of selected world cities, go to *www.lib.utexas.edu/Libs/PCL/Map_collection/world_cities.html*, which, strangely, isn't linked to the main map page. All I can say is, thank goodness for this Web site. Most of the maps were created by the Central Intelligence Agency, and a few come from other quasi-government sources. And although it's not comprehensive, this collection is one of the best single map sites on the Internet.

I don't know about you, but I find there's something...oh, I don't know...*erotic* about maps. You think that's strange? Well, I place the entire blame on *National Geographic*. As I recall from my adolescence, often it combined maps with, well, more titillating fare. The two have been inextricably linked in my mind since I was 10 years old. So when I need a cheap thrill, I log on to the map pages of the National Geographic Society at its Xpeditions site, at *www.nationalgeographic.com/xpeditions/main.html*. Let's see if we can't titillate ourselves by looking at a map of Bolivia.

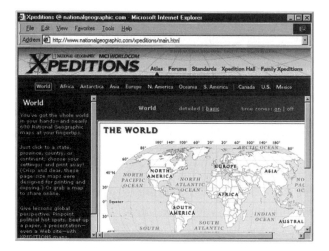

Point-and-click mapping makes the National Geographic Xpeditions site one of the easiest of all map sites to use.

▼ Try It Yourself

1. Log on to the Xpeditions main page and go to Atlas.

2. Bolivia is in South America (you *do* know that, right?), so either click the words "South America" at the top of the page or click the continent of South America on the map.

3. Go to Bolivia in the left margin, or click the country on the map.

4. Confess to yourself that you have never seen a nicer map of Bolivia than this one. Really, just a nice old map of a nice old country.

▲

Two much more commercially oriented map sites are MapBlast at *www.mapblast.com* and MapQuest at *www.mapquest.com*. At MapBlast, all you have to do is type in a state, city, or ZIP code to get a map of the area you want. (Use the pull-down menu to do the same for Canadian or other foreign cities.) At MapQuest, click the Online Maps link and find useful maps of U.S. and major foreign cities.

When it comes to map sites, the question is not which one works best, but which one works best for *you*? Open them up, play with them, *challenge* them. Discover which ones you feel most comfortable with. And always remember that a good traveler has good maps.

Distance Calculators

If you want to see a really cool map with zoom-in/zoom-out capability, stop by the Xerox PARC Map Viewer at *pubweb.parc.xerox.com/map*. It will amuse you for a few minutes before you realize that it's a serious mapping device that is geared more toward professional cartographers than simple travelers like you and me. But you should look at it because a number of easy-to-use distance calculators use the PARC server.

It's nice to know that someone has taken that highfalutin technology and dumbed it down for us to use. That "someone" is Bali Online, which has one of the Web's most straightforward distance calculators at *www.indo.com/distance/*. The interface is simplicity itself—you simply type in the cities that you want to measure the distance between and click the Look It Up! button. You get the distance in miles and in kilometers, and you get a link to the PARC server, which shows you the two cities highlighted on a world map. Bali Online is a one-stop marketplace of information on that Indonesian island paradise. Why it sees fit to offer this service is beyond me, but it certainly has my gratitude—and it should have yours as well.

You can get a pretty good list of other distance calculators by searching for "distance calculator" at *GoTo.com*, but I doubt you will find one that is more practical or easier to use than the one at Bali Online. You'll find calculators limited to distances within a single country, or calculators that require airport codes, or calculators that factor in air speed (which is great if you're a jet pilot).

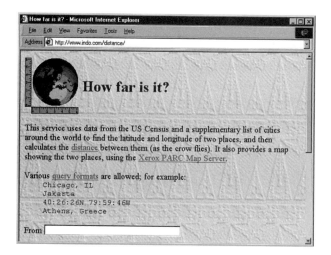

Using Bali Online's distance calculator is simplicity itself. You just type in the names of two cities.

Any distance calculator or route planner that requires airport codes or country codes ought to be shot. Who knows from those things? But sometimes you'll have no other choice than to use such calculators, so you'd best have the information you need. To find airport codes around the world, try the Airport Search Engine at *www.uni-karlsruhe.de/~un9v/atm/ase.html.* You just type in the name of the city and submit your request. If there is more than one airport, the site will prompt you to choose the one you want. The same sort of information is available from the World Wide Airport and City Code Database at *www.cowtown.net/users/rcr/ aaa/ccmain.htm.* This site is arranged alphabetically, both by city name and airport code (the latter is especially useful if you know an airport code but you don't know which city that airport is in).

Back to distance calculators: I wouldn't bet the farm on the accuracy of any of them. One of them may begin its calculations at the center of a city, while another begins at the city limits. Use them for general research purposes only. At the moment, the only distance I care about is that between my office and the dank, beer-stained interior of McSorley's Old Ale House, which I'll calculate by walking there and counting my steps.

By the Way

The airport code for Chicago's O'Hare International is ORD. It stands for "orchard," which is what the airport used to be.

Route Planners

Okay, I'm back from McSorley's. Now let's carry on...

The American Automobile Association used to provide members with a TripTik, a collection of neatly folded and spiral-bound maps on which a member's vacation driving route was neatly marked in felt-tip pen. Cumbersome but practical, these itineraries generally followed the major roads between the various points of a trip—Interstate 5 from San Diego to Los Angeles, Highway 101 north to Santa Barbara, Highway 1 north to Carmel, that sort of thing.

Remember

Distance calculators plot distance as the crow flies. Route planners use actual driving distance.

Today, anyone with access to the Internet can make his own driving itinerary using any of the numerous route planners available on the Web. Most route planners are limited to either North America or Europe. I have yet to find online route planners for Asia, Africa, or South America. Let's look first at the U.S. route planners, and then we'll tackle the ones for overseas.

North American Route Planners

AutoPilot, at *www.freetrip.com*, isn't particularly different from the several route planners available online, but it has a simple and clean interface and the query results are easy to read and understand. For instance, let's say you want to find the driving distance between Evansville, Indiana, and Williamsburg, Virginia. The planner prompts you to enter your driving preferences (such as scenic routes, interstate highways, parkways), as well as anything you'd like to avoid (toll roads, city centers, Britney Spears music). The results of your request show that you could cover the distance of 724 miles in 11 hours and 26 minutes if you maintained an average speed of 63 miles per hour and didn't make any pit stops.

Funny things happen when you enter the same information into different route planners. I used the factors from the previous paragraph on Yahoo! Maps and Driving Directions at *maps.yahoo.com/py/maps.py*. When I got my results, the mileage wasn't much different. Yahoo! came up with 729 miles versus AutoPilot's 724, but my anticipated driving time was given as 982 minutes. Not only is this a stupid way of saying 16 hours and 22 minutes, but it's also far more driving time than most people would require for that distance. (Or perhaps Yahoo! figures that people from Evansville, like my editor, are going to get lost for a few hours.)

Get the driving time and distance between any two North American cities at AutoPilot.

I like AutoPilot better, not just for its cleaner interface but also for its wider range of information (accumulated miles, elapsed time, remaining miles, and remaining time, all given at each change of direction, clearly and neatly listed). The Yahoo! route planner, unlike AutoPilot, offers a couple of map views of your itinerary, although they're more useful as locator maps than as anything more detailed.

1. From the AutoPilot driving directions page, enter your start and end cities and your driving preferences.

2. Notice that in Route Preferences, you can select up to three topics either to favor or to avoid.

3. Skip the section asking for your email address, and click Submit at the bottom of the page.

4. Notice that the left columns display the driving time and distance that have expired, while the right columns display the driving time and distance remaining.

▼ **Try It Yourself**

▲

There are so many other good U.S. route planners that it would take several chapters to cover them all. These include Microsoft Expedia Maps at *www.expediamaps.com/DrivingDirections.asp*,

MapQuest (discussed earlier in the chapter) at
www.mapquest.com, Maps On Us at *www.mapsonus.com*, and
more. Try them at your leisure. As an experiment, sample each of
them using the same factors and compare the various results.

Route Planners à l'Européenne

The European route planners are more problematic. The Easy
Tour Online Route Planner, at *easytour.dr-staedtler.de/*
routenplanung_engl.asp, requires you to choose destinations
using country codes (and if you're so smart, wiseguy, what's the
country code for Poland?), and you have to use the local spelling
of city names (such as Wien for Vienna and Roma for Rome).
Unfortunately, most of us don't have that kind of knowledge at
the tips of our typing fingers.

Similarly, the Shell Route Planner, at *shell.route66.nl/shell/*
route.html, requires you to use local spellings. The good part is
that if you luck out and spell the cities correctly, you get results
that include total mileage (in kilometers), driving time, and even
fuel consumption, plus a locator map showing your route.

CW Lease Routeplanner, at *www.cwlease.com/cwlint/*
selection.html, is by far the best of the Euro-bunch. Its interface is
very much like that of AutoPilot, and the results are similar, providing you with elapsed time and mileage at various route points.
Also, it includes a large map of the itinerary. You'll find other
European route planners in the appendix.

Currency and Time Converters

Money talks... but what language does it speak? If you've got
French francs and your next stop is London, do you know how
many British pounds you should expect in exchange? You don't
have to memorize conversion rates, because you can figure them
out in seconds with any of several currency converters available
for free on the Web. The Interactive Currency Table, at
www.xe.net/ict/, creates a table that cross-references your chosen
currency against the value of the world's other currencies. Easy to
use, yes, but it provides more information than most of us want or

need. The OANDA Currency Converter, at *www.oanda.com/ converter/classic/*, is far and away the best of the breed. Elegant in its simplicity, this is the most basic and user-friendly converter, IMHO. (For example, it took me all of 12 seconds to discover that one Albanian lek is equal to 1,437.34 Angolan New kwanzas, which is a really good piece of arcana for winning bar bets.)

Just as we travelers need to convert currency, frequently we need to convert the time of day from one part of the world to another. The World Wide Web is a 24-hour operation, but if you have to call someone on the telephone 6,600 miles away, it's good to know whether they just finished dessert or are in the middle of a deep sleep at 3 a.m.

The converter that I use most often is the Time Zone Converter, at *www.timezoneconverter.com*. Load it up on your screen and let's take a crack at it.

Money, That's What I Want

Do you know the currency names from the following countries? Aruba (the florin). Bolivia (the boliviano). Honduras (the lempira). North Korea (the won). Vietnam (the dong). Learn more currency names by logging on to the currency converter Web sites.

From the box on the left, choose the location where you are. From the box on the right, choose the location whose time you want to know.

1. From the home page, click any of the links to Time Zone Converter.

2. On the next page, choose the location where you are from the box at left. From the box at right, choose the location whose time you want to convert.

▼ **Try It Yourself**

3. If you want to use the current time, click the appropriate box as prompted. If not, change the current time in the form at the top of the page. Be sure to use the 24-hour format—1 p.m. is 1300, 8 a.m. is 0800, midnight is 2400, and so on.

4. Click the Convert button in the lower-right corner and review the results given on the next page.

For an incredibly simple site that allows you to figure out the current time in any country in the world instantly, see World Time Locations at *www.isbister.com/worldtime/wt-location.html*. All you do is choose a country from the list, and you're told what day and time it is in that place. It takes almost no time at all, which lets you spend more time planning what to do with your leisure time. But that's all for this chapter because, as you've probably guessed, we're out of time.

Wrapping It Up

Never let your travel tools get in the way of your travels. On the other hand, don't begin planning your travels without knowing which tools can help you learn more about your destination and the best ways to travel there. This chapter discussed the importance (and frustrations) of search sites, as well as the basic difference between search engines and Web directories. You added some goodies to your tool belt, including currency and time converters, route planners, and maps. Most importantly, you learned that there's more to getting started with e-travel than just logging on to a country's Web site. First, an e-traveler must have the solid foundations of travel research.

So now you know

- How to use search sites for travel research—by accessing both their search engines and their Web directories.

- The different kinds of maps available on the Web.

- The kinds of route planners available for North American itineraries, as well as those for Europe.

- How to use distance calculators, currency converters, and time converters, and where to find airport codes.

CHAPTER 2

Keeping Your Electronic Information in Order

Hundreds of Web sites appear throughout this book and its appendix. Some of them will be more pertinent to your needs than others, but none of them will be useful at all unless you have them organized and ready to use as *bookmarks* or *favorites* in your Web browser.

Whether you use Netscape, Internet Explorer, American Online's Web browser, or some other browser, you can create and maintain a list of favorite sites so that you can go back to them as frequently as needed without forgetting where they're located. But how do you go about doing that? Is there more to it than simply pressing the button that creates a new bookmark? To which I answer: Uh huh, yup, you betcha.

If you're of a certain age, you'll remember the old-fashioned card catalogs used by public libraries. Each drawer in the catalog cabinet held hundreds of 3×5 cards, in alphabetical order. Each card was printed with a book's title and author, as well as its location on the library shelves based on its number in the Dewey decimal system. You may not even know what the Dewey decimal system is because it's not taught in school anymore outside of library science classes. But those of us lucky enough to have started our library experience using the old card catalogs and the Dewey decimal system realized the benefits of a well organized system of information. All the history books are over there in that part the library, and all the sociology texts are over here. And within each of those larger categories are the minor topics, equally well organized.

Nowadays, of course, every book, CD, and video in a library's archives is catalogued on computer. It's all too easy to type in the

What You'll Learn in This Chapter

▶ Why a well organized and detailed list of Web favorites or bookmarks is important to you as an e-traveler.

▶ How to develop a list of the major travel topics based on your own interests and standard trade categories.

▶ How to efficiently use a category-within-category approach to indexing.

▶ How to edit your individual bookmarks so they'll make the most sense for the way you work.

title or author of a volume and be directed to the appropriate bookshelf almost instantly. But in so doing, you can't step back and get the larger perspective of the organizational structure, as you could when looking at the multiple drawers of the outmoded card catalog system. This chapter is going to blend the best of those two worlds, taking a comprehensive and category-within-category approach to bookmark organization, yet doing it in such a way that you still use the speed, ease, and search capabilities of your computer.

Creating Your Own Travel Bookmarks

How many times have you set something down, only to forget where you put it? I do that all the time with my money (until I finally remember that I didn't misplace it—I spent it). It's frustrating and time-consuming to hunt for something that you should have readily available.

Caveat

Your Web browser and hardware may work differently than that described in this chapter. If so, refer to your hardware manuals and your browser's help section for details on specific bookmarking and editing procedures.

Therein lies the beauty of Web bookmarks. Each time you discover a new Web site that might be useful in the future, you can add it to your list. But maintaining that list is not an easy thing to do. If you simply add bookmark after bookmark, you may end up with hundreds of Web sites on your list. If they aren't organized in some easy-to-use fashion, they're not going to do you much good. But before delving further into the fine art of organizing your Web favorites, let's go over some of the basics needed to create bookmarks in the first place and how to create folders in which to place them.

Let's look at the two most popular standalone Web browsers to see how you can create a list of Web sites that you may want to access regularly.

Try It Yourself ▼

If you use Netscape, do the following:

1. Open your Netscape browser and choose Bookmarks (from the Communicator menu in Windows or from the pull-down menu on the Netscape icon on a Mac). A new screen indicates which bookmarks, if any, are currently contained in that file.

2. Close that Bookmarks window, and then go to a Web site that you enjoy and would like to bookmark.

3. Once that page loads, choose Add Bookmark from the pull-down menu on the blue-green bookmark icon at the top of the screen.

4. Open your Bookmarks file again (as in Step 1) and verify that the newly bookmarked site is listed there. Then choose New Folder from the pull-down File menu at the top of the screen. In the pop-up window that appears, type in the broad subject listing that your new bookmark falls under. For example, if you've bookmarked an airline site, name your new folder "Airlines."

5. While still in the Bookmarks file, use the drag-and-drop method to place your new bookmark in the newly created folder.

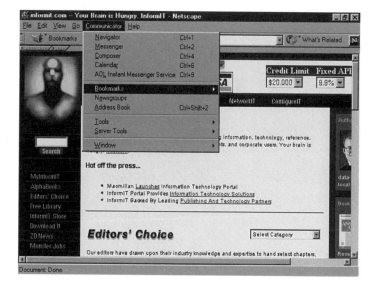

▲

Use the pull-down menu from the Netscape icon to access your bookmarks.

You have just completed 95 percent of what is required to make a detailed and comprehensive bookmark file that would make any Net surfer proud. Go back to this exercise and practice it twice more.

If you use Internet Explorer, do the following:

▼ **Try It Yourself**

1. Open your Internet Explorer browser and choose Favorites, Organize Favorites.... A new screen indicates which bookmarks are currently contained in that file.

2. Close that Favorites window, and then go to a Web site that you enjoy and would like to add to your bookmarks.

3. Once that page loads, choose Favorites, Add to Favorites....

4. Open Organize Favorites... again (as in Step 1), and verify that the newly bookmarked site is listed there. In that same dialog box, choose Create Folder. Give the new folder the subject name you want to use by typing it into the appropriate field next to the icon. For example, if you've bookmarked a cruise line site, name your new folder "Cruises."

5. While still in the Favorites file, use the drag-and-drop method to place your new favorite in the newly created folder.

It's easy to create folders for your Internet Explorer favorites.

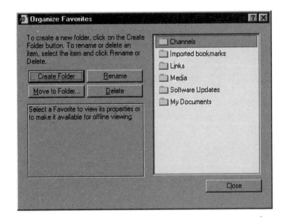

By the Way

You don't have to use the overly long names that sometimes come with bookmarks. You can rename a bookmark or edit it down to something shorter and more to the point.

Practice this exercise several times. You'll have it down pat in just a few minutes.

Just as you named your folders in a sensible way, don't neglect to rename your bookmarks as necessary. When you bookmark a Web page, it comes with its own name. Feel free to edit this name, because sometimes a default name doesn't clearly identify just what a Web page contains. (This is especially true if the page you've bookmarked is not the site's home page, but rather some subsequent page deeper into the site.)

In Netscape, you can change the name of a bookmark by opening your Bookmark file, highlighting the bookmark that needs to be changed, and then choosing Get Info from the Edit pull-down menu at the top of your screen. A pop-up window displays the name and URL of the bookmarked site. You can simply delete the existing name and create a new one. In other words, if a bookmarked Web site comes with the name *brown/destination-ppg. backfile/swiss/destination*, you might decide to rename it as something recognizable, like Switzerland (Brown's Travel Guide). Or perhaps the default name is Brown's Travel Guides Lead You All Around the World Including Switzerland and Of Course This Is the Main Page for the Switzerland Section of Brown's Travel Guides Which Lead You All Around the World. If you want to rename this—and I think you would be right to do so—call it Switzerland (Brown's Travel Guide).

Using Internet Explorer, it's even easier to change the name of a favorite. Open your Favorites file, place the cursor on the name of the favorite you want to rename, and click once. When a black outline appears around the name, you can type in a new name or edit the existing one.

Which Comes First—the Bookmark or the Topic Folder?

You'll develop your own habits and theories when it comes to good bookmarking, but you'll want to get started on the right foot right away. In the appendix of this book are numerous Web site addresses. You may want to add all or only some of them to your list of personal bookmarks. No doubt you have some bookmarks already entered into your favorites file (even if you created them by accident!). Most people have dozens of bookmarks or more, in no particular order, and you're probably no different.

If that's your situation, you should begin thinking about the kinds of folders you should be making. This is a book on e-travel, so we'll focus on travel topics, but this can apply to any subject matter you want to organize.

The first thing I want you to do is separate all your travel bookmarks from everything else. Open your bookmarks file and create a folder called Travel. Using the drag-and-drop method, move all of your travel-related bookmarks into this Travel folder.

At this stage, you shouldn't worry about keeping the travel-related favorites in any sort of order. For now, just keep them the

Tip
Don't begin your folder names with the word "travel" or they'll be hard to find. For example, name a file "Magazines (travel)," not "Travel magazines." Otherwise, most of your folders would begin with the word "travel."

heck away from all of those non-travel bookmarks by throwing them into their own folder.

Next, create some folders within that Travel folder. Think of big topics, broad categories: Transportation, Destinations, Publications, and Government Resources. Don't limit yourself. Create as many comprehensive folders as you can think of off the top of your head.

Remember

You can also use the drag-and-drop method to move folders into or out of other folders.

Then, within each of those folders, create new, more specific folders. Here's how to create a folder within a folder: In your bookmarks (or favorites) file, highlight the folder in which you want the new folder to be located, and then use the New Folder command as described in the preceding exercises. For instance, within your Transportation folder, you can make folders for airlines, cruises, car rentals, and other transportation topics. Same for your Publications folder. You might want to create folders for travel magazines online, guidebooks, Internet newspapers with good travel sections, and so on.

You get the idea. Start with the broadest categories for your major folders, and then create subfolders with more specific topics. There's nothing wrong with creating topic folders even before you have bookmarks to place inside them. At the very least, opening an empty folder will remind you that you should keep an eye out for good Web sites to bookmark and place in that folder.

You probably want to get a peek at my bookmark folders to see just how much I heed my own advice, don't you? Unfortunately, I didn't have the benefit of a book like *Sams Teach Yourself e-Travel Today*, so I had to learn efficient bookmarking habits by trial and error. Also, because I need to access a wide array of Web sites scores of times each day, I have fewer broad-category folders than you should have.

All right, enough stalling, Orwoll. Show 'em your bookmark file and let's move on to Chapter 3.

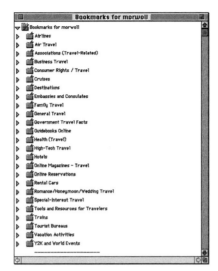

This is my travel-related book-marks file. Each of the topic folders holds other folders and folders within folders. Somewhere in there, according to rumor, are the actual bookmarks themselves.

Wrapping It Up

I suppose there are some people who actually thrive in a messy work environment. I'm not one of them, and I hope you're not either. This chapter discussed ways to keep your bookmarks where they belong so you can access them readily whenever you want them.

Here are the key points covered in this chapter:

- How to open your browser's bookmark file and create folders.

- How to organize a folder-within-folder index of favorites.

- How to change a bookmark's name so it makes more sense to your system or organization.

- How to develop a list of travel-related topics so you can reach your bookmarked Web sites quickly.

CHAPTER 3

Evaluating a Web Site's Accuracy and Validity

When the Internet was in its infancy, there was a radical, almost Utopian approach to its content. Basically, the premise was that there should be no censorship except for commercialism. Those of you who weren't paying attention when this whole Internet thing was still in diapers may not believe me, but it's true. If a company tried to advertise on the World Wide Web, especially on message boards, it was flamed by outraged Websters, spammed by Net surfers, and generally decried from every nook and cranny in cyberspace.

Those days didn't last long, did they?

Nowadays the Web is full of commercial content. And just as you look at television commercials with skepticism (at least, I hope you do!), so too must you venture into a commercial Web site with one unspoken but ever-present guiding thought: "What are these sneaky guys trying to sell me?"

Maybe what they're trying to sell you is something you want to buy. Or maybe you're just window-shopping. Being able to access commercial operations on the Internet is a good thing—as long as you can tell a commercial site from a noncommercial one, and you understand that most commercial sites use every tool at hand to sell you something. And these commercial sites sometimes look like innocent, well-meaning, noncommercial sites—an insidious approach to Web design that makes the smarmiest ad director on Madison Avenue look like a choirboy in comparison to his counterparts on the Internet.

What You'll Learn in This Chapter

▶ How to identify an official travel Web site.

▶ How to test the accuracy of a commercial Web site.

▶ How to find a Web site's fine print—and why it's important for you to read it.

Before we begin reviewing the many travel-related sites throughout the rest of this book, this chapter will show you how to put a
Web site through the validity test to determine if it really is what
it claims to be.

Official Sites vs. Official-*Looking* Sites

Did you ever see those commercials for the Columbia School of
Broadcasting? You know, the place that teaches you how to be a
radio announcer? What I always found interesting in those 60-
second TV spots was the rapidly spoken disclaimer that always
ended each commercial: "Not affiliated with the Columbia
Broadcasting System." On one hand, you gotta hand it to them for
being honest. But on the other hand, you have to suspect that
when the founders devised the school's name, they wouldn't have
minded too much if a few prospective students got mixed up and
thought they were enrolling in some official CBS broadcasting
school.

In a similar way, some Web sites look a lot more official than
they really are. I won't say that such sites are purposely trying to
fool you with their unmerited official appearance. Could be a
coincidence. Nor will I say that a faux-official site has less credi-
bility than its official counterpart. Its information could be very
good indeed, and often is. But I *will* say that you should always
be cautious when entering a site that purports to be more official
than it really is.

Remember

Just because a Web
site *looks* official
doesn't mean that it
is official.

Consider one such confusing example concerning Arizona
tourism. The State of Arizona has long been a major vacation destination, so it should be no surprise that the state's tourist office
would build a fancy, colorful Web site like The Ultimate Arizona
Vacation Guide—Official Site of the Arizona Tourist Bureau at
www.arizonatourism.com/index.html. There you'll find details
about hot air ballooning in Phoenix and resorts in Carefree, as
well as statewide information about transportation, shopping,
dining, and more.

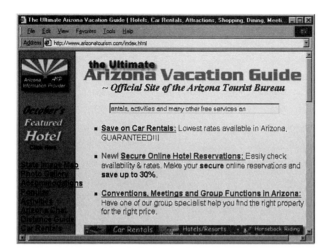

The Ultimate Arizona Vacation Guide is the official site of an unofficial agency. Huh?!

It won't take long, however, before you start to wonder about some quirks of this site. For instance, why does it advertise the lowest car-rental rates available in Arizona, "GUARAN-TEED!!!!"? Why does it have a page devoted to apartment rentals? Why are some notable Arizona hotels missing from the accommodations listings? The more you read through the site, the more and more it seems like a... *commercial* Web site.

1. Open your browser to the Ultimate Arizona Vacation Guide.

2. Count how many items on the page give the impression that this is a noncommercial informational site. (I came up with eight, including the Arizona Information Provider logo in the upper-left corner.)

3. Now count the items that look suspiciously like they belong on a commercial Web site. (I got only six.)

▼ **Try It Yourself**

▲

On balance, the site would seem to be an official site... of *some* sort. But perhaps you were able to discern some fine print at the bottom of the home page. You squinted, you managed to read it, and oh-ho, what have we here?! The Arizona Tourist Bureau is "not in any way affiliated with the Arizona Office of Tourism."

And what, pray tell, is the Arizona Office of Tourism? Use one of your search engines to type in that phrase. I used GoTo.com for my search, and the very first item in the list of results was for Arizona Guide—The Official Site of the Arizona Office of Tourism at *www.arizonaguide.com/*.

No need to feel squeamish. The Arizona Guide is as pure as the driven snow, an honest-to-goodness authorized government travel site.

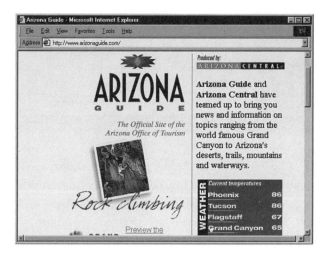

Try It Yourself ▼

1. Log on to the Arizona Guide and repeat the preceding exercise, looking for evidence of the site being either commercial or noncommercial.

2. Read about Arizona Central (which produces the site) in the upper-right corner of the screen.

3. Scroll down to the bottom of the screen and click on the link to Arizona Central, which leads you to the online version of the *Arizona Republic* newspaper.

Now, I don't know about you, but the first thing *I* did when I logged on to the Arizona Guide home page was to look for any fine print admitting that this site isn't in any way affiliated with the Arizona Tourist Bureau. Turns out that this site is produced by the *Arizona Republic* newspaper, a well-regarded publication, in partnership with the Arizona Office of Tourism, which in turn is a government agency created in 1975. So, this Web site really *is* official.

(I can hardly bring myself to mention the potential for even more confusion that arises from the second result of the GoTo search—the unimaginatively named Official State of Arizona Web Site. Not to worry, though. It's strictly a government site, with no tourist information.)

The Arizona Guide versus the Ultimate Arizona Vacation Guide. The Arizona Office of Tourism versus the Arizona Tourist Bureau. Goodness me oh my, what next? Perhaps The Official Guide to the Ultimate Arizona Web Site Developed by the Arizona Tourism Board in Association with the Arizona Office of Tourism?

Once you've discerned the difference between these two Web sites, a more pertinent question to ask yourself is: Does it really matter? The answer is an emphatic yes, but not because the quality of the information or presentation is necessarily better on one site than the other. It matters because, as information consumers (and that's what we are), it pays to be savvy data shoppers. You might prefer one of the two confusing Arizona sites while I might prefer the other, and that's okay. The important element here is not which site you choose, but rather that you make an informed choice. And that is why it is essential to differentiate between a *real* official site and one that merely looks or claims to be.

Ask Yourself

Do you trust a Web site that looks as if it's trying to fool you? Are you savvy enough to *know* when a Web site is trying to fool you?

Can You Tell the Official from the Unofficial?

Below are pairs of real Web site names. Guess which one of each pair is the official government-sponsored site. (*Answers can be found at the end of this chapter.*)

1. Hawaii State Vacation Planner or Hawaii, the Islands of Aloha
2. California Vacations or California—Find Yourself Here
3. Visit Florida or Florida.com
4. TravelTex or Wild Texas
5. Virginia Is For Lovers or Virginia Tourism Corporation

Web Site Accuracy: Putting It to the Test

Whether it's a commercial Web site or a noncommercial site, everybody is selling something. An authorized honest-to-gosh state tourism Web site is trying to sell you on the idea of vacationing in that state. That kind of sales technique may be a bit more subtle than, say, a Web site that tries to sell you airline tickets or vacation packages. Nonetheless, it's trying to sell you something, just like everybody else is.

As mentioned before, that's not bad in and of itself. But if you know what it is that's being sold, and you understand how it's being sold, you can place the information you receive into some sort of context. "That Web site is trying to sell me vacation packages," you might say to yourself, "but they have a great message board with postings from other travelers." On another Web site, you might feel that the only thing being sold is transportation arrangements and the rest of the site is apparently unfettered by direct commercial implications.

Remember

There's nothing wrong with a Web site trying to sell you something... as long as you realize that's what they're doing.

If you want to know whether a travel-related Web site is giving you the straight dope or is couching advertising in the form of objective information, you'll have to visit the site and look around. If you get burned by bad information, or you feel that a site's information is sullied by considerations of profit, you won't go back to it. So to a large extent, each Web site must prove itself to you, and you must put the Web site to the test. Let's try doing just that.

Try It Yourself ▼

1. Choose one of the booking services listed under "Online Reservations" in the appendix of this book. It doesn't matter which one.

2. How much advertising clutter is there? In how many different ways does the site try to sell you something by assaulting you with "special offers," or "last-minute discounts" or pleas to "book now"?

3. Find a link to information about a destination you know about—either a city or a country. Can you find clear, concise, and reliable information on that destination, untainted by salesmanship? Does there seem to be any advertising tie-in with the information provided?

4. Return to the site's home page and follow some of the site's other paths to hotels, restaurants, activities, what have you. Decide for yourself if this is a straightforward and reliable site that's honestly attempting to convey solid information, or a site that's interested solely in selling you something, even to the point of skewing its supposedly objective information. ▲

Ultimately, you must determine for yourself if the information supplied by a travel Web site is accurate and noncommercial. If you think it's good, based on your own knowledge and experience, lucky you! Add it to your list of bookmarks. But if you get the feeling that there's something fishy about a travel site, trash it and move on to the next one.

Reading the Fine Print

Part and parcel of a Web site's integrity—and integrity is the crux of this entire chapter—is its willingness to identify itself and its mission. Some sites do this with vigor and pride, but others seem to shrink from giving out any information about themselves. The following figure shows the home page of Mexico Online, a Web site that I've used many times for travel information on that country. Log on to Mexico Online to see how easy it is to find out who are the operators of this Web site.

Somewhere on Mexico Online's info-packed home page is a link to its ownership and mission... but how long will it take you to find it?

1. Look for a link to a page about the site's ownership. Often such links are at the bottom, indicated by phrases like "About this site."

2. In the left column, under the Services heading, click the Our Services link.

3. In the next window, select the most appropriate link for your goal. Specifically, click the one that says Company and Staff Bulletin: Who runs this site, anyway?

4. Bingo! You're sent to a page with the names and email addresses of the Webmasters and sales staff. It may not be everything you hoped for, but at least we know that there are actual human beings that you can contact.

▲

If you want to continue searching for details, try the press releases section, which gives even more background on the company that runs the Web site. I think we can all admire a firm that states clearly who runs the site, and the easier it makes that information to find, the happier we'll all be. Try this same exercise on some of your favorite travel-related sites and see how simply—or not—the information can be located.

Cause for Concern

If a Web site doesn't give you any contact information—no names, addresses, email addresses, phone numbers, or fax numbers—you might want to ask yourself just why they're hiding.

One of my greatest frustrations is when I come up against a site that seems not to exist outside of cyberspace. There's no street address or telephone number listed anywhere—nothing even to indicate from which *country* the Web site originates. Maybe that's an oversight on the part of an otherwise upstanding and honorable Web editor. She just forgot to add that information. But I can't shake the feeling that there's a reason—a slightly sinister reason—when a Web site shields its identity. And, equally, it's usually for good reason that a reputable Web site makes its ownership and its mission clear to all.

Wrapping It Up

Trustworthiness. Integrity. Accuracy. Truthfulness. These aren't necessarily qualities we expect in our political leaders, perhaps, but certainly they're traits that we hope for in our travel Web sites. This chapter showed you that a Web site is obliged to have its facts straight and shouldn't attempt to pass off advertising as objective information. You also learned what to look for to ensure that a Web site is not a fly-by-night operation—legal disclaimers, statements of ownership, and contact information that can lead you to a person who works for that Web site.

Here are the key points covered in this chapter:

- Now you understand what constitutes an official site, as opposed to one that just looks that way.

- You've learned how to test the accuracy of a Web site and determine whether its commercial nature interferes with the quality of its information.

- You've discovered that the fine print on a Web site can help you develop a better overall picture of a Web site's usefulness, its mission, and its trustworthiness.

Answers to "Can You Tell the Official from the Unofficial?"

Did you answer the questionnaire above? How well did you do? The official tourism Web sites are:

1. "Hawaii, the Islands of Aloha"

2. "California—Find Yourself Here"

3. "Visit Florida"

4. "TravelTex"

5. Trick question! They're both state-sponsored agencies.

CHAPTER 4

Guidebooks on the Web

You're no longer clueless. I suppose I should say you're no longer *totally* clueless. Now you know a little bit more about travel information on the Internet, you're prepped to catalog your discoveries in a filing system of browser bookmarks or favorites, and you have a hazy sense of what differentiates a commercial travel site from an official site. All you have to do at this point is find somewhere to go—both geographically and electronically. And just what are the best places to begin this consideration process? The online guidebooks.

In this chapter, you'll learn… uh, let me rephrase that… In this chapter, you'll be provided with the information that will enable you to learn how best to use the electronic versions of popular guidebook publishers (whew!). You'll begin by looking at the big dogs, the major guidebook publishers, most of which you should recognize by name. Then you'll take a peek at a couple of the younger publishers (both chronologically and in spirit).

Once you've completed this chapter, you should know how to assess the information available from each of these online publishers, identify the strengths and weaknesses of each, and find additional online guidebooks apart from those covered in this chapter. (Notice that I said you *should*. I didn't say you *would*. I can only take so much personal responsibility for your actions.)

Meet the Three F's

When I was but a beardless boy, it was easy to remember the top guidebook writers. They were the Three F's: Eugene Fodor, Temple Fielding, and Arthur Frommer. Those were the giants of the travel game whose names have been synonymous with guidebooks since the 1950s. While each of these authors had his own

Key Points in This Chapter

▶ How to get the best use of the major guidebook publishers.

▶ Which guidebooks are more appropriate for younger, adventurous travelers.

▶ Search tips for finding other guidebook publishers.

writing style, pet peeves, recommendations, and point of view, all of them performed a similar function—making travel fun, meaningful, and practical for the average American.

Since their initial guidebooks were published in the years after World War II, these writers transformed their names into franchises. They hired eager young bucks to research and write new travel books, they developed their own eponymous magazines, and they produced videotapes, television shows, and (you knew this was coming, didn't you?) Web sites. The beauty of tracking down Web info from the three F's is that, unlike the books and videos from these authors and their legions of globetrotting scribblers, the material on the Web is free.

Way Back When

The first European guidebook published in America for Americans was probably *The Tourist in Europe,* which came out 1838.

Beyond the Three F's, there are hundreds of travel guides both in print and on the Internet. To find them for yourself, try the search phrase "travel publisher." You'll be directed to such varied (and, in some cases, rather dubious) guidebook publishers as Boiling Billy Publications ("Travel guides for adventurers"), Intrepid Traveler ("Publisher of budget travel books"), and, for those of you with a microscopically narrow field of interest, Channel Tunnel Publications (with travel-related books and merchandise "relating to the Tunnel"). But beware of the scores of minor-league guidebooks that you're bound to stumble over on your searches. Many of these sites are little more than teasers for the publishers' printed line of guides. They place a greater emphasis on e-sales of their books than on expanding the travel knowledge of their online viewers.

Before you go gallivanting off to the more obscure online vade mecums, first you should become familiar with the major online guidebooks, if only for benchmarking purposes. They hold so much information that their Web sites have more pages than the NBC studio tour at Rockefeller Center. If I didn't hate the word so much, I'd say that these sites were "chock-full."

The online Three F's are happy to sell you copies of their printed books, to be sure, but that isn't the emphasis. They seem not to care if you only stop by to gorge on travel trivia, holiday hints, and trip tips. These sites are sturdy, reliable, and substantial. To be honest, they're kinda old-farty in some respects.

Fodor's Travel Online—Nuts 'n' Bolts Travel

The interface of Fodor's site, at *www.fodors.com*, is clean, colorful, and straightforward. To my mind, that's the best way to present the nuts and bolts of travel. And Fodor's has more nuts and bolts than your father's basement workbench.

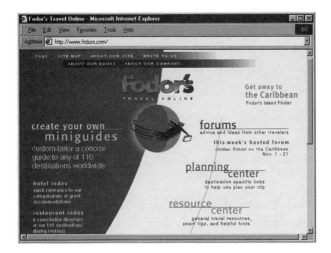

Fodor's is especially helpful, with restaurant and hotel listings in top destinations.

As a travel journalist, I receive more questions about hotels and restaurants than about any other topic (except for the oft-asked question, "When are you going to pay back that money I lent you, Orwoll?"). That's one of the reasons I find Fodor's so useful in my own research. Click on the site's Hotel Index icon for a searchable database where you can look for lodgings in 110 international cities, from Acapulco to Zurich. You can request the hotels either by name or by such criteria as price, location, and facilities. (By the way, if you're looking for a hotel in Calcutta with a $125-$200 price range and a beauty salon on the premises, Fodor's will point you in the direction of the Hotel Airport Ashok, calling it a "clean and fresh" high-rise that "offers little excitement." Hey, what can I tell you. There are some places in this world where you can have cleanliness or you can have excitement, but not both.)

Speaking of Foreign Languages...

Fodor's site lets you listen to and learn 500 phrases in four languages.

The Restaurant Index is similarly arranged, with descriptions of selected eateries in the site's 110 destinations. Let's take a ride through some of these eateries... more specifically, let's find a cheap place to eat in Brussels. Ready?

1. From Fodor's home page, click Restaurant Index on the left side of the page.

2. From that index page, go to the city menu and scroll down until you can find and highlight Brussels. Then, directly below that menu box, click the Search by Criteria icon followed by the Find button.

3. Then you're given a choice: Let Fodor offer its choices, or make our own selection based on price range. You're a cheapskate, so click the Under BF 1,500 box and then click the Find button.

4. Scrumpdeliumpcious! There are seven restaurants in your price range, from Adrienne ("Fun for the kids") to La Grande Porte, whose specialties include—get this—beef and onions stewed in beer! Now that's my kind of restaurant.

Moreover, on Fodor's site you'll find forums with comments from your fellow readers, a resource center that includes planning tips and links to other sites, and sections on B&B's, national parks, adventure travel, and foreign languages. There is a wealth of information there. If I were to complain about anything, it would be the somewhat limited nature of the city-oriented approach, as opposed to the often more useful and comprehensive country-by-country approach.

Fielding Travel Guides—Elegance with a Dangerous Edge

A sleek home page gives you the sense that something cutting-edge and exciting is happening at Fielding Travel Guides' Web site (*www.fieldingtravel.com/*), which titles itself, not unlike a Barbara Cartland bodice-ripper, "A Passion for Travel." Its attractive design invites you to investigate such intriguing sections as the Cruisefinder (with reviews from "the largest cruise-ship database in the world"), the Dangerfinder (for adventurous, off-the-beaten-mountain-bike-path travelers), and forums devoted to both of those topics. If you're planning a trip to one of the world's more dicey locales, or if you want quick access to cruise ship stats, the Fielding site is useful indeed.

The intriguing Fielding site mixes passion, cruising, and (gulp) danger.

Since I've always taken an interest in places where weasels might rip my flesh or tsunamis might unexpectedly wet my whistle, let's take a peek at Fielding's Dangerfinder, which you can access from the home page. Let's see what sort of unwanted things might happen if you go off the beaten track.

1. From the Dangerfinder's main menu, choose Dangerous Things.

2. Choose Diseases—Souvenirs from Hell.

3. From the frame on the left, choose Worms (I'm gagging already, yuck, yuck!) and read all about how these intestinal parasites—including my favorite, the Oriental liver fluke—will be even better than snapshots when it comes to remembering your last vacation.

▼ **Try It Yourself**

▲

Good information to have, as I'm sure you'll agree. On the other hand, of the Three F's, the Fielding site has the least amount of city and country information. It lacks the sort of comprehensive, all-purpose approach that might otherwise make this a definite bookmark. If what you really want to know is how to catch a bus in Istanbul or where to find the best roast-pig dinner in Pago Pago, you'll want to go elsewhere.

Arthur Frommer's Budget Travel Online—Spending Your Money Wisely

The only one of the Three F's still alive and well is Arthur Frommer, probably the best-known guidebook writer of the 20th century. He started his career over four decades ago with *Europe on $5 a Day*, aimed at Eisenhower-era Americans who thought travel was just for the wealthy. His oeuvre now includes a wide assortment of travel guides, but Frommer has never forgotten his roots—giving practical advice to frugal travelers.

By the Way

The Frommer's series now includes 270 travel titles—more books than there are countries in the world!

His Web site at *www.frommers.com* is organized around what Frommer calls "The 200 Places People Go" (take *that,* Fodor!), including islands and cities on six continents. Granted, the selection of destinations in some of the regions is pretty skimpy (Africa, for instance, lists only Cape Town and Nairobi), but the amount of information for each individual destination is good indeed, listing everything from top attractions and hotels to choices in evening entertainment. Frommer's Online is also full of opinions, suggestions, advice, and vacation ideas—just like Arthur Frommer himself. Of the Three F's, Frommer's site is the clear winner.

At Frommer's, you'll find money-saving ideas from the original budget traveler.

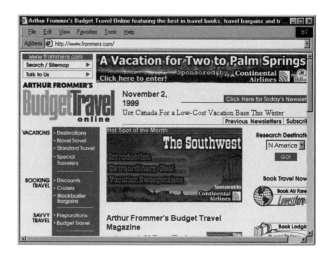

As a guidebook author, Arthur has always been close with a buck, so let's put him to the test and find out what sort of tips he has for saving money the next time you travel.

1. From the home page, move your mouse over to the left column that says Budget Travel and give it a click.

2. In the frame at left, choose Saving Money Wherever You Go.

3. Still in the new frame at left, choose Bathless Rooms for Less. (Personally, I like rooms with running water, thank you very much.)

4. In the main window, you are presented with an essay that explains why, in exchange for using a bathroom down the hall, you can have a decent hotel room for less than the price of dinner.

▼ **Try It Yourself**

▲

Online Guidebooks for the Young and the Restless

So you *do* think these traditional guides are sort of old-fashioned in their approach? Shame on you. Anyway, because I would hate for you to think that I'm an old fart too, this section covers two of my favorite "young" online travel guide series: Lonely Planet and Rick Steves. They're a bit more "with it," as the kids like to say nowadays when they "rap." They're a little bit "hipper" than the Three F's. These "groovy" books really "make the scene, man," and… Hmmm? Sorry? Was that *me* saying that? I dunno what happened. Something just came over me. Let's move on, please. (Audio clip: Peal of ceremonial trumpets and the clattering of horses' hooves as author charges forward with rather more substantial data.)

Lonely Planet Online—Over the Hills and Far Away

If you're eager to learn about the destinations your Auntie Griselda would never visit, those remote and touristless places that the Victorian Brits used to call "the back of beyond," naturally you'll lean toward a Web site aimed specifically at a like-minded breed of traveler. Lonely Planet Online, at *www.lonelyplanet.com*, is such a site. The site's motto is "All roads lead you astray." I've known a lot of women who should have worked for Lonely Planet—they were always saying things to me like "Get lost" and "Take a hike."

Don't Got Time to Wait

Lonely Planet's Web site has a text-only version called Text Express for readers who tire of waiting for the graphics to load.

Intrepid types log on to Lonely Planet for news from the back of beyond.

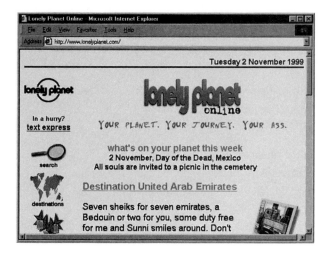

Lonely Planet is best known for its guidebook series featuring such godforsaken places as Malawi, the Gambia, Comoros, Lombok, and other real places that you probably didn't know were, well, real places. The LP Web site builds upon that immense storehouse of knowledge. Virtually every Third World destination you can think of is covered, if only in passing. Besides information culled from the pages of the printed guidebooks, the site also boasts straight-from-the-shoulder postings from other adventure travelers on Lonely Planet's popular message board, called the Thorn Tree, and from the messages it receives from on-the-road readers in the Postcards section.

Let's see what the readers of Lonely Planet are saying about... hmmm... about, er... well, New Zealand, the land of extreme sports.

Try It Yourself ▼

1. From the home page, click on Postcards.

2. On the Postcards page, look at the list of world regions and select Australasia & Pacific. On the next page, choose New Zealand.

3. You can choose the shortcuts at the top (in red) to go to a topic of your choice, or simply scroll down to read all the messages received on this destination.

4. If it's still posted, read the Jeffs family's warning about traveling the Whanganui River Road from Raetini to Whanganui. (Okay, so you weren't planning to take that apparently hellacious road. But if you ever did decide to drive that devilish track, the Jeffs' advice could save your worthless hide!)

The Postcards section is just plain fun reading, even if you're doing it for nothing more than armchair adventure. Add to that the sections devoted to photography, travel news, health tips, related links, and much more, and you have one of the most vibrant and active online travel guidebooks around. Lonely Planet Online may not be for everyone, but it's an invaluable resource for anyone who likes to get away from it all. And I do mean *all*.

Rick Steves' Europe Through the Back Door—Living Like the Locals Do

Rick Steves is the Arthur Frommer for the Baby Boomer generation. He's as well-known for his PBS television travel series as for his many guidebooks. His Web site Europe Through the Back Door (*www.ricksteves.com/*), which takes its name from one of Steves' most popular books, mirrors the author's travel philosophy. In a nutshell, he advises living like the locals, being an extrovert, and avoiding tourist traps. (That's Steves himself smiling brightly on his home page.) Like many such Web guidebooks, ETBD carries travel news, messages from other users, and archives of travel articles (in this case, listed by country). Unlike most of the other major guidebook sites, though, this one carries a more obvious dose of e-commerce. At the click of a mouse, you can purchase everything from fanny packs to entire vacations.

Did You Know?
On his first trip to Europe, Rick Steves visited piano factories with his father, a piano importer. He paid for later trips by teaching piano.

There's nothing fancy about Rick Steves' site... just a lot of solid travel tips (and a dose of e-commerce).

Well, while you're here, you might as well see what Rick is offering in his upcoming guided tours.

Try It Yourself ▼

1. From the home page, choose Our Tours for 2000.

2. You might be a bit peckish and could use a little snackie, so choose Turkey from the list of destinations.

3. You can read all about the Best of Turkey in 14 Days, which, at a price of $1,900, seems to include all the sightseeing you could hope for in a couple of weeks—and all with the Rick Steves touch. (Although I must tell you, Rick himself doesn't accompany these tours. He's too busy writing his books, shooting his TV show, and producing the Web site).

▲

Wrapping It Up

For me, the main attraction of all these online guidebooks is the combination of opinion and authority. Too many travel Web sites give you either one or the other, but not both. True, you don't have to go to these sites to find firsthand travelogues. If that's all you want, you can find a personal Web page in which a just-returned traveler gives you his POV on every aspect of his trip to Oslo. It's also true that you don't need these online guidebooks if all you want are the nuts-and-bolts details of a destination.

There are scores of plain-vanilla information sites that are strictly objective (read: boring) in their listings. But online travel guides are generally the best at combining solid information with opinions that can range from innocuous to incisive.

Online guidebooks are not designed primarily as booking services (see Part 3, "Booking Your Trip Online"), although they often have links to such reservation-oriented Web sites. And online guidebooks are never *quite* as comprehensive as you might want. Rarely do they focus tightly enough on a specific destination and give it the thorough coverage it might deserve. But when these guidebooks are used as a backstop resource (and thanks particularly to their public forums, in which travelers communicate with one another on a wide range of topics), they hold a valuable spot in any e-traveler's WWW bookmarks.

In a nutshell, here's what you now know about online guidebooks:

- The big three publishers (Fielding, Fodor, and Frommer).

- What distinguishes each of those major leaguers, and where they excel or fall flat.

- What some of the "younger" guidebooks have to offer—specifically, Lonely Planet's Web site and Rick Steves on the Internet.

Three Million Web Pages Is a Bit Much

If you have absolutely nothing else to do, try an AltaVista search for the phrase "travel + publisher." Although the total number of matching Web pages may vary slightly from day to day, you're apt to come up with as many as 3,513,400 Web pages, as I did recently. If you don't have, say, seven or eight *years* to read through the hundreds of thousands of listings, try to refine your search by adding such words as "guidebook" and the name of the particular destination and/or activity that interests you. If you input "travel + publisher + guidebook + snorkeling + Tahiti" instead of just "travel + publisher," you will reduce the results to as few as 20 Web pages. That may be fewer than you hoped for. Don't be afraid to play around with various search phrases until you start getting the number and type of results that most closely approximate your interests and needs.

CHAPTER 5

Regional and Foreign Newspapers Online

One of my favorite sources of up-to-the-minute news about a destination on my itinerary is the electronic version of the local print media. Most newspapers and magazines these days have Web sites, from the *Daily Graphic* in Accra, Ghana to the *Post Courier* in Port Moresby, Papua New Guinea. A guidebook might tell you what a destination was like six months to a year ago, when the author completed his manuscript. But a local newspaper can tell you what's going on in a destination as recently as yesterday—and, increasingly, you can access news about events on the very day they occur.

The easiest way to track down a periodical in your intended destination, whether it be foreign or domestic, is to use any of several online media directories. Basically, these are indexes of newspapers and magazines with hot links that connect you directly to the periodical you choose.

What you'll glean from these local rags and mags is the sort of secondary information that, while not necessarily crucial, is bound to make you a better-informed traveler. Imagine stopping at a roadside diner in Bisbee, Arizona, during a vacation and being able to chat with the locals at the counter about how federal mining subsidies could help reopen some of the old copper mines nearby. All right, so maybe you don't think that's as cool as I do. But avoiding the appearance of a full-on tourist is important to me, and one of the ways I do that is by logging on to local e-papers and learning a little about the local goings-on wherever I'm headed.

So that's what this chapter is about, in essence. You got a problem with that?

The Author's Obligatory Anecdote

Not long ago I was invited to be the International Judge of the annual New Zealand Tourism Awards, sponsored by the New Zealand Tourism Board. I knew that a good part of that trip would involve schmoozing—making nice with tourism officials, hoteliers, restaurateurs, tour operators, and the like. I was pretty knowledgeable about the country's major geographical features, cities, and attractions, having read plenty of guidebooks (online and otherwise) and magazine articles in the weeks leading up to my departure. I figured that if I was going to be hobnobbing with the leaders of the country's tourism industry, I'd better not come across sounding like a know-nothing (that is, the real me).

But until I began checking into the local newspapers in Auckland and Queenstown, I didn't know that recently there had been a significant political contretemps involving one of the country's top tourism officials. Thanks to several Kiwi newspapers, I got the latest news of the incident and was able to sound well informed. Equally important, this knowledge helped me avoid putting my foot in my mouth by inadvertently bringing up a touchy subject.

The chances that you'll need to avoid sensitive political debates are not as remote as you might think. These days, travelers are increasingly interested in delving into all aspects of the local culture. In so doing, they take the same risks that anyone takes who brings up such vital yet controversial subjects as politics, religion, education, economics, and human rights, to name a few. Let's face it, you'd better be up-to-date when it comes to local news if you plan to talk about anything other than the weather. Come to think of it, the Web news outlets are also a pretty darn good way to keep up on the weather!

How to Use the Online Media Directories

You can do a search for individual newspapers via the search engines discussed in Chapter 1, but that can be a long and not always fruitful exercise. Another method of tracking down online papers is to use the search engines' hierarchy lists, starting on their homepages. Try Yahoo! (go to Newspapers under News and Media), AltaVista (go to International News under News &

Magazines under Media & Amusements), or Snap.com (go to Newspapers under News & Media). You can follow similar paths on most other search engines.

But why bother to do all that when someone else has already done the work for you—the online media directories? The following are a few of the directories I find useful to one degree or another. I've tried them all, and I think that each is worth keeping in your list of travel-related bookmarks.

NewsDirectory.com—8,200 Publications to Choose From

One easily navigable Web site for international-news junkies is NewsDirectory.com at *www.newsdirectory.com*. This comprehensive resource, which bills itself as "A Guide to English-Language Media Online," allows you to track down news sites from around the world in such categories as newspapers by country, magazines by topic or region, broadcast TV stations and networks, and United States news links by region or area code. NewsDirectory.com (formerly Ecola.com) has links to some 8,200 newspapers and magazines from 105 countries around the globe, and it has been serving Net users since 1995. For a step-by-step walkthrough of how to use NewsDirectory.com, see the section "Becoming a Better Traveler via Online News Media" later in this chapter.

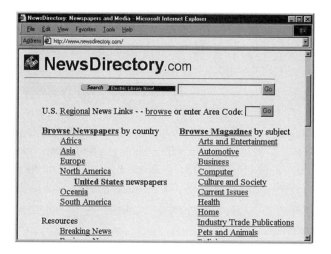

NewsDirectory.com's easy-to-navigate outline format enables you to choose where you want to go quickly.

By the way, I know it has publications from 105 foreign countries because I counted the links. However, I confess that I didn't count each of the 8,200 newspapers and magazines that the Webmasters claim are listed. You go ahead and count them if it makes you feel better. Write me a letter if they're wrong.

Internet Public Library—The Library That Never Closes

There are no overdue fines at the Internet Public Library, which calls itself the first "public library" of the Internet. Developed by trained librarians, the site has a noble mission—to serve the public by obtaining, organizing, and making available high-quality information resources. One of those resources is a compendium of international online newspapers from 132 nations, located at *www.ipl.org/reading/news/*. The design of the IPL Online Newspapers Collection is as simple as pie. Links to each of those 132 nations (yes, yes, I counted!) are listed under the world's continents and major regions. Open up your Web browser to the Internet Public Library and let's see how easy (or not) it is to use.

Try It Yourself ▼

1. From the Online Newspapers page, select something unusual. Scroll down to South Pacific, and then choose the link to Antarctica. (Way cool!)

2. The resulting page tells you that the *New South Polar Times* is indeed printed in English (which is great, since your conversational Antarctic is probably a bit rusty), that its URL is *205.174.118.254/nspt/home.htm*, and that it is published at the Amundsen-Scott Station. (Later you'll discover that sometimes it's also published at the Palmer Station, or aboard the research vessel *Laurence M. Gould*, or wherever the editor happens to be on any given day.)

3. Click the link for the newspaper to go to the NSPT's homepage, which is decorated with a photograph of a rather dreary igloo-shaped building that is apparently the home of the presumably lonely and homesick editor. Links take you to the local news, as well as to background sources on Antarctic

▲ research.

Granted, the NSPT is more of a news*letter* than a news*paper*, but when was the last time you read the current events—in *any* format—from the bottom-most chunk of land on earth? Besides, this periodical has solid roots—the first edition was written in 1901 by the crew of explorer Robert Scott's ship, *The Discovery*.

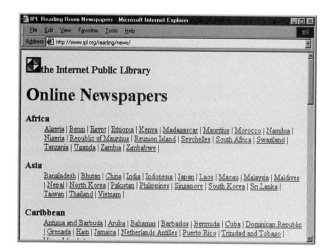

The Online Newspapers section is just one not-so-small part of the Internet Public Library.

The Largest Newspaper Index on the Web—But Who Has Time to Count?

In the category of online newspapers, who could fail to be impressed by the sheer bravado of a site that calls itself "The Largest Newspaper Index on the Web" at *www.concentric.net/~stevewt*? With newspapers from only 79 countries, though, one wonders how comprehensive this site might be. No doubt you'll like the site's pull-down menu of countries better than a simple list of links (as found in the Internet Public Library and NewsDirectory.com). The USA Newspapers section not only has a pull-down menu but also a clickable map. I keep this site bookmarked in case it holds an offbeat publication I can't find on any of the larger collections.

Some users like the Largest Newspaper Index's pull-down menus and clickable maps—but then, some people like pineapple on their pizza.

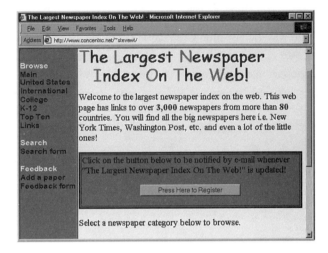

Newspapers Online—Using a Topical-Index Approach

Read All About It

More than 75 percent of daily newspapers on the Web have a circulation of less than 50,000.

Yet another index of Internet newspapers is Newspapers Online (*www.newspapers.com/*). This professional-looking site goes much further than the other newspaper compilations by including religious, business, and trade newspapers, college publications, online news services, and related books for sale, as well as the topic of interest to you—foreign newspapers. Disappointingly, Newspapers Online lists newspapers from only 64 countries. Moreover, many of the online newspapers listed are published only in their native languages—which is great if you speak Estonian, or Greek, or Spanish, or Hebrew, or… Still, Newspapers Online is one more resource to add to your ever-growing list of travel-related bookmarks.

Becoming a Better Traveler via Online News Media

Let's have a look at what you might expect from a typical English-language foreign newspaper. Use NewsDirectory.com as your source, and for your foreign newspaper choose—completely at random—the *Borneo Bulletin,* published in Bandar Seri Begawan, Borneo, in the sultanate of Brunei Darussalam. (Hey, you never know. You just might end up there one of these days! Stranger things have happened.)

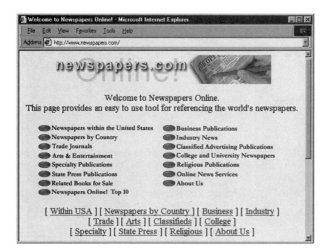

If you want to explore newspapers by topic, Newspapers Online may the best place to begin.

1. To find this newspaper using the NewsDirectory.com interface, simply select Asia under the Browse newspapers by country category.

2. You're taken to a new screen with a list of Asian countries. Although Sri Lanka and Bangladesh may tempt you with their exotic-sounding names, stick to the mission here and choose Brunei.

3. Your choice at this point is simple. The *Borneo Bulletin* is the only English-language newspaper listed under this rather small nation on the South China Sea. Click the link for that newspaper to electronically transport yourself to Brunei.

▼ Try It Yourself

▲

If you suppose that such foreign e-papers are fairly primitive, you're wrong. In the following figure, you see that the Web version of the *Bulletin* is as slick as a New Hampshire sidewalk in February. Choose from local news, national news, and sports items, read or send a letter to the editor, and learn more about the *Bulletin* itself, which became a daily paper in 1990 after 37 years as a weekly tabloid. If you read some of the news stories on August 27, 1999, you'd be delighted to learn that the Sultan of Pahang has taken a supermarket tour, there has been a call to revive the boat-making industry, and in sports, unfortunately, a Thai boxer is too strong for a Bruneian.

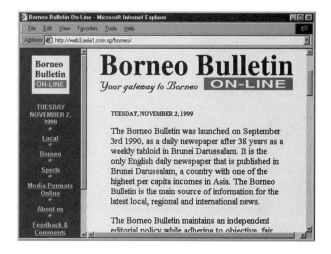

Crisp design, simple links, and stories about sultans in supermarkets—it could only be the Borneo Bulletin.

Will any of these stories make or break your trip to Brunei Darussalam? Of course not. Is it imperative that you be up to speed with local goings-on while you're on the go? Nah, not imperative, exactly. But will a basic knowledge of such news events enhance your trip? Absolutely, and I don't care whether your destination is Kennett, Missouri (see the Internet version of the *Daily Dunklin Democrat*), or Paramaribo, Suriname (see the English-language Web version of *De Ware Tijd*).

Can Web Newspapers Save Your Life? Mmmm, Maybe...

E-news Is Good News

Eighty-two percent of consumers who read online newspapers also read a print newspaper.

Much of the overseas news you'll read in this way will be either trivial or just plain irrelevant to your trip. However, there are plenty of times when the news from your planned destination arouses in you something more than amusement. You may even read news items that cause you to alter your plans, and wisely so.

When I was in college (before most of us had even heard of the Information Superhighway), I spent several months roaming around Europe, usually hitchhiking. I had been in Barcelona, trying to shake off the effects of a three-day drunk, and was thinking about hitting the highway through southern France to Italy. Sitting at a café table on Las Ramblas, near Barcelona's harbor, I picked up a local newspaper someone had left behind. It was in Spanish, of course, which I read only imperfectly. But I knew enough to recognize that some big news had hit northern Italy, literally.

According to the paper's lead story, a *seismo* (earthquake) had struck, there had been *mucho muerte* (much death), and the officials were now concerned about outbreaks of *colera* (cholera, obviously). All of which made me *miedo* (scared shoeless). Despite being a college student and therefore pretty stupid about most practical matters, I determined then and there that Morocco beckoned me with a more alluring hand than did good old Italy.

These days I could have gotten that information on a laptop with an Internet connection at my hotel, or on a borrowed computer at one of the Internet cafés springing up in the world's capitals. Sometimes, as in my decision to avoid Italy, the information you glean from foreign newspapers online is helpful in shaping your itinerary. At other times, it might prove essential to your very safety.

Take the case of the *Concord Times* (*www.oe-pages.com/ BIZ/Homebiz/concord/*), published in the city of Freeport in Sierra Leone, a small and troubled nation in West Africa. Imagine for a minute that you sell widgets for the XYZ Corporation in Peoria, and your boss, Mr. Dithers, has just charged into your office, awakened you from your nap, and said, "Johnson, we need you on the next plane to Sierra Leone because there's a widget shortage there. This is a big opportunity for someone like you, Johnson." If you were less intelligent than you really are, you might simply reserve an airline ticket to Freetown, book a hotel room, and go. But you're smarter than that, so you locate the *Concord Times* on the Internet and realize that doing so may have saved your life.

When you first log on, you note that, unlike the *Borneo Bulletin,* the *Times* has a rather… shall we say, rudimentary look. There's a silhouette drawing of some beachside palm trees in front of a full moon, a paragraph-long history of the young newspaper (founded in 1992), and a few paltry links, including the day's news stories. There's no design whatsoever to the staff-written articles—just black text on an off-white background. But you're unconcerned with the lack of bells and whistles because the stories themselves have reached out and grabbed you by the throat, something that no Java-enhanced Web design could ever do in the same way.

Online newspaper
pages don't come
any uglier than
this, but no mat-
ter. This is defi-
nitely the paper
you want to read
if you're traveling
to Sierra Leone.

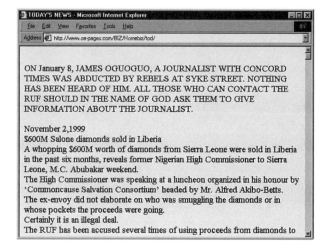

For instance: A notice at the top of the primary news page in a recent issue explains that one of the newspaper's journalists has been abducted by rebels on Syke Street. The notice goes on to say that anyone who can contact the rebels "should in the name of God ask them to give information about the journalist."

For instance: Heavy fighting broke out in the Makama section of the town of Makeni as rival groups of rebels battled each other over possession of some stray dogs. It turns out that starvation is rampant in Makeni. "This has forced civilians and rebels to eat all the livestock, so that dogs and cats are now the targets, with rebels getting the lion's share."

For instance: A member of Sierra Leone's parliament reportedly said that the citizens in the country's northern half are all rebels. Upon having said this in public, "the parliamentarian was nearly beaten up by the angry youths who were present at the scene."

Journalists being abducted by rebels! Citizens eating cats and dogs to fend off starvation! Members of parliament being chased through the streets by angry youths! Yikes! Not the sort of news you're apt to find in the *Peoria Journal Star*. In fact, not the sort of news that you're likely to read about even on the government-sponsored Sierra Leone on the Web at *www.sierra-leone.gov.sl/*.

Armed with details of these calamitous events in widgetless Sierra Leone, you march directly into Mr. Dithers's office and say with firmness and conviction, "My name isn't Johnson, you know." Oh, and don't forget to tell him what you think of the golden opportunity he offered you.

Wrapping It Up

John F. Kennedy lived in a small town in Westchester County, New York for a very brief time as a boy. When he became the nation's 35th chief executive, the newspaper in that small town ran an unlikely headline that said, "Local Man Elected President." News is important to everyone, but local news is the most important to us on a daily basis. Tidal waves in Japan are of concern, fiscal disasters in Germany hold some interest, but a news story that says your town is cutting back on garbage collection is going to make you sit up and pay attention.

For that very reason, it's helpful for you to read the local news in the destination you'll be visiting. In some cases, knowing the local happenings will help you enjoy your travels more. In other instances, such knowledge could actually help you in very real and practical ways. The best way to plug into the local news where you're going is to read the online version of the local newspaper.

Here's what you should have under your belt after reading this chapter:

- A knowledge of online media directories—what they are and how they work.

- An understanding of how online newspapers can make you a better person while traveling.

- A sence of the practical uses of online newspapers in planning your trip.

CHAPTER 6

Virtual Tourist Bureaus

This chapter, being an unusually polite chapter that does things the old-fashioned way, will introduce you to some of the more perfunctory yet often extremely useful government-backed tourism (and tourism-related) Web sites. Please be sure to smile and shake hands upon being introduced, because this chapter brooks no nonsense from mannerless readers.

Our first stop will be the foreign embassies and consulates on the Web; we'll examine three specific embassy-intensive Internet sites that will help link you to virtually every country on earth, saving you untold hours of agony in search-engine purgatory. (I would have used stronger language, but my editors have told me not to use the word "hell" if I can possibly help it, because this is not that kind of book.)

Next on our agenda are the national tourist offices on the Web. These are the electronic manifestations of the tourism-promotion agencies sponsored by nearly every country on the globe. You will learn why these sites are, if not always highly remarkable, at least usually highly *book*markable.

Finally, we'll touch on the more parochial aspect of this topic by examining what we can expect from the hundreds of state and local convention and visitor's bureaus found on the Internet. You'll understand why they offer abundant information but virtually no critical reviews—and why that ain't entirely bad.

What You'll Learn in This Chapter

► How to find and use foreign embassies and consulates on the Web.

► How national tourist offices differ from embassy and consulate sites, and why they are useful.

► How to navigate and find what you need: a case study of the British Tourist Authority's Web site.

► How to find useful information at state and local convention and visitor's bureaus.

Some Amusing Background Notes (No, This Section Is Not Optional)

Depending on when you last counted, there are anywhere from 193 to 207 sovereign nations in the world, and that's not even including Michael Jackson's Neverland. Almost all of those countries have an authorized governmental presence on the Internet—a ghostly presence in some cases, an annoying or useless presence in others, but a presence nonetheless. There may be a country without some sort of an official Web site; if so, I haven't found it yet.

But there are official Web sites and then there are…Official Web Sites. A country may have a strictly pro forma government site in its native language (snore), one developed by its mission to the U.N. (snore), or one created and monitored by an embassy or consulate (alarm clock starts to go off). What you don't particularly want, unless you're some species of international policy wonk, is a government-sponsored site that links you to the various branches of the bureaucracy (what the hey, let's sleep in this morning). The exception to that caveat, of course, is if one of those government branches has to do with tourism information (time to wake up!).

By the Way

The phrase "tourism information" is so broad as to be almost meaningless.

You need to figure out exactly what sort of "tourist information" you want before you decide which official government Web site is right for your needs. Do you want to know about visa requirements, opportunities for employment, and when the ambassador's next photo op is scheduled? Then an embassy or consulate site is what you need. Do you want travel recommendations along with a healthy dose of cultural information (national history, traditions, holidays)? If so, you'll want to look for a nation's official tourist office. For details on specific regions and cities, where you're likely to find more comprehensive lists of hotels, restaurants, area attractions, and calendars of events, your best bet will be the city- and regional-oriented convention and visitor's bureaus. Let's browse around some of these different types of official sites to see what we can expect from each.

Foreign Consulates and Embassies on the Web

We all know what an ambassador and an embassy are, but what's a consul? A consul is an official appointed by his or her government to live in a foreign country and represent his or her own country's commercial interests—sort of like an ambassador but without the attitude. The consulate is the consul's official premises, but, by extension, is used to mean the workings and responsibilities of the consul and his or her staff.

Most foreign nations have an embassy in Washington, D.C., and one or more consulates in the United States, especially in New York City, Chicago, and Los Angeles. Sometimes, when a country has more than one consulate in the United States, each of those consulates will have its own Web site.

Although the primary purpose of a foreign consulate is to represent its country's commercial interests; tourist information is a natural by-product of the consulate's mission. That's mainly because one function of foreign consulates is to provide visas (if required) to citizens of the host country. In other words, if you're an American citizen and you want a visa to visit India, you would apply to an Indian consulate based in the United States. (Turns out there are plenty of them, including locations in Chicago, New York, San Francisco, and Washington, D.C.)

A visa, used in conjunction with a passport, is simply an official endorsement allowing a traveler to enter a foreign country. Not every foreign country requires visas; some nations require them for tourists from certain countries but not from others. Those that do require visas have a specific procedure a potential visitor must follow.

For a nifty comparison of an embassy Web site and a consulate site, open your browser to the Embassy of Italy in Washington, D.C. at *www.italyemb.org* and, at the same time in a second window, open the Consulate General of Italy in San Francisco Web site at *www.italconsfrisco.org* (see the following figures). Let's see if we can get information from both sites on visas we might need to visit Italy.

By the Way

The quality, volume, and even accuracy of the information at consulate sites, despite the fact that they all claim to represent the same foreign country, can differ greatly from one to the next. An e-traveler would be well advised to do some comparison shopping to see which of the sites is the most useful.

By the Way

Try the Kingfisher brand of local beer once you get to New Delhi; it rocks.

For a further discussion of visas, see Chapter 20, "Online Info about Passports, Visas, and Customs."

The Embassy of Italy site is simple to understand and clearly designed...

...while the Italian Consulate of San Francisco site is...in Italian!

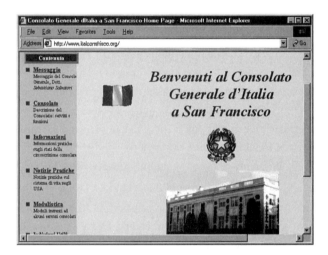

Try It Yourself ▼

1. Open two Web browser windows, and arrange them on your Desktop so you can see them both.

2. On the embassy site, click the icon that says Tips for Travelers. On the consulate site, which is apparently written completely in Italian (*mamma mia!*), click the lower-left link labeled English Information that will appear when you scroll down the screen.

3. On the embassy site, click Tourist Information, which takes you to a list of subtopics, where you can click Documents Required and then Visa Information. On the consulate site (now, thankfully, written in English!), follow the link for Entry Visa into Italy and then Tourist Visa for U.S. Citizens.

4. On the embassy site's visa information page, read the section on U.S. citizens, which says, in so many words, "Hey, Giancarlo, break out the Asti Spumante, 'cos you don't need a visa for visits of less than 90 days!" On the consulate's visa information page, you discover (gasp!) the exact same thing. ▲

Two different sites, same results—although it did take one extra click on the embassy site to reach the visa information. The point here is that there are numerous ways to access the same information. If you run into a roadblock in one direction, follow a different path.

If the consulate page doesn't have the details you want, try the embassy page, and vice versa.

Most online embassies and consulates also make at least a token gesture at providing basic travel information. But don't waste too much time on those generic tourism pages (unless they provide direct links to the country's official tourist board, which, as we will see later in this chapter, can prove exceedingly useful). Better you should limit your online time to a consulate's practical information on entry requirements.

You could do individual Web searches for the consulates of the countries you want to visit. Or you could look for Web sites that collect Internet links to the world's consulates. Or you could just read on and use the ones that I'm about to give you.

The Electronic Embassy—Inside-the-Beltway Chatter

The Electronic Embassy at *www.embassy.org,* shown in the next figure, calls itself "a resource of and for the Washington, D.C. foreign embassy community." As such, its emphasis is on fostering a kind of we're-all-in-this togetherness among the diplomats in the scores of embassies in the nation's capital.

Among the avenues you can follow on the site are erudite histories of some of the more notable buildings and monuments in the foreign embassy community; a compilation of diplo-quotes ("Peace, commerce, and honest friendship with all nations—entangling alliance with none." —Thomas Jefferson), which unfortunately, requires you to reload the page to get the next quote; bibliographies on such topics as diplomacy, espionage, and public policy; and a calendar of inside-the-Beltway events of interest to embassy staffers.

The Electronic Embassy makes you feel like one of the capital's embassy staffers while you track down links to consulate Web sites.

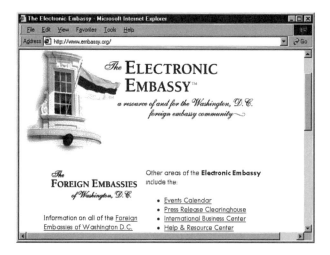

More germane to our purposes, the Electronic Embassy features an alphabetical list of 178 nations. By clicking a country name, you are taken to a fresh page that gives you the address, telephone, and fax numbers for the embassy, as well as (in most cases) a hot link to an informational government Web site sponsored by that country.

Whaddaya say? Let's give this baby a whirl. Somebody call out a country. What's that? Liechtenstein? Who said that? Throw that joker outta here. Come on, people, how about a serious country this time? Hmm? Mexico? Perfecto, hombre. Ready?

1. On the Electronic Embassy's home page, follow the Foreign Embassies of Washington, D.C. link. There you are presented with a quick alphabetical index, from which you choose the letter *M* and then Mexico.

2. At this point, the Electronic Embassy offers you several options, including links to the Embassy of Mexico in Washington, the consulates in New York City and Ottawa, Canada, and the Permanent Mission of Mexico to the United Nations. Follow the link to the embassy.

3. Arrive at the virtual embassy (please wipe the dust off your shoes), and, at your leisure, choose from the multiple links on the left side of the screen—everything from U.S.–Mexico Relationship to Mexico for Kids, along with pages devoted to travel.

4. You've earned a reward, so have a bottle of my favorite Mexican beer, Bohemia. If you want a Coke, ask the barman for a "Coca," as they call it south of the border.

▼ **Try It Yourself**

The Electronic Embassy's approach is not a perfect arrangement, though. The page given for information on the Embassy of the Republic of Zambia, for example, has a nice photograph of the embassy building, but no Web links. For the Embassy of the Democratic and Popular Republic of Algeria (try fitting *that* into the lyrics of a national anthem!), the only link on the page promises to take you to the Permanent Mission of Algeria to the United Nations—not the best place to get visa information. The Embassy of Austria page links you with the Austrian Press and Information Service in Washington, D.C. Too bad the links aren't more uniform in the kinds of agencies to which they refer the user. And yet, there's no denying that the Electronic Embassy's lists are one of the easiest ways to find out the location, phone, and fax of the major foreign embassies in Washington.

Embassy Web—More Info Than One Person Can Handle?

A site with a far larger database of original information and links is the Embassy Web (*www.embpage.org*). Actually, that's part of the problem from an e-traveler's viewpoint: There is so much information that one hardly knows where to begin. As with so many large Web sites, though, the best place to begin on the Embassy Web is the FAQ (see the following figure). There you'll learn that the site's goal is to compile links for as many embassies, consulates, trade missions, and national tourist offices from around the world as possible. We also learn the Webmasters' modus operandi in selecting links, which to my mind is the chief reason the site is worth bookmarking: The Embassy Web site limits its scope to official government Web sites (although occasionally, when an unofficial source is of unusually high quality, the Embassy Web will include it as a link, noting its unofficial status).

If you're not sure how the Embassy Web works or where to go once you do figure it out, stop in at the FAQ page first.

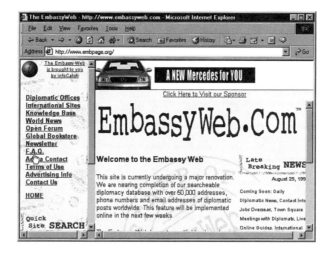

Open the Embassy Web so we can learn how to find out more about the site.

Try It Yourself ▼

1. From the home page, choose the F.A.Q. link at left, which takes us to the page devoted to frequently asked questions.

2. Select Question #5, which asks how the Embassy Web compiles its list of embassies.

3. Presto change-o, the answer arrives on our screen, telling us, in so many words, that the Embassy Web staff gets its information from embassy staffers and the major search engines.

The Embassy Web has many attributes worth exploring when you have free time (newsletters, forums, a bookstore), but the most useful section for e-travel planning is the one devoted to Diplomatic Offices. Diplomatic Web sites are listed according to the sponsoring agency's location; in other words, if you want to find foreign consulates based in the United States, you'd go to the United States section. There the site provides links to virtually every Web site sponsored by any foreign mission based in this country. For Argentina, as an example, the links include that country's embassy in Washington, its consulate in Chicago, and its Trade Promotion Center in New York. For Brazil, the site links to that country's Washington embassy, four consulates in various U.S. cities, and the Permanent Mission of Brazil to the United Nations in New York.

Drawback

The lists are far from complete. If an embassy or consulate does not have a Web site, it is not listed in the Embassy Web's database.

Embassy World—Simple and Cool Consular Searches

My favorite of the diplo-sites, because it has most of the consular links that a travel planner might need in an easy-to-navigate interface, is Embassy World (*www.embassyworld.com*).

At Embassy World, you can choose from among well-categorized lists (embassies and consulates of the world, embassies of other nations to the U.S.A., United States embassies worldwide, and United Nations Permanent Missions) or use the brilliantly simple search function, in which you first choose the guest country and then the host country. The following figure gives you an example.

When you apply that search function for, say, Great Britain as the guest and the United States as the host, you are directed to three Web sites, including the San Francisco-based consulate. You can also connect to Embassy World's index for Great Britain, where you can find links for U.K. embassies around the world.

Before you know it, you'll get carried away and start searching for weird combinations, like how many Mexican consulates might there be in Japan, and whether Switzerland has any trade missions in Zambia.

If you've ever wondered how many Bangladeshi consulates there are in Bolivia, Embassy World might hold the answer.

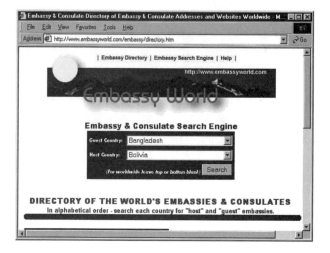

The most useful section of the entire site is the aforementioned index of embassies of other nations to the U.S.A. There you will be presented with the names of 226 sovereign nations, self-governing territories, and overseas dependencies, along with links to their U.S.–based embassies and consulates. It is a trove of consular contacts.

National Tourist Offices

It's no secret among the world's governments that tremendous potential revenues can result from tourism. While it's true that no two tourists are alike, there's one thing that every tourist does—spends money. Some countries have developed their tourism business to such a degree that tourism revenues have become the country's principal source of income.

What that means to you as a traveler is that most places in the world want you to come for a visit. And just as it's no secret that huge profits can come from tourism, the governments also know that their countries are in competition with one another for your travel dollars.

You want to lie on the beach? You will have every tropical island-nation on the globe, from Aruba to Zanzibar, urging you to spread your beach towel across their soft sands. Want to see Old World architecture, search for your family's roots, ski, trek, imbibe, partake, bike, hang-glide, relax, wine and dine, swim, become intoxicated, shop, get healthy, dance naked in the moonlight, hear an opera, party till dawn and sleep till noon, turn left at the fountain, stay in a castle, or any other possible vacation activity? There are scores of countries vying for those traveler's checks in your money belt.

How do they tempt you with their attractions? Increasingly via the World Wide Web, which is fast supplanting the old-fashioned tourist brochure. And the authorized agency that usually promotes a place's tourism efforts is its national tourist office. For a straightforward phone and address book of national tourist offices in the United States, visit *www.armchair.com/bureau/inttb.html*, sponsored by the Web site called Armchair World. But that's only a fallback resource to request travel information via snail mail, if for some reason you can't locate a specific country's tourism Web site.

National tourist office sites have some built-in drawbacks. Because they are funded from the public coffers, they have to be circumspect in their opinions and recommendations. Because they are quasi-governmental organizations, the information they supply can be subject to the shifting winds of politics. But as all-purpose sources of general travel information, there is nothing to beat a good national tourist office Web site.

Hard-to-Find Tourist-Office Links Sites

Web sites with comprehensive links to foreign tourist offices in the United States are few and far between, though. The Travel-On Web site has a list of addresses and phone numbers for about 100 such offices at *www.tvlon.com/International.html*, but only 41 of them are hyperlinked to Web sites.

Travel & Leisure's online magazine has about 60 links to national tourist offices at *www.pathfinder.com/travel/TL/links/tour.html*. You'll find a list of 190 countries, dependencies, and self-governing territories at *www.mbnet.mb.ca/lucas/travel*, the Tourism Offices Worldwide Directory. But it's hit or miss whether the country that you're researching will have a national tourist office Web site listed.

Unfortunate But True

Often, the best way to find a national tourist office is through Web search.

Tourist Offices—What's in a Name?

When searching for the all-important official tourist office in your chosen destination, remember that those organizations bill themselves in different ways. The following are some of the many names for those groups, which you can use in your searches and in identifying the most appropriate resulting matches. For foreign countries, the word "national" used with any of these phrases is another good indication that the site is officially sanctioned.

- Convention and Visitor's Bureau (sometimes shortened to ConVis or Con/Vis Bureau)
- Tourism (or Tourist) Bureau
- Convention (or Visitor's) Bureau
- Office of Tourism
- Tourist Board
- Discover [name of destination]
- Historic [name of destination]
- Tourist Authority
- Travel and Tourism Council

Once you've tracked down the Web site you want, what can you expect from it? The basics of any good tourist office site include information or links on weather, lodgings, history, attractions, public holidays, and transportation. A better-than-average site will also give you such extras as maps, FAQs, audio and video files, and age- or interest-appropriate attractions—and sometimes a lot more besides.

Case Study: British Tourist Authority Online

Consider one of the better national tourist office Web sites, the one at *www.usagateway.visitbritan.com/BTA-USA.htm* operated by the British Tourist Authority. Right off the bat you know you're in for a treat when you read the home page introduction: "Grab a cup of tea, turn off the telly, and get your mouse ready for a virtual tour of the UK!"

And what a tour it is! Under the Plan Your Trip section (shown in the following figure) are details on all the earlier-mentioned attributes of a good site (maps, lodgings, transportation, and so on), as well as information on tickets and tourist discount cards.

The Facts & FAQs pages include everything you may want to know about British currency, insurance, passport and visa requirements, taxes, and weather. Fun Stuff is just that—notes on "funky" festivals, British cuisine (is that an oxymoron?), and places to go when the sun goes down. Travel agents will want to visit the Travel Trade pages (an IATA number is required to enter that area), and media types can check out the Public Relations section.

About the only question the BTA site doesn't answer is why Prince Charles always has such bad haircuts. On second thought, we don't want to know.

Just point at the map and click your way to your favorite part of the U.K., courtesy of the British Tourist Authority.

Shall we try it? Need a cuppa tea first? Then let's carry on. We'll challenge the site to give us some fairly obscure information—not the name of the Cavern Club in Liverpool where the Beatles gained early fame; that would be too easy. Let's try for something harder, like the name of the street where the Cavern Club sits.

1. On the left of the home page, find the menu and click Fun Stuff.

2. Here we're offered a few choices, the most promising of which is Brit Pop. Go ahead, try it.

▼ **Try It Yourself**

3. Now we're getting closer! Here, under Brit Pop, we have a slew of choices, including The Beatles. Click it.

4. The third item on the Beatles page is something called Cavern City Tours, the description of which informs us that the Cavern Club is on (ta da!) Matthew Street.

State and Local Convention and Visitor's Bureaus

First off, don't confuse convention and visitor's bureaus with chambers of commerce. The latter are, for the most part, private organizations made up of local business owners to further their mutual commercial interests. Sure, those interests can, and probably do, include tourism, but any tourism promotion they underwrite and any tourist information they provide will likely be limited to members of the chamber.

A convention and visitor's bureau, on the other hand, is almost always sponsored by the state or local government. As such, it is charged with the responsibility of luring as many meeting groups and tourists as possible who will spend lots of money and pay lots of sales and hotel taxes. This, in turn, allows legislators to justify voting themselves big fat pay raises.

Remember

Con/vis sites are trying to sell you an image of their destination the way they'd *like* it to be, not necessarily how it really is.

Convention and visitor's bureaus implement their primary duty in many ways: They sponsor entertainment events, maintain information booths, produce and distribute tourist brochures, make travel and meeting arrangements for large groups, run a hotel referral service, handle inquiries from the media, and just about anything else that will help make a state, region, or city visitor-friendly. One of the major components of their jobs is to give individual tourists the information they need to plan a vacation. And, of course, one of the chief ways they do that nowadays is via the Internet.

Let's have a look inside a few of these con/vis sites to see how best we can use them in our plans. But before we do, a caveat: These bureaus are out to prove to you that their destination is fantabulous, better than any other destination imaginable, the best dang destination you could possibly go to on your vacation.

They are trying to sell you something—specifically, they are trying to sell you an image, the way they want their destination to appear to the public. You may buy that image or not; that's up to you. But don't expect critical reviews or even-handed descriptions of the attractions being touted on the con/vis Web sites. These are happy-face Internet pages, where the sun shines all day long, where handsome men and women lounge next to every swimming pool, where fruity drinks with tiny paper umbrellas are served on silver trays, and where your cares will melt away.

Pennsylvania Visitors Guide

The Pennsylvania Visitors Guide (*www.visit.state.pa.us*), to pick one site at random, is sponsored by the Commonwealth of Pennsylvania—which explains why there are so many pictures of the governor and his family.

You're presented with a clean, one might even say spare, home page featuring a charming Pennsylvania-in-a-nutshell, naïve-style illustration and eight paths to follow, from seasonal events and attractions-by-region to tour itineraries and activities for children.

In the Fresh Ideas section, you are invited to follow links to official information about the state's amusement parks, museums, festivals, and much more. The Kids' Club department is written for the under-12 set and covers the kinds of attractions that appeal to youngsters—everything from pretzel-factory tours to fun facts about Punxsutawney Phil, the famous groundhog (whom you can see in the following figure). If your personal passions lie in the direction of culture, history, the outdoors, sports, or shopping, the By Interests pages will provide you with lots of ideas about where to go in the Keystone State.

Then comes Reservations—literally and figuratively. Sad to say, but the presentation and information for the listed accommodations are lackluster. To a great extent, this is because no government-sponsored travel site wants to give the appearance of critiquing the hotels and resorts in its region. The problem is that, in trying to be even-handed, such official sites are either uninformative, boring, or both when it comes to lodging recommendations.

The Pennsylvania Visitors Guide helps you learn more than you ever wanted to know about the world's most famous groundhog, Punxsutawney Phil.

I Love New York

The official I Love New York site (*www.iloveny.state.ny.us*) handles the situation with equal delicacy but through a different approach—the Web editors simply provide accommodations links to hotel and resort booking agencies, as well as to local-based business groups and chambers of commerce. Some of these make up for in overwhelming praise what they lack in objectivity; others are as skittish as the state-run sites when it comes to giving full and revealing hotel recommendations.

Rather than recommending specific hotel and resorts, the I Love New York site links you to hotel chains and reservation agencies.

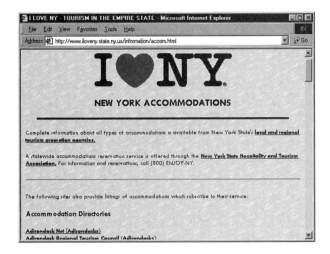

Where the con/vis sites shine is in their glowing praise of everything their state or region has to offer. They make you want to visit, to dream, to enter a vacation paradise where everything is just peachy, all the time. We know that the picture they're painting is phony, a ruse, a twenty-dollar strumpet in a hundred-dollar dress, but you know what? Sometimes it's nice to look at life like little Mary Sunshine!

Bottom Line

Don't visit con/vis sites for lodging recommendations—lists, yes, but not recommendations.

Semantic Antics

Convention and visitor's bureaus are valuable resources for travelers. The information they provide can help you decide whether their destinations are the right places for your vacation and, if so, make it easy for you to plan your trip. But sometimes, in their efforts to put a positive spin on some not-so-positive aspects of their region, they must resort to some creative terminology. For instance...

Turn-of-the-century atmosphere—The area's buildings haven't been repaired or painted in nearly a hundred years.

Nonstop nightlife—The street noise is so loud you can forget about getting any sleep.

Up-and-coming neighborhood—Don't walk there after dark.

Nearby attractions within an easy drive—Too bad they don't have any such attractions in their own city.

Affordable accommodations—Bathroom down the hall.

Local crafts—Well, local if you live in Taiwan.

Wrapping It Up

For those of you who didn't actually read this chapter yet, but who skipped to this section to get a summary of what you should have learned, shame on you. But since you're here, I'll go ahead and tell you anyway.

You should know by now

- The differences between foreign embassies and consulates, how to find them on the Web, and the sort of information they offer travelers.

- How to track down a country's official tourism site, usually sponsored by its national tourist office, and how to use that information in planning your own travels.

- To Appreciate the valuable information available on the Web from state and local convention and visitor's bureaus—but also to remember that they're trying to sell you the best image possible.

PART II

Planning a Vacation on the Internet

CHAPTER 7

Quiz: What's Your e-Travel Type?

Time for a little self-analysis. Have a look inside that mainframe taking up space between your ears, be honest with yourself, and describe your goals as a traveler. It's perfectly acceptable to say that all you want to do is lie on a beach somewhere and vegetate. Not everyone was meant to conquer Mount Everest during vacation. Or maybe you want to meet people from different cities and foreign lands. Or view the world's great artworks. Or add another country to your destination list. Or smuggle a salami out of Italy. Whatever the answer, the most important thing is to be truthful with yourself. Otherwise, you're just going to be miserable on your next holiday.

At times, you probably see yourself differently in your mind's eye than the world sees you. Perhaps you envision yourself as a dashing, world-weary foreign correspondent—even though your last five vacations involved amusement parks and lots of Raffi tapes to amuse the kids during the long car trips. Perhaps you've grown somewhat timid because you aren't fully mobile. You fear that your wheelchair or your advancing age will keep you down on the farm instead of seeing Paree. Maybe you want to go on a cruise, but you never travel without your Labrador retriever Leaky. These are all challenges, realities, issues to be addressed. But you can't address them until you understand what they are. What *you* are.

Ask yourself, "Why am I going to [wherever it is you're going]?" I've met many people in my travels who were visiting someplace because they thought it was where they *should* visit. This is a rather unintelligent method of choosing a vacation destination. In fact, choosing a destination based on the place itself will lead you to a far less enjoyable vacation than choosing a destination based on your personal interests.

What You'll Learn in This Chapter

- ▶ How to make a realistic appraisal of your travel needs, desires, and goals.
- ▶ How to determine your e-travel type by matching your self-appraisal with various Web sites.
- ▶ How to marry your travel ideals with your travel realities by using appropriate Internet content.

Let me explain. Besides doing shooters and playing beach volley-ball, what do you like to do? Do you like to paint and look at the work of other artists? Are you a born beach bum who wants nothing more than to bodysurf all day and do the shimmy-shimmy-shake-shake all night long with whoever you happen to meet at the singles-only luau? Are you an adventurer who likes to canoe, raft, kayak, dive, jump, bungee, ski, run, play, or anything else that works up a solid adrenaline rush? Then go with the flow, Moe. Think of what you like to do in your leisure time, and then find some great places where you can pursue your passions. Don't do so at the expense of everything else your destination may have to offer, but certainly milk that destination for all it's worth. Don't choose a place because you feel it's where you *should* go, or because it's fashionable, or for any other reason except one—it has what you want.

In this chapter you'll be prodded to assess what kind of traveler you are. If you're even halfway-intelligent, you'll learn how to put that self-realization to work for you.

10 Questions to Ask Yourself

If you know who you are as a traveler, all the information that follows in this book, all the tips and advice, will have some meaningful context. However, I won't suggest that you can be pigeon-holed as this type or that type of traveler. Each of us is unique. Especially you. Not only that, but we're constantly evolving, improving, growing. (Okay, not *all* of us, but you catch my drift.)

Remember

No matter what kind of traveler you are, there are probably dozens of Web sites that are just right for you.

The questions that follow don't lead to the sort of add-up-your-score-hey-you're-a-sex-fiend quiz you often find in *Cosmo*. Instead, they're designed to prompt your thought processes. You have to pick and choose which parts of the discussion are most appropriate for you personally. And as a bonus, in each answer I've listed a Web site that's designed to match the travel profile. Consider these Web sites a bonus, my gift to you, because you mean so much to me. You're like my children. You don't call, you don't write. No, no, don't bother yourself. I'll just sit here in the dark, by myself...

#1—Do You Plan for a Vacation Like It Was the D-Day Invasion?

Are you a planner, a nonplanner, or something in between? Are you a Type A, anal-retentive, ducks-in-a-row, currency-lined-up-in-your-wallet-according-to-denomination-and-of-course-all-bills-facing-the-same-direction sort of person? Or are you a can't-decide, road-less-taken, figure-it-out-when-you-get-there kind of traveler? Unless you're truly a candidate for psychotherapy, you probably have elements of both of these travel types with a tendency to lean more in one direction than the other. That's good. That's healthy. And no matter which way you lean, it's probably the right way for you (although you should try to stand up straighter, like your mother told you).

But a word of caution. If you're an uptight, by-the-book, hurry-up-we're-gonna-be-late person (in other words, like me), don't fight it. Go ahead and make your endless lists. Feel free to read and reread the tourist brochures to make sure you don't miss a thing. It's okay to do lengthy computations of the exchange rates before you finally swap your greenbacks for dirhams at the *bureau du change*. Don't fight who you are. Make the most of your normal inclinations in organizing your vacation. But at the same time, remember: You're only planning a vacation, for Pedro's sake, not Sherman's March.

On the other hand, you may be among those lucky people who would rather wander down the narrow lane than follow the well-marked highway, who does what feels right rather than what's on the day's itinerary, who doesn't know the meaning of the word "schedule" (but then, you don't know the meaning of a lot of words, so what's that prove?). If so, don't lose that explorer's spirit, that ability to shift directions when the opportunity presents itself. But do try to give yourself some structure, even if it's a simple list of the main things you hope to do in a given city or during your overall vacation. At the very least, if you decide not to do something on your list, at least you'll know what you're missing.

By the Way
Even if you're not an organized person, you can still make a simple to-do list to prepare for your travels.

If you feel that too much planning isn't enough, there's a travel checklist from the folks at Black Mountain Travel in Henderson, Nevada, at *www.blkmtntrvl.com/trvltips.html*.

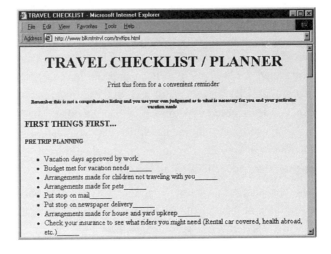

Worried that you forgot something, that you didn't plan enough? Just check your list against this one from Black Mountain Travel.

Try It Yourself ▼

1. Write up a comprehensive packing and pretrip to-do list.

2. Open your web browser to *www.blkmtntrvl.com/trvltips.html* and read through the items in that large list.

3. Compare your list with theirs. If you have even half the items on your list, you win the Field Commander of the Week award.

▲

#2—Are You a Newbie, a Novice, a Travel Beginner?

In the coming chapters, you'll learn about many sources of travel information. You'll deal with general research practices so you can use some basic strategies to find even more information. The question is whether you'll take advantage of all that information. Good guidebooks, printouts from the best Web sites, emailed details of airfare and hotel discounts—none of that will do you any good if you don't sit down and read the material.

Do you remember those students in high school and college who would eagerly go through their textbooks with a highlighter pen, marking line after line, page after page, until you wondered what good it was doing them, considering that virtually every word in the book was highlighted? Hmm? What'd you say? Oh, that was *you* doing that?! Sorry. Anyway, those students had the information they needed, but they didn't really pay attention. They figured that by virtue of having the textbook and splattering its pages with yellow ink, somehow the knowledge within those pages would transmigrate through the cosmos and discreetly enter their brains. Usually it didn't work. They didn't synthesize the information, didn't digest it, didn't take a brainwave version of Alka-Seltzer to help channel the informational gas welling up inside them.

The point is that you need to read, ask questions, look at pictures, get all the information you can get, and let it penetrate that thick skull of yours. Then, when you travel, you're much more likely to know what you're doing.

One of my favorite sites for just browsing around, trying to learn something new, is the travel section of a site called 100hot at *www.100hot.com/directory/lifestyles/travel.html*. Based on a proprietary measuring system, travel sites are listed in 100hot according to how popular they are with other Web users. The rankings change frequently, as do the sites listed, but you can always expect to find travel sites for a wide variety of interests—everything from the usual suspects (airline Web sites, online booking services, major hotel chains) to the seriously odd (Roadside America, which recently featured articles on haystack sculptures and a Jell-O museum).

Advice for Newbies

If you're new to e-travel, play around with as many travel sites as you can find—and have fun doing it.

Just close your eyes and choose a site, any site. It's bound to be popular if it's on the 100hot list.

Try It Yourself ▼

1. From the travel section home page of 100hot, review the list of the most popular sites.

2. Scroll down to the very bottom of the screen and click the 100hot Methodology link.

3. Convince yourself that the way 100hot creates its lists is statistically legitimate (or not). Then click the Back button and have fun playing with the various Web sites on the list.

#3—Are You a Fast-Paced, Get-Up-and-Go, If-It's-Tuesday-This-Must-Be-Belgium Traveler?

Fast or slow? Soft or hard? Go, go, go, or slow, slow, slow? There are few things worse for a traveler than a) not doing all that you had hoped for, and b) doing way too much. Like the Type A versus Type B debate, the question of pacing your vacation is one of balance. If you push too hard for one extreme or the other, you'll regret it. Maybe not now, maybe not tomorrow, but soon, and for the rest of your life.

In my experience, most travelers try to do too much. One correspondent recently sent me an email about a trip he was planning to the Southwest. He wanted to land in Albuquerque, head up to Taos to see the pueblo, proceed to the Colorado/New Mexico border for a ride on an antique railroad, and drive through the Zuñi Pueblo to buy some kachina dolls before continuing into Arizona, where he wanted to see the Grand Canyon, the red rock country around Sedona, the saguaro cactus preserve near Tucson, and the Old West town of Tombstone. His question was whether there were any other important destinations he should be sure not to miss during the course of his ten-day vacation.

That man was a plain fool, and there's nothing you or I can do for him. His wife will leave him, his kids will renounce his name, and his pet dog will pee on his leg, because he's going to drive them all mad with his obsessive need to see everything and do everything. It's insane to cram in so much.

Yet it's not much better to do the opposite—say, spending two hours at an art museum and then leaving the rest of the day for leisurely strolling. You can stroll back home in Sheboygan whenever you want, but you can't see the Eiffel Tower there. There's no Madame Tussaud's Wax Museum in Omaha. You're unlikely to run into anything resembling the Coliseum in Salt Lake City. The point being, you shouldn't waste an opportunity to see as much as you *reasonably* can... without running yourself ragged.

Do you insist on packing as many sights into one trip as you possibly can? Boy, do I have a Web site just for you. Check out the Round-the-World Travel Guide at *www.travel-library.com/rtw/html/faq.html*.

Remember
Planning to do more than you're able to do on your vacation is just as foolhardy as not planning enough.

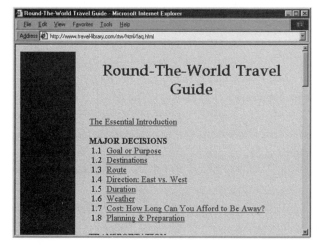

It ain't pretty, but for a no-nonsense description of how to circle the globe and see as much as possible on a single trip, go to the Round-the-World Travel Guide.

1. Open the page and pick out a topic that looks as if it has nothing to do with going around the world. Try Television Shows & Videos.

2. There's a list of shows with links, all of which have to do with traveling around the globe.

3. Choose the link to Going Places, a PBS program. Grow frightened at how quickly host James Avery changes costumes in a bit of home-page animation. Then return to the main page.

▼ **Try It Yourself**

4. There, read in earnest all that is involved in an around-the-world journey—a journey in which you truly can exercise your desire to "do it all."

#4—Do They Call You "Wild Man" (or "Jungle Jane")?

By the Way

For another information-packed adventure site, go to GORP at *www.gorp.com/.* (Is GORP an acronym, or some sort of edible trail mix?)

When you think of exotic adventure, you probably think of African safaris. Now, even though much of this book has to do with planning a trip on your own, I don't recommend trying to follow that route when it comes to safaris. On safari, you need the assistance of many people. Unless you usually hang out with bearers, porters, guides, animal experts, jeep drivers, and the like, you'd do better to put your yourself in the hands of a company that specializes in safari tours.

There are numerous firms that can do this, including Park East, Abercrombie & Kent, and private hotel "camps" like South Africa's Mala Mala Game Reserve, but one of the highest-rated safari specialists is Ker & Downey. The firm has its own fleet of light aircraft, which it uses on many of its safaris to whisk you from one area to the next, thus maximizing the amount of game-viewing time on the ground. It also houses guests at the various destinations in either deluxe tents or upscale lodges. You can visit its info-packed Web site at *www.kerdowney.com.* Log on and see what kind of animals you'll meet on one of the company's more unusual itineraries.

Hemingway wannabe's can book themselves a safari on the savanna through the respected firm of Ker & Downey.

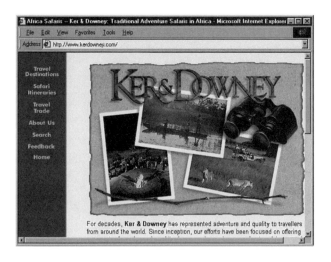

1. From the site's main page, click the Safari Itineraries link.

2. On the right side of the new page, choose whichever safari appeals to you most. Try Great Rivers of Life.

3. There's a description of the trip up the Zambezi River to Victoria Falls, during which you'll see lions, hyenas, and jackals (sounds a bit like some of the magazines I've worked for), as well as other game.

4. Return to the home page and drool over the many other African itineraries available.

▼ **Try It Yourself**

▲

#5—Do You Need a Lot of Pampering?

Have you ever slept in an irrigation ditch on a farm in France? How about in a flea-covered bed in a Mexican sporting house? Or in a California king-size bed in a five-star luxury resort? I've done all three. Trust me—choose the resort if you have any say in the matter. The point is that I can make myself comfortable in a Motel 6 or in a Ritz-Carlton. In certain ways and on certain days, I can enjoy a McDonald's double cheeseburger with the same gusto as when I rip into a medium-rare aged sirloin at the venerable (and expensive!) Keens Chophouse in Manhattan.

But I ain't everybody. Plenty of people I know would cringe at sleeping at a Motel 6, and would gag before they could wolf down a burger at Mickey D's. And still others find fancy hotels and haute cuisine restaurants to be very off-putting. They'd rather spend their mazuma on something other than highfalutin resorts and big-bucks eateries.

You'll need to establish what sort of comfort level you require. If you're a high-maintenance traveler, the sort who can't even enter a hotel room unless there are Crabtree & Evelyn amenities in the bathroom, it may make more sense to either stay fewer days so you can spend more money on the hotel room or wait until you've saved up enough money to travel in the style to which you're accustomed (or would like to be). Whether you prefer to travel like a baron or a backpacker, you need to deal with this question head-on before you proceed any further.

Be Honest with Yourself

Have you reached the 3F stage of travel—fat, forty, and first class? Don't fight reality. Maybe backpacking isn't for you.

I advise people never to spend more money than absolutely necessary, except on those things that are important to them. For instance, at one time I felt compelled to stay in fancier hotels because I figured I had reached a stage in my life where I was *supposed* to stay there. I wised up pretty soon, though, realizing that I'd much rather stay at a more moderately priced lodging. Any money that saved on the cheaper hotel could be spent on the things that carry some deep, existential meaning to me (Hawaiian shirts, pints of Guinness, full American breakfasts, Sinatra CDs... that sort of thing).

But if you're a luxury traveler, someone who can't get enough pampering (and is willing to pay for it!), there's a Web site just for you called SpaFinders at *www.spafinders.com/*.

Let's say you live in the Mid-Atlantic region of the country, and you want to find an expensive spa to soothe away your cares. Try to find what you need at the SpaFinders site.

If you need a spa that specializes in aromatherapy, massage, fitness training, or just lounging in a whirlpool, the SpaFinders Spa Source will help you find one.

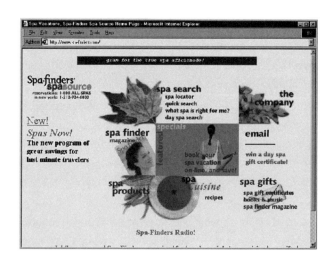

Try It Yourself ▼

1. Go to the home page and choose Spa Locator under Spa Search.

2. In the new window, click Mid-Atlantic in the Location pull-down menu, and then click on Search By Criteria.

3. Notice that the search results are listed in terms of cost, using dollar signs. Choose one of the expensive ones, the Greenbrier, in West Virginia.

4. You're taken to a page with a highly detailed description of the resort's spa facilities, along with some package vacation deals offered by SpaFinders.

#6—Do You Mainly Travel on Business?

Most of the people on the road or in the skies on any given day are poor slobs traveling for their masters. Look across the aisle there. She looks like a regional sales manager from Bend, Oregon, returning to her home office after a less-than-successful trip. The man in the seat next to you is on his way to a big meeting with clients in San Diego. Business travelers are all around us. Unfortunately for them, they usually don't have the time to look out the window and enjoy the scenery, or even to start up a friendly conversation with any of their fellow passengers. They have to get their notes in order, compile their figures, finish their sales projections, or any number of other business tasks.

Combining your work with travel has its own special problems. If you travel frequently for your job, you know what sort of difficulties business travelers face every day. What you may not know, however, is that there's a Web site just for you, called Biztravel.com at *newhome.biztravel.com/*.

Biztravel.com is the road warrior's friend, packed with great information, news, and advice from its many columnists. It also has a first-rate booking system aimed at business travelers. The site is worth a look at least once a week, if only to read the savvy, good-natured ranting of Joe Brancatelli, the lovable columnist who is upset about almost everything.

If you become a member, there are many benefits, including a system to track your frequent flyer miles and other planning services and discounts. But even for the casual visitor, there's plenty of information available without having to join. For instance, see if Biztravel.com can help you find out how to get into downtown Atlanta from the airport.

Did You Know...

...that 40 percent of all business travelers today are women? (Source: Travel Industry Association of America.)

You don't have to be a frequent business traveler to use Biztravel.com, but if you are, this site should be high on your list of bookmarks.

Try It Yourself ▼

1. On the right side of the Biztravel.com home page, select Atlanta from the pull-down menu in the United States section of City Information.

2. Read the Atlanta city profile, and then click on Executive Summary in the left-hand menu. Then click on Arriving By Air.

▲

3. Here you get an explanation of all your transportation options from the airport, including hotel courtesy vans, taxis, commercial shuttles, and the MARTA subway trains.

#7—What Special Needs Do You Have?

So you haven't yet been to Europe, something you've been dreaming about for most of your adult life. Now imagine that you're confined to a wheelchair, or you can't get around on your own very well because of your age, or you're blind, or deaf, or in some way other-abled. Maybe you don't have to imagine, because you deal with that reality every day. Does your dream have to go up in smoke? Of course not! Will traveling in Europe be easy for you? Probably not. There are realities to face, after all.

Most of us don't care how wide a bathroom door is. But if it's not at least 32 inches wide, many wheelchair users won't be able to get to the toilet. If you don't know that what they call the first floor in Europe is what Americans call the second floor, you may be in for real problems when you check into your hotel only to find out that there's no elevator and only a flight of stairs to your room.

Imagine what it must have been like traveling around the United States 25 or 30 years ago, before the Americans with Disabilities Act was introduced, and you'll get a sense of what Europe is like for the disabled traveler today. In other words, you can do it, but it won't necessarily be easy. But hey, you're looking for adventure, right?

Global Access: A Network for Disabled Travelers (*www.geocities. com/Paris/1502*) is a great resource for anyone in this situation. It's a regularly updated Web site that covers worldwide destinations, including Europe. You'll find useful first-person accounts of wheelchair travelers' experiences on the road, helpful tips, and a selection of disability-related travel links.

In a section called Trip Tips and Resources, the Web site addresses points like these:

- Most (but not all) hotel rooms are on the second floor (which in Europe is called the first floor) or higher. It's imperative that you or your travel agent contact the hotel directly to ensure accessibility to the room itself, through the doorway, and into the bathroom.

- If you use trains in Europe, don't expect accessible restrooms.

- If you can cope without a motorized chair, bring the narrowest, most lightweight chair you can. Global Access also suggests bringing along a narrowing device, a quarter-inch-thick chain with a clip that can be strung through the chair's wheels, pulled, and clipped tight to make the chair narrow enough to pass through a narrow door.

- Consider new tires for your wheelchair. Traditional air-filled inner tubes provide more shock resistance on the cobblestone streets of Europe.

Unfortunate Reminder

The Americans with Disabilities Act doesn't pertain to Europe.

This is great stuff! Who would even think about these things?! Other disabled travelers who have been there and who are willing to give you the benefit of their experience, that's who.

Rolling down the river... or across Europe... or wherever you want to go. Travelers with disabilities will find a community of interest at Global Access.

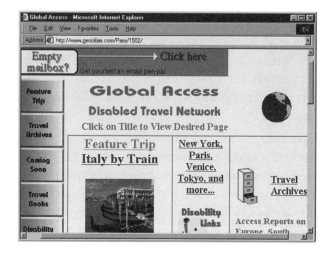

Try It Yourself ▼

1. You want to go to London, but you have to use a wheelchair. Log on to the Global Access site.

2. In the screen's upper-right corner is the section on Travel Archives, with access reports about destinations around the world. Follow that link.

3. On the new page, below the world map, find the link to London and follow it to a story written by a disabled Anglophile who knows the city—its joys and drawbacks—like a local.

4. Take note of all the access-related resources provided in the article.

▲

#8—Are You a Pet Person?

If you're one of those people who won't leave home without your pet hare, Harvey, your guinea pig, Gidget, or your tabby, Tina... Well, you may have lost your mind, but at least your heart is in the right place.

Traveling with a pet is difficult, to say the least. They aren't allowed in restaurants. Most hotels have a strict policy against them. Airlines make them fly in uncomfortable crates in the storage hold. Cruise ships won't take them at all, crated or not. But if you're a big-hearted person who loves animals, your Uncle Mark has a Web site just for you. It's called Taking Your Pet Along, from the American Veterinary Medical Association, at *www.avma.org/care4pets/safetrav.htm*. Let's put the site to the test and find out what advice it has for someone who is taking a dog on a camping trip by car.

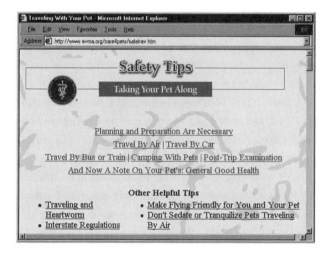

Whether you're flying with Fido or you're on a road trip with Rover, follow the safety tips from the American Veterinary Medical Association so your pet stays healthy on the road.

1. From the Safety Tips page, select the Travel By Car link.

2. Make note of the good advice here (especially the part about not letting your pooch stick his head out the window of a moving car!). Then return to the previous page.

3. Choose the Camping With Pets link.

4. Well, the advice here is kinda wimpy ("Keep your animal in sight and on a leash"), but at least it makes sense.

▼ **Try It Yourself**

▲

#9—Are You a Woman Who Prefers to Travel on Her Own?

I've been on the road by myself for as long as four months. I fly solo, baby, and Jack Daniels is my copilot. But that's me. As I mentioned, I'm an obsessive planner, and when I travel with someone else, I usually drive them up the wall with my lists, sightseeing strategies, and demanding schedules. I do travel with my family, of course, but I'm generally so busy keeping my kids from conking one another on the head with empty root beer cans and picking their noses in restaurants that I don't have time for my usual compulsive traveling style. Besides, my wife would throttle me in my sleep if I didn't control my otherwise obsessive behavior.

You may be entirely different. Maybe you really go for the idea of you and a pal on the road. Like Hope and Crosby. Martin and Lewis. Lemmon and Matthau. Thelma and Louise. Funk and Wagnall. You and your good bud rely on one another when necessary, and leave one another alone when called for. You work as a team, two halves of a traveling whole. (By the way, people talk about you two behind your back, in case you didn't know.) If that's your situation, you may be miserable traveling by yourself. So why bother? Find a traveling partner, even if you have to advertise in the personals. (Well, try not to be *that* pathetic about it. I'm sure you must have one or two friends, at least.)

Obvious But True

If you're a woman and you're planning to travel on your own, get advice from other women who have traveled on their own.

Then there are those travelers who want or need a group. Whether it's because of physical requirements, or for the perceived security of a group setting, or for whatever reason, thousands of travelers prefer to travel with... well, thousands of travelers. Go figure. I've been on such group excursions, and I could never shake the sense of being on a high school field trip but with better shoes. If you've never traveled, or you just simply like a group atmosphere and the convenience of a tour leader to smooth your way, don't try to pull an Indiana Jones solo act. Do what feels right—whether it's in a group, with one other person, or by yourself. (Ooh, that *does* sound kinky, *non*?)

But if you're a woman traveling alone, you have certain concerns that I don't. You want to know where the bottom-pinchers are lurking. You want to know the cultural status of women at your destination. You want to know how easy or difficult it will be for you to travel alone on your next trip.

That's why you should check out Journeywoman, the Premier Travel Resource for Women, at *www.journeywoman.com*. It's a site for women travelers, where women share tips about the various countries they've been to and the activities in which they've taken part. This site is lighthearted yet informative, well-rounded yet focused on women. You'll find details on destinations for solo travelers, as well as on organized trips for those times when you'd like to travel in a group. One of my favorite sections is the Women's Travel Tales, which has first-hand reports from women who have just returned from all over the globe.

Let's say you'd like to take a trip to a fundamentalist Arab country. That would call for some good advance information, don't you think? Open the Journeywoman site to see if you can find such info.

The Journeywoman site is a regular laff riot—but never short on practical, "gal-friendly" travel news.

1. From the topics at the bottom of the page, choose the Women's Travel Tales link.

2. The topics that show up on the new screen aren't comprehensive, but there is a link to something called She Dresses Smart in Iran.

3. In a detailed description of mandatory clothing laws that affect even foreign travelers, the writer points out that women must wear long boxy coats at all times, but that "you can wear whatever you want underneath, including jeans or black nylons." I guess you can leave your halter top at home on your next visit to Tehran.

#10—Are You a Family-Vacation Traveler?

Ah, the good old days, when the two of you would run away together for a romantic weekend at the drop of a chapeau. Remember those days when you could spend a week in San Francisco, or New Orleans, or Rome, go to any adult restaurant you wanted, and treat yourselves to a meal that would etch itself in your memory? Of course, that was in the days before you started using phrases like "adult restaurant."

Now you know why minivans are so popular. Now you understand why your father got so upset on your vacation car trips all those years ago. Now you see the humor in the sentence "'Shut up,' he explained." You're a parent. Therefore, you've given up any hope of doing what *you* want to do on vacation so that the children can do what *they* want to do. God bless you. You're a hero, a martyr, a schmuck… like me!

Don't Give Up Hope, Mom and Dad

At least one Web site, Travel & Leisure Family, proves that sophisticated travel and family travel can still go hand in hand.

Wouldn't it be nice to be able to travel as a family, to go somewhere that would appeal to the whole group but would still allow Mom and Dad to have a sense of sophistication? To actually feel that they're not giving up their travel desires for the kids' sakes, but rather sharing with their children the very finest of what travel has to offer?

Travel & Leisure Family, a spin-off of *Travel & Leisure* magazine at *www.pathfinder.com/travel/TL/family/index.html*, does all that and more. I know, because I was on the editorial team that started

T&L Family. And as a father who loves to travel, I can tell you that it's a magazine for every parent who has ever longed to travel in style even though they have kids in tow.

Stylish travel and family travel aren't mutually exclusive at T&L Family.

▼ **Try It Yourself**

1. Start at the home page of Travel & Leisure at *www. travelandleisure.com.*

2. Under the Related Sites link, choose T&L Family.

3. On the T&L Family home page, read the table of contents of the current issue so you can come back later and read the stories.

4. Return to the main Travel & Leisure home page and search for additional family-related stories using the page's search engine.

▲

Wrapping It Up

Perhaps none of the travel types discussed in this chapter accurately reflects the kind of traveler you are. In fact, I'd be surprised if anyone reading this book fell under just one of those travel types. Instead, most of us are a mix of travel types depending on what's happening in our lives at the time, where we're traveling, and who we're with.

If you take away anything from this chapter, I hope it's the sense that there's a Web site for everyone, a place where you can become part of a larger community of travelers who share your interests and values. This chapter should have given you some ideas of just what's out there and inspired you to look for more sites that are even better suited to your individual desires.

Here's what this chapter helped you do:

- Understand that you, as a traveler, are an individual, and yet you can join a community of like-minded individuals through the wealth and variety of travel content on the Internet.

- Categorize yourself, even in a broad, generic manner, in order to search out Web sites that are designed to appeal to your travel type.

- Challenge your idealized self-image by camparing who you think you are with reality-based travel sites geared toward others who share your travel point of view.

CHAPTER 8

Serendipitous Travels on the Hyperlink Trail

You're going to try something different in this chapter. You're going to be a risk-taker, an experimenter (don't inhale!), a pioneer. You're taking a ride on the train called Chance, just around the bend from a town named Fortune. Let's see if by following the twists and turns of the Information Superhighway, you can discover new avenues of travel information. And if you're lucky, maybe you'll find some fresh and intriguing ideas about where and how to travel.

Before you do anything else, figure out *why* you want to go somewhere. That will make all the difference in the world when you decide specifically *where* to go.

When in Doubt, Start with an Internet Directory

Submitted for your approval: A dry and dusty day in a dry and dusty town, a place so hot that even the mirrors sweat. On the horizon, a car appears. Behind the wheel, a sad and lonely man, a salesman, his sample case full of shoe polish, his heart full of pain. He's looking for direction, a place to hang his hat. He chose this state, this road, and he's narrowing down his options. He sees a sign up the road. The sign for a dry and dusty town. Population: Less than yesterday, more than tomorrow. This traveling salesman, this man in whose heart hope is a hollow thing, has entered a place beyond time and imagination. A place we call… the Internet Zone! Ta da daaaa, dud-duh-duh.

Find your own dry and dusty town by logging on to About.com at *www.about.com.*

What You'll Learn in This Chapter

▶ How to use an Internet directory as an idea bank for travel destinations.

▶ Why a search engine can get you to the heart of the matter faster than anything.

▶ How online reservations sites can be useful in planning your travels, even if you don't use them to make your reservations.

Try It Yourself ▼

1. Use the Internet directory rather than the search engine. Go to Travel (the last item listed under Channels).

2. Scroll down on the next page. Near the bottom, under Of Special Interest, go to Just About Twisted Travel. (Why not? Sounds curious.)

3. When I visited this page, there was a story about the Mile-High Club with a link to a site written by a former flight attendant for MGM Grand Air. Click on whatever twisted travel story appeals to you. Any ideas for *your* next vacation?

▲

If you've ever been curious about the Mile-High Club, you can get all the facts at About.com (or contact the author of this book directly for even more details).

By the Way

Tradition has it that the Mile-High Club was founded by a stunt pilot and his socialite passenger in 1916.

The goal here is to follow links on an Internet directory, starting with the most generic topic (travel) and working your way down to something much more specific (the Mile-High Club). If you're looking for travel ideas, let the Internet directories of the major search sites lead you to new and unexpected ideas. Come fly with me, baby!

A Search Engine Cuts to the Chase

Chapter 7 discussed the different kinds of travel types. Among them is the traveler who just can't wait for an answer, the one who has to get moving—now!—and isn't interested in spending time on research to bear out his inclinations. If that's you, forget the Internet directories. What you want is a search engine. You want to get to the point, and right away. So give it a shot and see what you come up with.

▼ **Try It Yourself**

1. Hop aboard the HotBot search site at *www.hotbot.com*. In the search engine form, next to Search Smarter, type the words "sun fun vacation" (unless you have a better idea!) and then click the Search button.

2. The results of such a search can change from one day to the next, but go to the result that appealed most to me: Surf and Sun Beach Vacation Guide at *www.surf-sun.com*.

3. Under the Main Menu, go to Beach Guide, then to Thailand, then to Phuket.

4. Notice that you've been transferred to a different Web site called *Phuket.com*. Click Phuket Photo Tour, then Beaches, then any of the thumbnailed photos for a full-size picture.

▲

If you haven't already begun packing your valise for a quick trip to Thailand, clearly you aren't a beach lover, because this place looks like it was made for beachcombers like me.

Go ahead and tell me this doesn't look attractive. I dare you. Thailand, islands, oooh.

What you should have learned from this exercise is not how to find out about great beaches in Thailand. No. Instead, you should have developed another skill to find out more about the kinds of vacations that appeal to you. Instead of typing "fun sun vacation" into your search, you could have entered "ski young nude" or "horses California gambling" or "hermaphrodites on parade" or any of a zillion and one other phrases.

Pronunciation Guide

No, Phuket is definitely *not* pronounced the way it looks. You pronounce it *poo-KET*.

Online Reservations Sites

The online reservations sites, which are covered in the "Major Online Booking Engines" section of Chapter 12, are another rich source of answers to the question "Where should I go on vacation?" Don't feel like you have to use these sites to actually make your reservations (although I'm sure they would love you to do just that). Instead, take advantage of all their free information about international activities and destinations.

Let's pull one out of the hat. Oh, whaddaya say? How 'bout Travelocity at *www.travelocity.com*? Log on and let's see what you come up with.

Try It Yourself ▼

1. From the top of the Travelocity home page, go to Destination Guide.

2. On the next screen is a map of the world's countries. Choose something exotic. Go to Indian Subcontinent, and then click Sri Lanka—or, as I like to think of it, the corn on the toe of India. (Perhaps you don't want to think of it that way, which is understandable. Click it anyway.)

3. Read the brief overview of the country, as co-opted from the Lonely Planet guidebook series. (I can also tell you from personal experience that the most exotic place you will ever go is the Temple of the Tooth in Kandy, in the Central Highlands of Sri Lanka.)

▲

Exotic Advice

You can make any destination sound more exotic by preceding its name with the phrase "the central highlands of...", as in "I just got back from the central highlands of New Jersey" or "We're on our way to spend a week in the central highlands of Omaha."

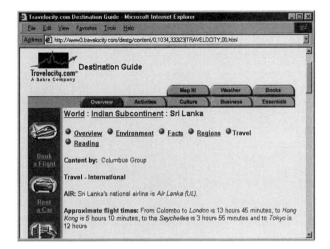

The information
may not be beau-
tifully presented,
but for an easily
assimilated precis
of Sri Lanka, have
a look at
Travelocity's site.

What have you learned from this? That there are online reservations sites with travel information? No, you already knew that.
That the Temple of the Tooth in Kandy is exotic? Of course not—
you could as easily have selected some other country in your
serendipitous search. The key thing to remember from this section
is that each of the major online reservations sites has a whole
lotta shakin' goin' on—destination guides, firsthand reports, news
from the travel world, and information that can affect your travel
decisions.

Wrapping It Up

If only one point makes its way out of the cosmos and filters its
way through your brain, I hope it would be that the world is your
erster, as my father-in-law would say.

So if nothing else, in this chapter you've learned that...

- Just playing around on the Web's travel pages can generate
  new ideas for your own vacations.

- Internet directories, search engines, and online reservations
  sites can all be used for serendipitous surfing—which is
  especially useful when you don't know what you want to
  find.

- My father-in-law pronounces oyster as *erster*.

CHAPTER 9

Using Web Sites for Specific Countries and Cities

You'll surely recall reading the elegant and sophisticated Chapter 6, which discussed virtual tourist bureaus—things like online convention and visitor's bureaus, state-run tourism sites, and the like. Most of them are pretty good sources of information, but as you learned, they're on a mission to entice you. They play down the negative and, as the song says, accentuate the positive. One of the truths of travel, though, is that no place is perfect. Crime lurks around dark corners. Roving bands of terrorists prepare their next attack. Policemen here or there are corrupt. Taxi drivers in that other place will rob you. As much as you'd prefer not to think about it, horrible things sometimes lie in wait... Out There. Whether they happen to you is, to a great extent, up to you. Like the Boy Scouts do, be prepared. Forewarned is forearmed and all that.

My primary source for that kind of information, available for virtually every destination on earth, is the U.S. State Department. In this chapter you'll find out how to access the State Department's travel-warning site. You'll also have a look at information from another part of the U.S. government, and therefore also underwritten by the American taxpayer: the Central Intelligence Agency. (Hey folks, you paid for this stuff, you might as well use it!)

You'll then look at other noncommercial Web sites that may lead you to quirky and highly personal information about specific destinations. And finally, rounding out this chapter, you'll poke around a few sites where you can access affinity groups—people who share a passion for a specific place or vacation activity.

What You'll Learn in This Chapter

▶ How to mine the destination-based resources of the U.S. State Department's travel-warnings site.

▶ How the CIA can make you a better-informed traveler.

▶ What to look for in noncommercial destination Web sites.

▶ Finding travel affinity groups online.

State Department Advisories and the CIA World Factbook

Among savvy travel editors, the most commonly used Internet address is probably *travel.state.gov/travel_warnings.html*, otherwise known as the State Department Travel Warnings & Consular Information Sheets. Whenever a terrorist incident occurs, when crime is particularly egregious, or when war breaks out, the State Department posts the latest status reports, with an emphasis on how Americans abroad might be affected. No travel editor worth his carryons would consider publishing a story about a place without first looking it up in the Travel Warnings. Nor should you, as a savvy traveler, decide to go overseas without first checking the State Department site.

By the Way

Some detractors claim that travel warnings issued by the State Department are sometimes motivated more by politics than by actual conditions.

The site contains a list of every country on earth. The descriptions of those countries come in three categories: Travel Warnings, Public Announcements, and Consular Information Sheets. Every country has a Consular Information Sheet. Only those countries with dangerous (or potentially dangerous) conditions receive announcements or warnings.

Consular Information Sheets are the mainstays of this site. They provide overviews of a destination's current status regarding customs and immigration, medical facilities, transportation, crime, currency matters, and, in countries where war or terrorism is present, a section called Areas of Instability. You can imagine that if a country you plan to visit has such an area of instability, you'd do well to know where it is so you could avoid it.

The State Department also issues Public Announcements from time to time when a country has a "perceived threat" of terrorism, natural disaster, or some other short-term potential danger to traveling Americans.

Travel Warnings, the most serious of the three categories, are posted when the State Department believes, "based on all relevant information," that Americans should avoid traveling to a particular country.

Clicking the names of individual countries takes you to their Consular Information Sheets. Some countries have Travel Warnings or Public Announcements as well.

1. Log on to the Travel Warnings and Consular Information Sheets at *travel.state.gov/travel_warnings.html*. (There is no *www* in the Web address.) As you scroll down the page, note that you can either use the alphabetical shortcuts to a specific country or continue scrolling to see each listed country.

2. Go to Bolivia and skim over the kinds of information offered—a brief description of the country, entry and departure requirements, customs regulations, medical information, high-altitude health risks (La Paz, the highest capital of any nation on earth, is more than 12,000 feet above sea level!), safety and security, crime information, and other legal issues.

3. Go back to the previous page, choose one of the Public Announcements, and read it. Go back one more time and do the same for one of the Travel Warnings.

The information you find through this service can prove to be invaluable. If nothing else, it will at least confirm information that you have learned elsewhere.

Another good source of government information about specific countries, although not quite as timely as the facts found in the State Department site, is the CIA World Factbook at *www.odci.gov/cia/publications/factbook/index.html*. Only a policy

▼ **Try It Yourself**

▲

Bottom Line

You'll find information about every country—from its economic statistics to curious facts about the locals—in the CIA World Factbook, which was declassified in 1971 and has been updated annually for the public ever since.

wonk would be interested in reading the entire history of the Factbook, but suffice it to say it had its genesis in World War II when Wild Bill Donovan, chief spook of the Office of Strategic Services or OSS (which begat the CIA), began searching for a way to assemble all the tidbits of intelligence assembled by military spies. The Factbook was a classified document until 1971 but has been made available to the public every year since then, along with a collection of maps.

Each entry in the CIA World Factbook, as with this one on Thailand, begins with a map and a picture of the country's national flag.

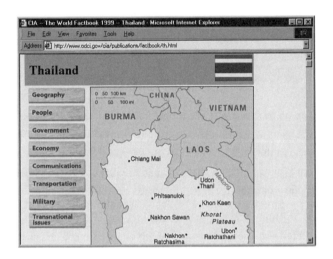

Did You Know?

President Harry Truman created the Central Intelligence Agency when he signed the National Security Act on September 18, 1947.

The key component of the Factbook is its country descriptions. Written much in the manner of a textbook (as opposed to the lively, persuasive, fun-lovin' style you've come to know and adulate in the famous *Sams Teach Yourself e-Travel Today*), with oodles of statistics, the descriptions begin with a brief introductory overview and then go into quite some detail about a nation's geography, people, government, economy, communications and transportation systems, and military.

Much of this information isn't germane to the average traveler, but then again, much of it is. For example, you may not care to know that Pakistan's industrial production growth rate is 2 percent. But you probably should be aware that although English is the official language, it is spoken by less than 10 percent of the population. Planning a trip to Sri Lanka? Well, you could proba-bly live your whole life without needing to know that its external debt is $8.8 billion, but only a fool would ignore the "occasional cyclones and tornadoes."

Pick and choose the information you want from the CIA World Factbook. You may walk away with the perfect nugget of knowl-edge that turns your trip from tragedy to triumph.

Noncommercial, Nongovernment City and Country Sites

The French island of Corsica is wild and mountainous, with rocky shores—the kind of place where you would expect to find lots of cork and cheese, two of the island's chief products. I learned this from a Corsica-devoted Web site that, sadly, no longer exists. This site was a work of the heart, with no advertising, no subscriptions, no e-commerce of any sort. It was a love letter to Corsica, exist-ing for no other purpose than to share the island's beauty with the world via the Internet.

It was not a perfect site, however. Ham-fistedly translated from French into English, the quasi-poetic descriptions of the villages, beaches, and mountains enchanted me with their incomprehensi-bility. One passage in particular so perplexed and delighted me that I copied it down for posterity: "Face to Ajaccio as to invite its inhabitants to come from the very summertime to frequent its long and beautiful beaches, Porticcio at the foot of the rock which dominates it, offers the swimming and the water activities lovers all the ressources (sic) whose they can dream of." Not unlike Symbolist poetry, or perhaps a shopping list written under the influence of hallucinogens.

There are literally thousands of similar sites on the Web devoted to almost any destination you care to name, from the big boys like Belgium and Boston to the backwaters of Botany Bay and Bahía Blanca. Let's see if you can't find one such site. Any suggestions for destinations? Costa Rica? Okay, Costa Rica it is!

Sad But True

Many private Web sites devoted to specific destina-tions are under-funded, one-man operations, and thus they go out of existence with dreadful frequency. But for every site that goes offline, you can bet that two or three more will take its place.

1. Go to Yahoo! at *www.yahoo.com*. Remember the difference between a search site's search engine and its Internet directory from Chapter 1? Use the directory. Go to Travel under Recreation and Sports, and on the next page go to Travelogues.

2. Next, follow the link to By Country and Region, then to Central America, then to Costa Rica.

3. Here you're presented with a small but intriguing selection of Web sites. Go to Costa Rica Adventure, described as "Erika, Irene and Sarah go whitewater rafting, learn about sloths, and run down iguanas in this adventure of a lifetime."

4. Read through portions of the site—an unvarnished, amusing account of three women who careened around the country for 10 days.

I don't recommend that you use these sorts of personal home pages as the basis for your vacation planning. But my oh my, do you get opinions! In Costa Rica Adventure, the women describe the sights you might see driving down the highway: "We saw absolutely gorgeous haciendas with gates and gardens right next to old crappy houses made out of rusty corrugated metal." This is not the local chamber of commerce speaking, people. This is straight-from-the-shoulder reportage by the folks who know, the travelers who have been there and have returned to share their experiences with you.

What if you don't care to use Yahoo!? HotBot will lead you to such traveler's tales when you go from Travel and Recreation to Travel to Personal Travelogues. At Lycos, you'll find what you need by bouncing from Recreation to Travel to Personal Travelogues. You get the idea. You can do the same thing at most search sites by using their Internet directories, although you'll probably be disappointed by how difficult it can be to find the travelogue category on some sites.

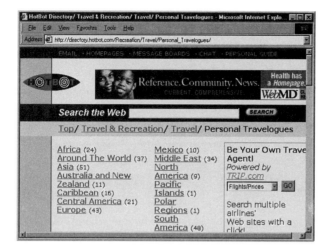

HotBot, like other search sites, will lead you to personal travelogues via its Internet directory. Note the hierarchy (that is, the directory path you followed) directly below the search engine form.

Affinity Groups—Chats and Message Boards

If you really have a passion for a particular destination, if you want to hang with people who eat, sleep, and dream a certain city or island or country, you'll want to investigate the various travel sites devoted to chats and message boards.

There are two kinds of chat sites—the kind where you can log on and talk with anyone else who happens to be logged on, and the organized chats sponsored by certain Web sites on a scheduled basis. The former are hugely popular at America Online, where you can even create your own chat rooms on the most narrowly focused topic (Very Short and Thin Women Looking to Talk with Very Tall and Fat Men About Vegetarianism in the Gobi Desert). If you have any of the latest Web browsers, you can also access such live chat rooms on the World Wide Web. Do a search for "travel chat rooms" and you will get links to such narrowly focused chat groups as New England for Visitors, Sedona (Arizona) Online Chat, MaineChat.com, Cruises Chat, and Disney Chat, among many others.

Scheduled chats generally feature a moderator, along with an expert who takes queries from an online audience. For instance, *Travel & Leisure* magazine (*www.travelandleisure.com*), where

I'm the managing editor, sponsors hour-long chats every Tuesday afternoon with travel writers and editors, as well as other industry insiders. Many of the online guidebooks have their writers attend chats so they can answer questions in real-time. Look up any of your favorite travel sites and browse around the home page to see if any mention is made of chat schedules.

At Travel & Leisure's *Web site, online chats are archived so visitors who were unable to attend the event can read the transcripts later.*

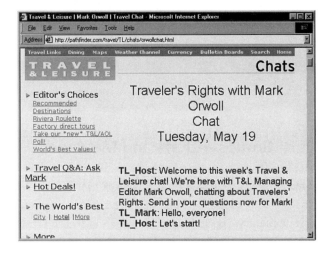

In the meantime, if you want to trade news, opinions, and travel gossip with others who share your interests, the best thing you can do is head for the message boards of the major travel sites. Again, there are message boards on an array of travel topics at magazines like *Travel & Leisure* and online guidebook publishers like Frommer and Fielding, as well as booking sites like Trip.com (in its TripTalk section). You can also do a search for "travel message board" on the search engines.

Let's have a look at one such collection of travel-related message boards, Bwana Zulia's Kenya Travel Guide at *www.bwanazulia.com/kenya/*.

Try It Yourself ▼

1. From the home page, follow the link to Message Boards in the left margin.

2. On the next page, you're presented with four different message boards, each focusing on a different topic having to do with Kenya. Go to General Questions on Kenya.

3. To read a posted message, just click on its name. Look for one called Mnarani Club Kilifi and click it. After reading the message, scroll down to see if there were any follow-up responses. In this case, there is one. Click it, read it, and then go back to the General Questions page. Note that at the bottom of each message, you can post a follow-up of your own by typing in your message and clicking the Submit follow-up button.

4. To post a message of your own (as opposed to a follow-up), go to Post Message at the top of the messages list. Peruse the requested information, but don't fill in the boxes (unless you really want to be part of the Bwana Zulia Internet family!).

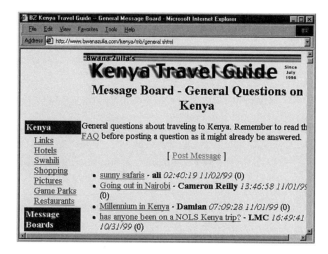

Bwana Zulia's Kenya Travel Guide has several message boards, including this one for general questions and answers aimed at first-timers to the country.

Bwana Zulia's message boards are typical of other boards on the Web, although many sites have a dozen or more different boards on various travel-related topics. Message boards, especially those that are very active, are a good way to get answers to your travel questions. A word of advice: Be sure to review the message board and its parent Web site before you post a message of your own. If you're on a message board for experts and you post a question that is perceived as too simplistic, you may end up getting a few flames for your efforts.

By the Way

In Kenya, the language known as "kitchen Swahili" has no future tense or past tense.

Wrapping It Up

I'm not a huge fan of the CIA, but it's nice to know that when they're not out toppling unfriendly governments, they're putting together useful travel information that you can use on your next vacation. And it's reassuring to know that if the U.S. government is advising Americans to stay away from a particular place, the State Department will tell you about it on its Travel Warnings site. Highly idiosyncratic sites, such as the personal travelogues posted around the Web (found easily on many search sites), may not be the best places to get hard facts on a region, but they are often lively and outspoken in their reviews of world destinations. And finally, there are online chats where like-minded travelers can get together and share their thoughts with experts and with one another, and there are message boards sponsored by many of the large travel sites.

Here are a few things you know now that you may not have known before:

- The State Department's Travel Warnings site is one of the best travel news spots on the Web.

- The CIA has taken much of the material it has gleaned over the years about foreign countries and compiled it into the online CIA World Factbook.

- Some of the funniest, most in-your-face, and most honest appraisals of travel destinations can be found in the personal travelogues that individuals have posted on the Web.

CHAPTER 10

Internet Resources for Seasonal Vacation Activities

Where are you going next winter? What about next summer? What about next spring and fall? It's funny how much of our vacation planning is geared toward the seasons. And why not? It makes sense. If you want to go skiing in July, it'll cost you a lot more (you'll have to fly to South America or New Zealand) than if you behaved like a rational human being and just went to Steamboat in January instead. Nothing beats a car trip in the fall—the weather is nice enough to keep the windows open, the foliage is ablaze on the hillsides, and a hint of woodsmoke fills the air.

Whether you're off to the seashore next summer or looking for a place to party during the upcoming spring break, you can always figure that your travel plans will be affected, if not outright dictated, by the seasons. But how can you put the World Wide Web to good use in planning your seasonal travels? The answer to that question is as simple as typing the name of the season, followed by the word "travel," into a search engine form and clicking Search.

Winter—Bringing New Meaning to the Words "Ouch, It's So Bloody Cold I Can't Stand It!"

Whether you want to strap on your skis or start shredding the mountain on your snowboard, let's hit the powder this winter. (Of course, the only way I hit the powder is flat on my ass.)

What You'll Learn in This Chapter

▶ How to compare seemingly similar Web sites covering similar topics and decide which one is more appropriate for your needs.

▶ How to take something you've learned from an earlier chapter and figure out how to apply it to your real travel needs.

▶ Why going straight to the source is usually your quickest and most direct way to get travel information.

▶ How to use two completely different Web sites in conjunction to plan your next vacation.

Oh, but wait. Let's say that you have kids now, and they don't know how to schuss. (Although one of them schussed all over the back seat on the way to your skiing vacation, and it still smells bad.) Where to go to teach those tykes how to slip down the slopes? Head for Utah. More specifically, head for the Ski Utah Web site, the official site of the Utah Ski & Snowboard Association, at *www.skiutah.com*.

At the Alta Ski Area, the Children's Ski Adventures program for ages 4-12 takes kids no matter how much or how little skiing they've done before. Before you know it, they'll be skiing along nature trails, taking part in a race day, and topping it off with an ice cream party on Friday. Deer Valley Resort has several ski-school programs for kids from 3 to 12. Participants are placed according to ability. There are races (in which everyone wins), something called a Snow Safari Terrain Garden, and an Adventure Pin on which the kids place a sticker for each new adventure they take part in. Snowbird Ski Resort likes to claim that it has the best value for skiing families, thanks to its "kids ski free" program. At the Ski Utah site, you'll also find info on lodging, dining, and activities.

Looking for something a little more generic, with ski destinations across the country? Then give Ski Guide a whirl at *www.ski-guide.com*. This site is a skier's delight, with more than 570 American and Canadian resorts described and mapped to help you make the best decision possible. What's it like to use this site to plan a winter trip? You're about to find out. But first, set some parameters for yourself. For instance, what say you try to find a nice resort somewhere in the Rocky Mountains? Of course you'll want good skiing, but also snowboarding. One of you is a beginner, and the other is an intermediate-level skier. Ready? Sounds good to me!

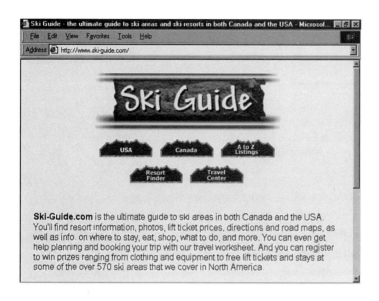

The *Ski Guide Resort Finder* will help you choose a lodge based on several guidelines, including destination. Ever wonder how good the skiing is down south... say, in Alabama?

1. From the home page at *www.ski-guide.com/*, click Resort Finder.

▼ **Try It Yourself**

2. On the next page you're asked for your preferences. Fill in the boxes using your agreed-upon guidelines, and then click Submit Query.

3. On the next page you'll get a long list of results. Did you get Buttermilk Mountain on your list? If so, click it. If not... you lose!

4. Read the description of the ski terrain, and then click Lodging in the left margin. Browse the various properties and note that if you wanted to book one of them, you could do so via the hotel's Web site or via email.

5. In the left margin, note all the other material you can obtain about the ski area—everything from shopping and dining options to a map of the ski trails.

Compare the depth and variety of information on this site with what you'll find at SkiResorts.com. Log on to the site at *www.skiresorts.com/* and poke around. It has features on ski resorts in Europe and elsewhere, not just North America. Also, you can book trips through the site or directly with the individual resorts. It has lots of news about skiing and resorts, special travel deals, and chat rooms for ski-heads.

Lot of Lodges

At SkiResorts.com, you can access information on more than 700 winter resorts around the world.

But which site is easier to use, SkiResorts.com or Ski Guide? Which one has a friendlier flavor? Do you feel more comfortable with one than with the other? "Flash and dash" sometimes goes hand-in-hand with solid content and an efficient interface, but sometimes simple and straightforward Web sites are easier to negotiate and just as informative as their flashier cousins. These are the sorts of considerations you should make when you compare Web sites on similar topics—whether it's looking at two ski sites side-by-side or two online reservations sites.

But look… I see some green buds on the trees. I hear a robin singing. I'm getting hay fever. Ah-choo! Ah-choo!

Spring Flings

When the sap starts to rise in spring, college students across America begin searching for that one perfect place to party down—where the party goes on till dawn, the cops are cool, the opposite sex is drop-dead gorgeous, and the hotels don't mind if you stick 20 people in a room to save money. Yes, folks, this is why American parents slave their lives away, saving their hard-earned salaries to spend on tuition—so their kids can boogie down and throw up for a week at spring break.

As you probably know, Fort Lauderdale used to be America's spring break capital. But since the city fathers clamped down a few years back, the scene has shifted. Cancun, Mexico, is huge with the spring break crowd, and so are Miami Beach and New Orleans. But Daytona Beach, Florida, has probably taken the title of Spring Break Champeen. Using the tools you've learned so far, how would you find out more about that college holiday in that particular city? I'd suggest that you think back to the virtual tourist bureaus you learned about in Chapter 6. What do you suppose the Daytona Beach promoters have to say on the topic of spring break?

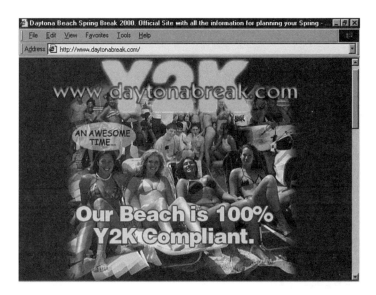

The Daytona Beach ConVis Bureau's Spring Break site is attractive enough to make you get plastic surgery, dye your hair, and act like you're 20 years old again. (What's that? You really are 20 years old? Would you leave, please? Just... leave.)

Where Are They Now?

The 1960 film *Where the Boys Are*, starring Connie Francis, popularized Fort Lauderdale as the top spring break destination for the nation's college students.

1. Let's use USA CityLink at *usacitylink.com/*. In the box called Select A State, click Florida, and then click Daytona Beach under Major Web Cities.

2. Click the link for Daytona Beach Visitor Guide, click Click to Enter, and then click What To See, Do, Eat.

3. You're just flying by the seat of your pants here, so try the link that says Festivals and Events, and then click Festival and Event Guide.

4. Whoopee! There, under Spring Break, is an unnamed link at *www.daytonabreak.com/*.

5. Yessir, that's right. You're taken to the Daytona ConVis Bureau's official Spring Break page, from which I quote the

▼ **Try It Yourself**

following: "With 23 miles of sandy beaches filled with Spring Break activity, hundreds of hotels, pool deck parties and lots of hot nightspots ready to rock, Daytona Beach is a great choice for your Spring Break experience."

My feeling is that the leaders of Daytona Beach are a very understanding group of people who don't mind a little free-spirited horseplay among half-naked college students. (Frankly, we could use a little bit more naked horseplay in this world, if you want my opinion.)

The point of this exercise is to give you the sense that you can take something you've learned about (virtual tourist bureaus) and use it for your own purposes, for your own travel needs. In the meantime, could someone turn up the air conditioner? It's starting to get a little hot in here. My goodness, is it summer already?

Summer Sun and Fun, on the Run with Your Hon and Your Son, Eating a Bun (Sorry... I'm Done)

I am a huge believer in getting my tax money's worth out of the U.S. government. When the government offers me a service, I generally try to use it, just on principle. As you've seen, and as you'll see in later chapters, the federal government has made a good start on transmitting information and services over the Internet. The State Department has its travel advisories and passport services, the Customs Service has its useful details of what you can and can't bring across various borders throughout the world, and even the National Park Service has gotten into the act.

In fact, for your summer travel plans, the National Park Service is *especially* helpful. Something I've always wanted to do is spend a few nights at the famous Ahwahnee Lodge in California's Yosemite National Park. Let's see if you can get the details and book that sucker through the NPS Web site.

Try It Yourself ▼

1. Log on to the National Park Service at *www.nps.gov*, a site it calls ParkNet. Click Visit Your Parks. Here you have a choice of all sorts of information, from entrance fees and park maps to special travel features. Under Find a Park, click By Park Name. Then, on the next page scroll down and click Yosemite NP.

2. You're taken to the NPS's Yosemite page. Scroll down to Lodging and Camping Facilities, and then click Yosemite Concession Services Corporation, which operates the lodging in Yosemite. Notice that after you click that link, you're told that you're now leaving ParkNet. Then you're automatically taken to the Yosemite National Park home page. Click Yosemite Lodging in the left margin.

3. At the top of the lodging page is a picture of the stone-and-log Ahwahnee Lodge. Drool. Then scroll down to near the bottom of the page and click On-Line Reservation Request Form.

4. Notice that the reservation form is similar to many others you've seen in previous chapters. Using forms and pull-down menus, you can choose the Ahwahnee and the specific nights you want to stay there. "Just book me in there for a week, please, and put the bill on my charge card."

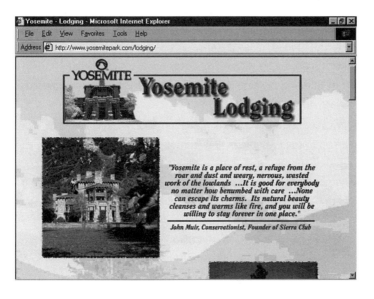

Maybe you don't like beautiful and gracious stone-and-log lodges in the to-die-for Sierra Nevada mountains. Well, don't stay at the Ahwahnee, you weirdo.

Your Tax Dollars At Work

The National Park Service's ParkNet Web site lists more than 400 national parks, recreation areas, monuments, and historic sites.

What does all this prove—that you can book a room at the
Ahwahnee by prowling through the National Park Service Web
site? Well, partly, yeah. What of it? But more importantly, you
can often find exactly what you need most efficiently by going
straight to the source. You wanted a lodge at a national park, and
by going to the National Park Service, you found the lodge you
wanted to stay in. The same procedure should help you plan your
next trip the same way, whether you're looking for a pousada in
Portugal or a B&B in Britain.

But the days are getting shorter now. Time to start thinking about
getting your woolens from the attic closet, stoking the furnace,
and maybe, just maybe, getting away for a long weekend to wit-
ness the change of the fall leaves.

Fall Scenic Drives

I may be in the minority here, but to me there's nothing more
exciting than hitting the road with a full tank of gas, a good map,
a Thermos of coffee, and some early Kinks on the sound system.
I'm with William Least Heat-Moon, the roving author who coined
the term "blue highways," those secondary roads (often colored
blue on road maps) where you never knew exactly what you
would find, although you were certain to discover some unusual
facet of America.

There's no better tool for planning a road trip than one of the
interactive route planners you learned about way back in Chapter
1. But even more important is having somewhere to go. That's
why there's no more important Web site, perhaps in the history of
America or even the world, than Roadside America, which
devotes itself to such things as mirages in the desert, mystery
spots, and gator farms—in other words, profound and meaningful
and weird things. So before you use one of the route planners,
pick a couple of places worth going to via Roadside America.

Nebraska Wonder

You can't say you've been there and done that until you've been there.
And done that. At Carhenge, that is. Its circle of upended and half-
buried autos brings to mind Stonehenge—with antilock brakes.

▼ **Try It Yourself**

1. Go to the home page at *www.roadsideamerica.com/*. In the interactive illustration, place your cursor on the Electric Map and click it.

2. Choose Nebraska, because that's where my grandfather was born (in North Platte, just down the street from where Buffalo Bill Cody lived). Now read about the world's largest ball of stamps at Boys Town in Omaha. Then, in the right margin, click Carhenge in the town of Alliance. Looks relatively cool, no?

3. Now go to the Autopilot route planner at *www.freetrip.com/* and type in the names of the towns where you'll find the ball of stamps and Carhenge (Omaha and Alliance, respectively), and use the pull-down menus to show Nebraska. You can also use the other pull-down menus for your route preferences. In box number 7, click Submit.

4. As if by magic, Autopilot replies to your request and tells you that the drive from Omaha to Alliance is 451 miles, which will take you 6 hours and 47 minutes to complete (that is, if you take Interstate 80 the whole way).

▲

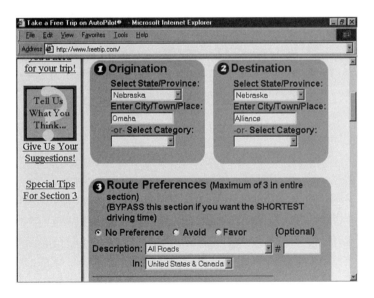

After leaving the giant ball of stamps in Omaha, where else is there to go but to Carhenge in Alliance, Nebraska?

What you're learning in this book—hey, stay with me here, this is important—I say, what you're learning in this book is not just a series of meaningless exercises or individual chapters without continuity. You must understand that everything you learn in each chapter can support and embellish what you learn in the other chapters. Just as in this exercise you paired Roadside America with Autopilot to help plan a fall driving trip, you can use two or three or more Web sites together to plan any kind of trip you want, from something as simple as a drive across Nebraska to something as potentially complicated as a year-long round-the-world trip.

Wrapping It Up

If there's one thing that I want you to take away from this chapter, it's that none of the exercises you're doing, the Web sites you're reviewing, or the techniques you're practicing are just to kill time. You're learning the building blocks, the fundamentals, the basics that will allow you to create your own vacations, research your own destinations, and be your own travel agent. Knowing these Web sites and how to use them is empowerment. You can put yourself in control. I'm making this sound like a Tony Robbins infomercial, I realize, but I have faith that what you're learning here will make you a better traveler, a more well-rounded human being, and one of these days, if you mind your p's and q's, maybe even President of the United States of America. Remember: Weirder things *have* happened.

Before you take the oath of office, please remember that you've arrived at the following conclusions in this illustrious chapter:

- Using Ski Guide and SkiResorts.com, you saw that two seemingly similar Web sites can offer nearly the same information in different ways—and you may prefer one Web site's tone over the other's.

- Thanks to the example of USA Citylink and Daytona Beach, you saw how it's possible to take the academic knowledge I've imparted (that is, get your information from a ConVis Bureau) and use it with solid results (and lots of near-naked college students).

- If you're going to Yosemite National Park, try to get a room at the Ahwahnee Lodge. No, that wasn't actually the point. The point was to go right to the source for your information and to make your own bookings, if possible.

- By using two different Web sites with two different purposes, you can build a database of information that will lead you to giant balls of stamps, cars stuck into the ground to resemble Stonehenge, and—seriously—practical tools to build not just a driving vacation, but any kind of travel plans.

CHAPTER 11

When and How Long to Go

In my role as a daily travel-advice columnist on the Web, every once in a while I'm obliged to actually read the hundreds of emails I get each week. At least one in every 10 questions sent to me begins, "What's the weather like in…?" Frankly, those questions start to get boring really fast.

On the other hand, travelers take their weather concerns seriously. In prepping for a recent family vacation to Narragansett, Rhode Island, I found myself monitoring the weather reports with greater and greater frequency as our departure date approached. I wanted blue skies and warm waters. It occurred to me that perhaps all those emails I'd been receiving for so long, asking me about the weather thither and yon (but mainly thither), weren't written entirely by morons.

The importance of your concerns about the weather at your destination shouldn't be overemphasized, however. I've heard people fret that New York in October might be rainy, or that there could still be snow on the sidewalks of Stockholm in May. Those kinds of worries border on the peculiar, because you can enjoy New York in wet weather and you can have a grand time in Stockholm whether it's snowy or dry. In fact, weather rarely needs to be an overriding concern in your travel plans. A concern, yes—just not an overriding one.

The trick is to figure out what kind of weather to expect (if only so you know what clothing to pack), but not to stress over it. And if you want to know what kind of weather to expect, you should become familiar with some of the key weather Web sites.

This chapter will also discuss the terms *high season*, *low season*, and *shoulder season*. It'll help you figure out how long your trip

What You'll Learn in This Chapter

▶ Where to go for online weather information, and how to adapt it into your travel plans.

▶ The definitions of *high season*, *low season*, and *shoulder season*, and what they should mean to you.

▶ How to find out about and plan for major events that coincide with your trip.

▶ How many days your destination is "worth."

should be. Also, you should know about events of interest at your destination—how to plan for them, or possibly how to avoid timing your vacation when major events are scheduled.

Everybody Talks About the Weather...

From time to time throughout this book, I'll treat you as if you're an audience of thousands. I'll walk among you, microphone in hand, racing up the aisles to reach you so you can ask a question of me, the Jerry Springer of travel. You, sir, there, in the lime-green sports jacket. Give me a destination... Rome? Okay, Rome. What season? Hmm? Early spring? Gotcha. Here goes:

The average high temperature in Rome in March is about 62 degrees Fahrenheit, rising to 68 degrees in April and 72 degrees in May. As for rain, you can expect slightly more of the wet stuff in April and May than in March.

Now you, ma'am. Yes, you, the chubby one. What's that you say? Istanbul in April *and* in November? All right. Here's your answer:

The average temperature in Istanbul (not Constantinople) in April is 52.7 degrees Fahrenheit. In November, it's 53.1 degrees Fahrenheit. You can expect average rainfall of 1.7 inches in April and 3.6 inches in November. My recommendation: Go in April.

How about the little boy in the back, the one picking his nose. You want to know the weather for which destination? Oh, come on, now. Athens and Bombay in November, *and* Tangier in April?! All right, kid. Just for you. Ready, set, go:

Athens will have an average temperature in November of 59.5 degrees Fahrenheit and a rainfall of 2.2 inches. For Bombay during that month, you can expect an average temperature of 81.1 degrees Fahrenheit (which is about the annual average) and slightly more than a half-inch of rain. Figure on it being cool and wet in Athens, so take along a mac. In tropical Bombay, the climate will be hot and dry, so bring your pith helmet (kinda like B-movie actor Jon Hall in all those 1950s jungle movies). As for Tangier, the average temperature in April is 60.4 degrees Fahrenheit (going up to an average of 63.9 degrees Fahrenheit in May) and the average rainfall is 2.5 inches.

Name Change

Bombay has changed its name to Mumbai, though both names will continue to be used for the near future.

How in the world does Orwoll *know* all this stuff, you may well ask yourself! Is he some kind of *übermensch*, a man of ultrasuperior brainpower, or just an incredibly bright guy? The answer, of course, is all three. But none of that has anything to do with how I learned this weather junk. I just plugged into any of several weather sites on the Internet.

Most of us who need to learn about the weather in some distant land are mainly interested in the long-term expectations. In other words, if it's February and you're planning a July holiday in St. Tropez, you don't particularly care what the current weather is. You want to know what it will be like four or five months down the road. Obviously, no one can predict the weather that far in advance. But for that kind of planning, there are weather resources that can give you historical averages for temperature and precipitation at your destination.

You can find this kind of info for cities all over the globe from WorldClimate at *www.worldclimate.com*. WorldClimate's Web site is not a traditional weather site—its purpose is not to give you the local weekend forecast. Rather, the people at WorldClimate collect data on temperatures, rainfall, and barometric pressure from sources in the public domain and then put together charts that are simple and easy to read. This site won't satisfy weather weirdoes and storm chasers, but for the majority of us who simply want to know the average temperature and precipitation, it can't be beat for comprehensiveness and ease of use. As this book was being written, the WorldClimate site was preparing for a major overhaul and updating.

As you get closer to your departure date, historical averages will have less meaning to you than the actual real-time weather, not to mention the predictions for the next week or more. For this kind of detailed weather information, your choices are many. I like the online USA Today Weather Page, as well as the Weather Channel's Weather.com (see the appendix for a list of weather resources), but my fave is Intellicast at *www.intellicast.com*. It has clear and succinct five-day forecasts for virtually every major city in the world, with temperatures given in both Celsius and Fahrenheit. As I'm writing this chapter I'm preparing to leave for a speaking engagement in Galveston, so let's check out the weather conditions in that historic Gulf Coast city. And while you're at it, try to remember the real lyrics to that wonderful song by my friend and yours, Glen Campbell: "Galveston, oh Galveston, la la hmm hmm la la dee dah…"

Basic, unadorned charts, like this one for San Francisco International Airport, are what make WorldClimate an easy-to-use vacation-planning tool.

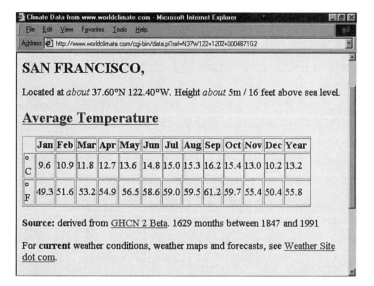

What's today's weather in…? The Intellicast site can answer that question and more for thousands of destinations worldwide.

1. From the Intellicast home page, click on the United States section of the world map, and then click on Texas.

▼ **Try It Yourself**

2. The next map shows only the larger cities in Texas and adjacent Louisiana. To the right of the map, click the hyperlinked word Texas, and then click Galveston in the list under Available Locations.

3. You're taken magically to a weather page for Galveston, with a simple, well-designed forecast that tells you thunderstorms may be on the way.

4. How close are those thunderstorms? Find out by clicking on Satellite Imagery under Local Weather. Cool! A satellite photo of Texas and the surrounding states appears, showing exactly where the storm front is at this moment.

5. From the satellite page, click Radar Imagery under Local Weather. Way cool! You get a radar shot of Texas, dissected by counties, showing the exact location of every bit of disruptive weather.

How they can put this kind of advanced space-age technology in the hands of any old idiot off the street (that is, yours truly) is totally beyond me.

(No doubt you realize that instead of clicking and clicking on the maps in order to get to the Galveston page, you could have simply typed in "Galveston" in the Quick Search box at the top of the home page. Well, that's true, but it wouldn't have been nearly as much fun, would it?)

Timing Is Everything

The timing of your vacation is important as it relates to the weather, but there's more to good timing that just knowing whether it will be sunny or rainy when you arrive.

Seasons—Hi! Feeling Low? Then Cry on My Shoulder

First, get your definitions straight. The *high season* is a destination's most popular period of the year for tourism. Some cities and resort areas have more than one high season—a Rocky

Mountain ski resort would certainly have a high season in the wintertime, but increasingly such resorts are developing a second high season in the summertime for visitors who want to camp, hike, and mountain bike in warm, dry weather.

Next comes the *low season*, sometimes called the *off season*. As you can imagine, this is when the fewest number of visitors arrive. It may have to do with bad weather at that time of year, or a lack of open attractions, or any number of reasons.

Finally there is the *shoulder season*, which falls between the high and low seasons.

One of the oddities of the travel industry is the almost arbitrary demarcation dates between a place's high season and its shoulder or off season. Prices can change a lot from one season to the next—and not always in your favor—even though the weather might be more or less the same. As a result, changing your vacation dates by just a week or two might save you a bundle by placing your reservation dates in the off season price range instead of the high season price range.

Seasons Matter

At many Caribbean resorts, rates drop by 40 percent when the low season starts in April.

Most countries have a high season and a low season. For instance, it doesn't take a rocket scientist to figure out that most travelers want to visit the Caribbean in the winter, when it's cold back home but warm in the islands. That's the Caribbean's high season. And you don't have to be a Mensa member to realize that the peak cruising season in Alaska is from June to September, when the weather is warm enough to prevent the passengers from turning into tourist-sicles. But I get more requests for information about Europe than any other destination, so let's look at the seasonal situation there.

Europe's tourist year is divided into the high season (mid-June through August, or through September in Italy), shoulder seasons (May through early June and September through early October), and the low or off season (mid-October through April). You'll find higher prices and larger crowds—but the best weather—in Europe's high season. The low season is the least crowded time of year (except at the ski resorts and during some holiday periods), but the weather is pretty dismal in most European nations during the winter.

I prefer to travel during the shoulder seasons, when the crowds are something less than swarming, the waiters at popular restaurants don't hiss at you in disdain, and the prices aren't as high as a college sophomore after a six-pack of Colt 45 malt liquor. You'll probably find that some attractions have limited hours outside the high season or are closed entirely, so make a list of your own personal "must-sees" to figure out if they'll still be open. Even the low season has its appeal—hotel prices may drop 20 or 30 percent or more, and you're less apt to feel like some anonymous character actor in a Cecil B. De Mille spectacular featuring a cast of thousands.

Another thing to bear in mind is that there are traditional vacation periods at some of the world's most popular destinations. That is, there are times when the locals head off on vacations of their own. Visiting one of those places at such times can leave you feeling as if all the inhabitants fled the city moments before you arrived. For example, August is when Parisians traditionally decamp for the countryside and the seashore on their annual four-week vacation (although more and more locals are leaving in July). You'll probably have fewer choices in restaurants because of summer-holiday closings at that time, but you also may find fewer crowds at the museums and parks than you would at other times. Reading up on your intended destinations can lead you to information about whether your vacation spot will be similarly affected.

Planning for (or Around) Major Events

Always beware of events going on at your destination. On one hand, the functions might be the sort of thing you'd like to attend: local fairs, street parties, concerts, exhibitions, what have you. On the other hand, you might find that 50,000 fat guys will be descending on your intended destination for a convention of the Large and Lovely Men's Society. You may not have anything against large and lovely men. In fact, in word and deed, you may encourage them to be all that they can be. But let's face it, it's a convention of the Large and Lovely Men's Society. If you plan your vacation to coincide with that, the chances are slim that you'll be able to get anywhere *near* the all-you-can-eat shrimpfest at the local Sizzler.

Take Las Vegas as a real-life example. There are really two sets of "best times" to go to Las Vegas—first, when the weather is bearable, and second, when the prices are most affordable. Fortunately, those two cycles overlap at least part of the time. The best prices at hotels are usually found in May, June, and July, as well as November and December. On the other hand, you might want to avoid Vegas when the big SEMA and COMDEX conventions are held there in parts of November and December. You won't get good deals in Vegas, or in a lot of other cities, when major conventions come to town.

Vegas in Summer

All around Vegas, when it gets really, really hot, you'll find "misters" on the sidewalks, shooting out a fine spray of water to keep the tourists from melting into colorful puddles.

The local tourist bureaus (see Chapter 6) usually have calendars of events posted on their sites. Also, there's a fine Web site that catalogs events great and small in cities throughout the world. If you're planning a vacation, you'd be foolish not to log on to EventsWorldWide at *www.eventsworldwide.com* to see what kind of events are planned for your destination at the time of your visit.

Try It Yourself ▼

1. Let's say you want to go to your favorite country next summer. Log on to the EventsWorldWide home page to begin your search.

2. Click Events Around the World. On the left side of the next page, click on all four event categories (Arts, Sports, Entertainment, and Special). On the right side, in the green box, choose the country you want to visit. Using the pull-down menus below, choose the dates, beginning next June 1 and ending August 31 of the same year. Click the button for Location (under Events Listed By), and then click OK.

3. A new screen appears. How many events are listed? Are there any goings-on that might possibly interfere with your travel plans? Are there any events that you would like to attend? What's that? The annual clown convention isn't in town?! Jeez, I guess you'll have to wait until next year.

Check out wuzzup where you're going and when you're going there by skimming over the happenings listed in EventsWorldWide.

How Long Do You Want to Be Gone?

We're living in what I call the Classic Era Of The Short Attention Span. Humanoids seem unable to focus their attention on one thing for more than 20 minutes. The MTV Generation has been trained to lose interest in anything that cannot be digested in the time it takes to read a *People* magazine article. With that in mind, I think a lot of simpletons out there could do the grand tour of Europe in about 12 minutes. On the other hand, those of us who have managed to retain a certain amount of brain function will realize that you couldn't fully absorb a grand tour of Europe even if you devoted a lifetime to it.

How do you go about planning the length of your vacation, then? Frankly, the bottom line has nothing to do with the Internet, and nothing to do with travel gurus like myself. It has more to do with how many vacation days you have at your job, and how many of them your supervisor will allow you to take at one time.

Good Advice

Build your vacation itinerary around the number of days at your disposal, not around everything there is to do at your destination.

The other consideration regarding the length of your trip is whether there will be enough—or too much—to see and do during the amount of time you have. For that reason, I recommend that you build your touring plan around the number of days you have to spend. Don't adjust the number of days to conform with the needs of the destination or, as happens more often, try to cram three weeks' worth of sightseeing into a one-week vacation.

Let's say you want to go to Rome. If you derived the number of vacation days needed to visit the Eternal City based on how many attractions and other attributes it has, you would probably need 3,000,017 days of vacation. On the other hand, if you decide that, realistically, you have 10 days of vacation, the next question is how you can best fill those 10 days during a sojourn in Rome. It's all just a matter of how you approach the equation.

Before you make a final decision about how much time to devote to your vacation, learn everything you can about your destination. Ask yourself what you most hope to do while you're there, and then factor in the number of days you have available. Maybe there will be time for only two museums instead of five. Perhaps you'll have to forgo a side trip that sounded appealing. But you know what? There's always your next vacation to do everything that you couldn't fit into this one.

Wrapping It Up

Time and weather... we place so much emphasis on them when planning our travels. That's why this chapter has discussed exactly those topics—weather, because it's helpful to know whether you'll be swept away by a hurricane, and time, because the month during which you travel and the number of days you travel can affect the cost and enjoyment of your trip.

But let me reiterate that neither of these topics is of paramount concern for most vacations. The more important thing is to get up and go, pack your bags and travel, whether you have two full weeks in the sunny month of July or nothing more than a long weekend during a rainy November.

Here's what you learned in this chapter:

- Getting your weather information online—both long-term climate details and short-term forecasts—can help you plan your travels.

- The different tourist seasons (high, low, and shoulder) can make a difference in terms of vacation cost and activities.

- You should find out what events are planned at your destination—for better or worse—during your stay.

- Use the number of vacation days you have as the basis for building a realistic tour itinerary.

PART III

Booking Your Trip Online

CHAPTER 12

Online Travel Agents

At the risk of undermining the premise of this unbelievably useful and well-written tome and having you rush back to your local bookseller to ask for a refund, I don't see why everyone is so all-fired eager to book their own trips instead of letting a travel agent handle all the hassles. Travel agents have more resources than most of us. They generally travel more often than the average person, thanks in large part to discounted "fam" (familiarization) trips available only to agents, and so they have a wider knowledge of destinations, hotels, and activities. They have access to agent-only reservations systems. They have a network of information sources. They have relationships with their counterparts at the airlines, cruise lines, and hotel chains that can lead to better deals for the client. They work like the dickens (and if you know what a dickens is, please drop me a line), and they get only modest remuneration for all their efforts.

And they're willing to book your entire vacation, for which they charge you little or nothing at all.

And yet here you are, right in the middle of this book about booking your own trips online, because you'd rather do all the work yourself! Go figure.

Thankfully, I've grappled with this issue long enough to have found a rather good reason why this book is still valid, even if you choose to use an online travel agent. To wit: Travel agencies have gone online in a big way, giving you the same sort of service as the travel agency down the block, but without your having to get up out of your comfy Barcalounger and walk down the street. In fact, the online travel agency you access on the Web may very well *be* the storefront travel agency down the street.

Key Points in This Chapter

▶ Find and identify an online travel agency.

▶ Learn how an online agency can help plan your travels.

▶ Know some of the major trade organizations with which many online agents are affiliated.

▶ Judge the legitimacy of online travel agencies.

In this chapter, you'll learn what exactly constitutes an online travel agency, how to locate one on the Internet, and what it can do for you, as well as some of the major trade groups that can refer you to affiliated travel agents. You'll also learn about your rights as a consumer, because the last thing you want is to be ripped off by some unscrupulous scam artist posing as a legit agent.

Defining "Online Travel Agency"

We all know what a travel agent is, right? She (or he) has that little shop on Main Street or in the mall, usually with travel posters plastered in the window and some semi-schmaltzy name like Worlds Away or Togetherness Travel. You walk through the door, tell the agent where you want to go on vacation and approximately how much money you want to spend, and in a day or two (sometimes longer) the agent mails you an envelope with airline tickets and resort reservations. That's one kind of travel agent.

An even better agent might actually give you advice on where to go, which hotels to stay in, the best season to visit, and the like. And then she would make all your reservations for you, based on your informed choices.

The first kind of agent is nothing more than an order-taker, except instead of asking, "Would you like fries with that?", he asks, "Would you prefer a window seat or an aisle seat?" You won't be dealing with that sort of agent in this chapter. And if you're lucky, you'll never have to deal with that sort of agent at all. Instead, you'll focus on travel agents who can offer you the benefit of their experience in the profession, who can give you advice, who are travel counselors more than simply travel agents.

Questions to Ask an Online Agent

Before conducting a financial transaction over the Internet, whether it's with a tour operator, a travel agency, or a firm selling wholesale widgets, ask the following questions:

- How long has the company been in business? A firm that has been around for 20 years ought to give you more confidence than one that started up last month (although this isn't foolproof).

- Is there a list of past clients that you can call for references? If the company won't give you any such names, it's already suspect.

- Is there a list of the firm's professional affiliations? Call those organizations to ensure that the firm is indeed a member in good standing.

An online travel agency of this sort is likely to be a member of one or more professional organizations, has been in business (or is owned by an agent who has been in the business) for a decade or longer, and will treat you as an individual, whether you're filling in forms on its Web site, sending email, or talking to one of the agency's employees on the telephone. (And when it comes to online travel agencies, you'll probably end up using all those forms of communication.)

A reputable online travel agency will be able to

- Communicate with you as an individual through any of several media, including email, fax, and telephone.

- Offer you solid, well-researched advice about your intended destination, including activities, lodgings, restaurants, and transportation.

- Arrange all necessary reservations, including airfare, car rental, and accommodations.

Yet another kind of travel agent (and here I use the term a bit loosely) is what the trade calls a *tour operator*. This kind of agent specializes in package deals (that is, airfare, hotels, sometimes meals and activities) for one price. Often tour operators specialize in one kind of activity (such as outdoor adventure) or in a certain destination at large. Reputable tour operators can be every bit as useful as the better travel agencies, although their destinations and/or activities might be more limited.

Finding a Good Travel Agent Online

There are any number of ways to locate a travel agent or tour operator, including the Internet search engines. Let's try to find a travel firm that specializes in, say, fishing trips. Use the Yahoo! site at *www.yahoo.com/*.

1. On the home page, scroll down and click the link that says Travel under the heading Recreation & Sports.

2. From the list of choices on the Travel page, choose Travel Agents.

▼ **Try It Yourself**

3. Read through the bewildering array of agencies listed there until you come across an agency called Fishing International, Inc. Follow that link.

4. The firm's home page tells you about the company's 25 years in business and about the various fishing vacations it can plan for you.

There's something fishy (if you're lucky) about Yahoo's Travel Agent listings.

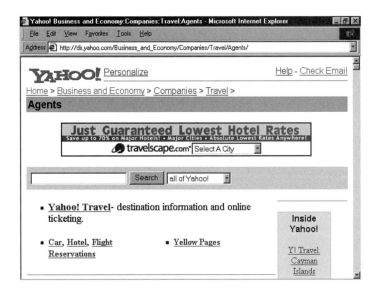

That's a lengthy way to find what we're looking for. It's also a gamble because there's no assurance that one of the agencies listed there will have "fish" in its name! So try it again. This time, if only for variety's sake, try using the WebCrawler site at *www.webcrawler.com*.

Try It Yourself ▼

1. Come up with a good search phrase and plug it into the site's search form. I had some success with the phrase "fishing vacation," but you can experiment with similar words and phrases.

2. Using "fishing vacation," you should find a list of results that includes "fishing lodges — fishing lodges for your next vacation." Follow that link.

3. You're taken to the piscine pages of TourWorld, a company that books fishing (and other) trips throughout Canada.

Experiment with other activities and destinations on the other major search engines to get a better idea of the array of agencies and operators ready to do business with you.

The Major Online Booking Engines

I'm reluctant to call the major online reservations Web sites "travel agents." It's sort of like calling the Trilateral Commission "a group of decision makers" or calling the Mafia "wayward youths." It's accurate, but it's not really to the point.

You've heard of them: Expedia, Travelocity, Internet Travel Network (ITN), Trip.com, 1travel.com, Biztravel.com, and the rest. Most of them are powerful, wide-ranging sites. One of them, Travelocity.com, merged with Preview Travel not long ago to become the largest online travel agency of all—50 percent bigger than its closest rival, Microsoft's Expedia.

American Express, at *www.americanexpress.com*, the largest travel agency in the world, is also a presence on the Internet, but I place it in a different category from these others. American Express has been helping travelers for 150 years or so, while these other guys didn't even exist 10 years ago. I've worked for American Express, the parent company of Travel & Leisure, for many years, so it wouldn't really be fair of me to spend much time singing the praises of that splendid organization. It might look too much like brown-nosing! But this is a good time to say, short and sweet, that no other travel company in the United States can boast the volume of travel agency business or the same travel-related history as American Express can. And if that results in my getting a big bonus in my next paycheck, well, that's a risk I'm willing to take.

As for the other major online travel agencies: Occasionally in this book I've used one or another of them to illustrate a point, and I'll continue to do so. You should feel free to use these sites (their URLs are listed in the appendix), but I want you to know my feelings about them.

First off, most of these sites (and there are dozens of them) use one of four airline-fare search engines—Sabre, ITN's FlightRez, Galileo/Apollo, or Microsoft's Flight Wizard. After you've searched for the best airfare on two or three of the major online booking sites, you'll start coming up with the same results again and again.

To some extent, the way I feel about these sites is the way some Internet users feel about AOL—that they're a simplified way to use the technology for people who are unwilling or unable to use the more advanced methods.

But don't ignore the major online reservations Web sites. Some of them have decent travel features, advice, and good links to unrelated travel sites. Most of them have sections devoted to travel news. But don't rely on them completely. Don't let them filter your travel information. The point of this book is for you to learn to do it yourself—not to go the lazy route and have someone else do it for you.

A Practical Walkthrough: How to Book Through a Good Agent or Operator

Carlson Wagonlit Travel is one of the largest travel agencies in the United States, with hundreds of outlets across the country. Let's log on to the firm's Web site at *www.carlsontravel.com/* and see what it takes just to register with an online agent. Most companies that deal in online financial transactions require a customer's personal information, and online travel agencies are no different.

You'll find tons to choose from at the Carlson Wagonlit site— but you'll have to register to get full use.

A Travel Pedigree

Carlson Wagonlit's roots stretch back to 1888, when its predecessor was founded under the name Ask Mr. Foster.

Although there's plenty of intriguing travel information on the home page, let's focus on the registration process as if you're ready to begin dealing directly with an agent. So go to the Carlson Wagonlit Travel home page.

▼ **Try It Yourself**

1. On the menu bar across the top of the home page, choose Online Reservations.

2. The next page prompts you to register as a new user, so click on the New User Registration Button.

3. Fill in the customer registration form, submit it by clicking the button at the bottom, review the confirmation screen that comes next, and click the Continue button.

4. This brings you back to the sign-in page, but this time you can sign in as a registered user. Type in your username and password, and then click the Reservations Login button below.

5. The new screen instructs you to select an agency from a list. Choose one in your home state and click the Submit button at the bottom of the page.

▲

Time Out to Talk About Privacy

Grab a soda and a sandwich, and let's chat for a moment about online privacy. Most firms with which you voluntarily share your email address and mailing address are bound to use that information to send you unsolicited information (unless their privacy policy expressly says otherwise). In some cases, you can prevent that from happening by sending an unsubscribe reply to an unsolicited email. In other cases, you may end up on a hundred undesirable mailing lists, only to discover that nothing you do stops the spam from flying down your email chute.

Most legitimate Web sites have a privacy statement or privacy policy somewhere on their site. Because we're spotlighting Carlson Wagonlit Travel, let's take a gander at its privacy statement...

"We collect the domain name of visitors to our Web pages, the email addresses of those visitors who volunteer them, user-specific information on what pages visitors access, and information such as survey information that you provide voluntarily. Like many other commercial Web sites, the Carlson Companies, Inc. Web sites may employ a standard technology called a 'cookie' to collect information about how our site is used.

"We use the information that we collect to understand your individual preferences and history. With this information we can better tailor our services and special offerings to provide superior levels of convenience and service on a one-to-one basis. We also use the collected information to improve the design of our Web pages.

"If you provide us with your email address, we may occasionally send you email offers, informing you about products and services. If you provide us with your postal address, you may receive periodic mailings from us with information on new products and services or upcoming events. These offers may be based on information you provided us in your responses to our surveys and on your history with us as a customer.

"If you do not want to receive posted or email offers from us, please let us know by sending us an email message, calling, or writing to us, telling us that you do not want to receive offers from our company. Our emailed offers include instructions for unsubscribing from emailed offers. If you want to be removed from our postal mailing list, please provide us with your complete name and address."

This is fairly serious stuff, folks. You don't want to register with an online travel agency (or an online *anything*) unless you're willing to have your email address and, possibly, your phone number and postal address available to lots of people who want to sell you things.

You May Resume Your Exercise Now

Your next step on the Carlson Wagonlit site is booking a trip. Pick up where you left off, having selected and accessed a local Carlson Wagonlit agent.

1. After you register, using your username and password, you go to a page that prompts you to select one of four paths. Choose New Itinerary.

2. At the Trip Planner page, click the Add Air button.

3. As instructed, fill in the dates and times you want to fly, click Show selected flights, and choose the particular flights (by airline and departure time) you'd like to take on both legs of the itinerary.

4. Click on the Price itinerary button to find out how much the airfare will be. In my case, I was told it would cost me just over $2,000 to fly round-trip between New York and Los Angeles. No thanks.

▼ **Try It Yourself**

If the price had been a little closer to what I wanted (like about one-fourth the price I was given!), and if I really was interested in such an itinerary rather just doing an exercise, I would have been given the choice of either sending my reservation to a reservation agent or filing it for future reference. The latter would allow me to access that flight information later, perhaps after thinking about it overnight.

Using Trade Organizations to Find an Agent

You know that there are rotten enchiladas in every sombrero, as my eighth-grade Spanish teacher was overly fond of saying. But you're less likely to come up against a rotten travel-agent enchilada if you consult the following professional membership organizations, each of which can help you track down one of its members near you.

At the top of my list is the American Society of Travel Agents at *www.astanet.com/*. ASTA's Web site, large portions of which are open to the public, can provide users with unbelievable amounts of information—everything from the latest travel news to careers in the travel business to forums where travelers can share their recent experiences. Also, it can help connect you to a member travel agency. Go to ASTA's home page and see if you can find an online agent near, say, midtown Manhattan.

What's an ASTA?

ASTA, the American Society of Travel Agents, is the world's largest and best-known travel agent organization, with more than 26,500 members in 170 countries.

With its prominent code of ethics and consumer affairs division, ASTA stands head and shoulders above most travel organizations.

1. From the sleek home page, with its rotating globe, click Travelers.

2. In the far-left margin, scroll all the way down to a box labeled Find ASTA members in your area, type in your ZIP code as instructed, and press Enter on your keyboard.

3. The new screen displays dozens of travel agents, with their mailing addresses, telephone numbers, and email addresses.

Try It Yourself ▼

The United States Tour Operators Association at *www.ustoa.com/* is another one of my favorite travel organizations, thanks particularly to its $1 Million Consumer Protection Plan. If you do business with a member company and it goes bankrupt after you've paid your money, you're protected by a bond that each tour operator must post in order to become a member in the first place. The Web site will help you find USTOA members for the kind of vacation you're planning.

The USTOA is the place to learn about tours and packages.

Stiff Requirements

To become a member of the USTOA, a tour operator must have 18 references from various industry sources and financial institutions, must have been in business at least three years, and must carry $1 million in professional liability insurance.

Determining If an Agency Is Legitimate

One of the "little people out there" who recently asked me for advice had a very good experience booking a trip to Italy through an online travel agent. But when it came time to actually hand over the mazuma to pay for the trip, the traveler started getting cold feet. "How do I know I'm not being ripped off?" he cried. "What if this travel agent is just a big scam artist?" he whimpered. "Mommy, Mommy! Help me, Mommy!" It was pathetic. And no, of course I didn't slap him. Instead, I gave him some advice.

Have you ever spent any time in a chat room, especially the seamier ones that you might find on AOL? Let's say you're having an arousing conversation with someone who uses the *nom de computer* of LoadoLuv. The two of you have really hit it off. This is more than two computer chips passing in the night, you say to yourself. Then LoadoLuv comes up with a brilliant idea—why don't you send him $2,000 for airfare so the two of you can get it on in person?! Whoopee! Best if you send cash, LoadoLuv says, to avoid the hassle of cashing a check.

Hoooold on there, Babalooey! If you did anything of the sort, you'd be dumber than… than… well, dumber than someone who spends all day in chat rooms. That holds true when you're dealing with commercial firms on the Web as well. You should never, ever send money or conclude a binding business deal with any company that you know nothing about beyond its home page on the Internet. Always investigate its professional affiliations, as well as several client references, before proceeding.

Wrapping It Up

You've learned the differences between a tour operator and a travel agent. But whether the company you want to use is one or the other, remember the professional groups discussed in this chapter. If the company is a travel agency, ask if it's a member of the American Society of Travel Agents (ASTA). If it's a tour operator, find out if it is a member of the United States Tour Operators Association (USTOA). Membership in a professional organization is not a complete measure of reliability by any means, but it's an initial indication that you're probably in good hands. Both ASTA and the USTOA have demanding membership requirements, as well as some facility for handling consumer complaints against their members.

You know now how to find a travel agency online through the major search engines. And once you've found an agency, you know that you must assess its legitimacy. So I'll bet you five bucks that you understand the following:

- How to track down an online travel agency or tour operator.

- What an online agency can do for you in planning your travels.

- How to access and use the Web sites of ASTA and the USTOA, two of the major travel industry organizations.

- How to tell if an online agency or tour operator is legit.

CHAPTER 13

Learning to Be Your Own Electronic Travel Agent

I know you. You're a DIY traveler, right? That is, a do-it-your-selfer. You don't want to put yourself in the hands of an online travel agent because you get a kick out of making all the plans yourself. You enjoy ferreting out all the details, reading the fine print, doing the dirty work, never delegating authority because Lord knows nobody else could do it as well as you can.

There's now medication that can help SOB's like you. And you might also want to consider therapy, too.

I must admit to being more or less a Type A personality myself. Whenever someone gives me the price of a hotel room or a plane ticket, something gnaws at me from inside, a nagging feeling that I probably could have gotten a cheaper price, a more convenient flight, a larger room, or whatever—if only I had made the arrangements myself.

To a great extent, this entire book is about learning to be your own travel agent. But in this chapter, you'll learn about some of the available travel industry resources that are constantly used by travel agents, including tons of free government information about your destination. You'll also learn a bit about consumer rights and how to complain if you feel you've been ripped off. By the time you finish this chapter, you'll be able to make a professional and useful itinerary—a basic component of being your own travel agent.

Now that I think of it, rip this chapter out of the book and frame it. This chapter is worth every penny you paid for the entire book. Frankly, I've got goosebumps.

Key Points in This Chapter

▶ How to plan a vacation itinerary.

▶ How to think like a travel agent.

▶ Knowing your rights and how to complain.

How to Make an Itinerary (Even If You Can't Spell "Itinerary")

Before you make any of your reservations, a good travel agent (and even most lousy ones) will ask you a series of questions—things like what time of the day or night you prefer to fly, what sort of lodgings you're looking for, the kinds of activities you hope to take part in, side trips you want to make, and the various destinations, besides your arrival point, in which you plan to stay overnight. Reservations are then made for the various components. This is very important—if the reservations are planned well, they won't conflict with one another. The best method to ensure that all the aspects have been addressed, and that your various reservations are not in conflict, is to prepare an advance itinerary even before you begin making the bookings.

Chapter 11 discussed when you should plan your trip and for how long. That's the fundamental building block of an itinerary. Next comes transportation to your destination, followed by nights of lodging, specific activities on certain days, side trips (including location, transportation, activities, and so on), and secondary destinations, if any. The last item on the itinerary, of course, is transportation back to your point of origin.

I prefer to use Excel to make up my own itineraries, but you can use any spreadsheet program, or any program that allows you to use a column format. In fact, you can even use a simple word processing program, like Word 98. Let's try a little exercise—preparing an itinerary for a short business trip.

Try It Yourself

1. In the left margin, type "Day 1" on one line, "Day 2" on the next, and so on for the number of days you plan to travel.

2. Across the top of the page, in a column style, enter the following categories: Transportation, Lodgings, Activities.

3. Fill in the blanks for each day of your trip.

	Transportation	Lodgings	Activities
Day 1	UA 18	n/a Depart LAX 2200	n/a
Day 2	Arrive JFK 0616 taxi to hotel	Algonquin single w/king early ck-in	meetings 9-5; Lion King 2000 p/u tix @ b.o.

	Transportation	Lodgings	Activities
Day 3	Amtrak Depart NYC 0900 Arrive Bos 1245	R-C Boston single w/king	meet reps 1600 followed by dinner
Day 4	Amtrak Depart Bos 0930 Arrive NYC 1315 car svc p/u 1600 UAL 905 Depart JFK 1830 Arrive LAX 2128		meeting 1400 at home office

To most people this looks like a lot of gobbledygook, but you know differently. You know your airport codes and your military timekeeping. You've got a rhythm thing going on here, baby, and it feels good. Here's what's happening:

On Day 1 you board United Airlines flight 18, leaving Los Angeles International Airport at 10 p.m. (Because it's an overnight or "red eye" flight, you won't need to plan for accommodations or activities. They're n/a, or not applicable.)

On Day 2, you arrive at John F. Kennedy International Airport at 6:16 a.m. and take a taxi to your hotel, the Algonquin, where you requested an early check-in for your single room with a king-size bed. You have business meetings from nine in the morning to the end of the workday, after which you managed to get a seat to *The Lion King* on Broadway, where you'll pick up the tickets at the box office. (Okay, that last part is what you might call pie-in-the-sky itinerary planning.)

Because this is mainly a business trip, Day 3 sees you going up to Boston for another meeting. Your Amtrak train leaves New York at 9:30 a.m. and arrives in Beantown at 12:45. You check in at the Ritz-Carlton Boston Hotel (again, a single room with a king-size bed) and prepare to meet with some sales reps at 4 p.m., after which a few of them have invited you out to dinner.

On Day 4 you take the train back to New York (you have a 2 p.m. meeting at corporate headquarters), and then a local car service picks you up at 4 p.m. for the ride to JFK airport. United Airlines 905 leaves at 6:30 p.m. and gets into La-La Land at 9:28 in the evening, local time.

This is a pretty simple itinerary, of course, but the same approach can be used whether you're planning a weekend trip to Grandma's or a two-week tour of Civil War battlefields.

How to Think Like a Travel Agent

I'm not a professional travel agent. I'm just a travel editor. But I've dealt with enough agents to realize that the good ones all have something in common—they think like travel agents. What exactly does that mean? Mainly, that they're well-informed about the travel business. They read the trade magazines and the latest government statistics. They can place the daily obligations of their vocation in a broad context of industry knowledge.

> **The Real Thing**
> If you want to become an honest-to-goodness travel agent, enroll in one of the schools endorsed by the American Society of Travel Agents. You'll find them under Travel Careers at *www.astanet.com*.

That's a trait well worth striving for. Don't get me wrong; I don't expect you to have the time or inclination to turn into a travel-industry groupie. You probably don't care whether the airline industry's on-time record improved by 2 percent last month... but you should know what an on-time record is, at least. You may not care that a man had his wallet stolen in Acapulco... but you should be able to access crime information on Mexico if you plan to go there. You don't have to wallow in the minutiae of the industry... but you should know how to access it and use it when necessary to help you shape your travel plans.

Travel Industry News: Read All About It!

Reading the travel news is the easiest and most important way to think like a travel agent. You already know how to access newspapers worldwide (see Chapter 5) and therefore the travel sections of those papers. But you should also read the "travel trades," as travel-industry trade publications are called. Let's have a look at one of the best: Travel Weekly Crossroads, at *www.twcrossroads.com/home.asp*, which bills itself as an "online community for travel professionals." And although you need to register as a member, there's no cost. So let's take a trip through TWC's pages.

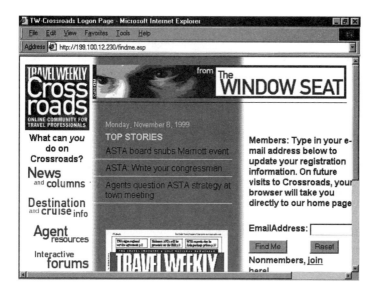

Travel Weekly Crossroads, the travel agent's friend, is a great source of travel news.

▼ Try It Yourself

1. Enter your user name and password, which brings you to the home page.

2. Read the headlines under the Top Stories heading, click on one of them, and then return to the home page.

3. Back on the home page, click on the link to the Destination Spotlight (today it's Switzerland; tomorrow it might be Zimbabwe). After reading the article, return to the home page.

4. Before logging off the site, read the menu bar across the top of the page—leading to such topics as news, cruise, directories, and resources—and familiarize yourself with these other sections of Travel Weekly Crossroads.

▲

See the appendix of this soon-to-be-prize-winning book for other travel industry news sites, and consult them regularly—not just when you're planning a trip. Being a good traveler means being a good travel *planner*, and the best way to do that is to keep yourself regularly updated.

Government Statistics—Hey, Stop Yawning!

The amount of information offered for free from local, state, and federal government agencies is truly mind-boggling.

Unfortunately, this means that the effort to find the exact information you need can also be mind-boggling. But luckily for you, I've collected some of the major travel-related government sites in the appendix of this book so you don't have to track them down the way I did—through instinct, rumor, and sometimes just plain luck.

The information the government provides is the sort that a good travel agent must know. Is the sanitation on a luxury cruise ship slipping? Do you need malaria medicine to visit Namibia? Such health-related questions can often be answered through the Centers for Disease Control (see Chapter 22). Can you expect your airline to get you to your destination on time (an important consideration for travelers who have to make tight connections)? You can find out through the on-time statistics available from the Office of Airline Information, a branch of the U.S. Department of Transportation (see the appendix under "Air Travel: Laws, Advice"). Let's say that you're going to visit France and you want to bring back a case of Bordeaux wine. You can find out if that's allowable by logging on to the U.S. Customs Service Web site, which explains the kind and amount of goods you can bring back with you to the U.S. (see Chapter 20).

One of the most useful government Web sites, and one that I use almost every day in my role as a travel magazine editor, is the U.S. State Department's Web site for Travel Warnings & Consular Information Sheets at *travel.state.gov/travel_warnings.html*.

A foreign country's travel conditions can change from year to year, or even from day to day, so the example in the following exercise might have changed by the time you access the Web site. But take a look at how the Travel Warnings site might help you in planning your vacation to a far-flung corner of the globe.

Try It Yourself ▼

1. Access the Travel Warnings Web page and read the description of Travel Warnings and Consular Information Sheets.

2. Choose a country to visit—let's say Morocco. Scroll down the page. You can either click on the letter *M* listed in the alphabet shortcut or continue farther down the page to where Morocco is listed by name. Notice the date in parentheses

next to each country's name, which tells you when the last announcement was released. Click it.

3. You're taken to a page that gives you an overview of the country in a nifty nutshell—country description, entry requirements, aviation safety, areas of instability (gulp!), medical facilities, crime statistics, and more.

Your tax dollars at work—the U.S. State Department tells you all about your foreign destination, including how safe (or not) it might be.

This info sheet tells you that Morocco is a parliamentary monarchy, Americans don't need visas for visits of less than 90 days, there are thousands of unexploded mines in the western Sahara (Attention camels: Watch your step!), you can expect adequate medical care, and annoying "guides" can pester you until you're ready to scream. If you rattle all that off to some guy on the street, you'll sound like the world's greatest travel agent. And in fact, you're well on your way to being just that. (Well, not really. That was false praise just to keep you slogging through the rest of this text.)

Power to the People, Right On! Know Your Travel Rights

If you're going to be your own travel agent, the only one who's going to stick up for your rights is you. So you'd better realize what they are and where to find out more about them.

Most (but not all) travel-rights Web sites have to do with airlines. Several upstart, in-your-face groups, like PassengerRights.com (*www.passengerrights.com/*), have sprung up in the past few years, and they're worth looking into. Perhaps the granddaddy of airline-passenger rights groups is the Aviation Consumer Action Project (*www.acap1971.org/*), which was founded by consumer advocate Ralph Nader in 1971.

> **Remember**
>
> Don't expect the Web's travel-complaint sites to solve your problem for you. Their purpose is to file your complaint with the appropriate parties and, if the site is a good one, give you advice about solving the matter on your own.

Such Web sites, while providing some information, are equally interested in getting you to sign up for a newsletter subscription or buy other publications. They may be good publications and well worth the money, but I'm a cheapskate. That's why another Web site is dear to my heart. Airline Complaints, at *www.airlinecomplaints.com/*, is the least commercial of the travel-rights sites, and it provides plenty of information at no charge and without membership.

If you have nothing else to do at the moment—you know, if *Wheel of Fortune* isn't starting in five minutes—maybe you could bring yourself to log on to the Airline Complaints site so you can consider its ramifications. Thanks. Thanks a lot. I appreciate your participation.

Try It Yourself ▼

1. Read the menu at left and choose a topic—say, Search the Complaints.

2. The pull-down menus ask you to select which airline, airport, and dates you want to search for. Leave everything set to All to get the comprehensive list of complaints, and then click the Search Now button at the lower-right.

3. Scroll through the scores of listed complaints and find one that compares to a similar complaint that you might have had in the past.

4. Marvel at the organized way the complaint information is given—airline name, problem type, airport name, incident date, and a brief summary of the complaint. (Note that each complaint file has a space for a company reply, almost all of which are labeled "no response.")

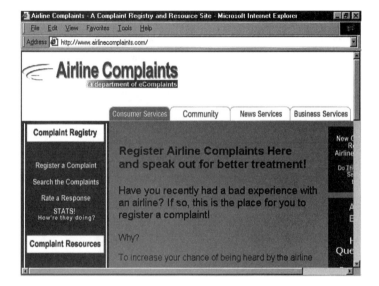

No airline is going to mess with your head—not with Airline Complaints on your side.

The Web site also provides you with information on how and where to make your own complaint, of course.

Obviously, there's much more to traveler's rights than simply air travel. There are also some general precautions that you should take if you're going to act as your own travel agent—whether it be for airfare, train tickets, hotel reservations, or an entire vacation package.

- Never agree to any travel "deal" that requires you to make an instant decision. If the salesman won't give you time to think about the purchase, it's most likely because he doesn't want you to think about it or you'll realize you're being bamboozled.

- Investigate the firm and ask for references. If you plan to book a trip through a tour operator or travel agent, ask if they belong to any professional organizations (see Chapter 12). Then check that they're indeed members in good standing.

Ask for the names and phone numbers of three satisfied clients, and then call those people.

- Get everything in writing before you agree to anything. Then read the fine print. If the salesman tells you that you'll be staying in a suite, but the written contract stipulates a standard room, trust the contract.

- Pay with a major charge card. In almost all cases, the card companies will retract a charge if you make a valid claim against a company that failed to provide the goods and services you paid for. Personally, I'm reluctant to pay cash in advance for travel arrangements. I'm even willing to pay a 2% or 3% premium for the security that comes with using a charge card, although I would make an exception by paying cash to a well-known company of long-standing repute, if absolutely required.

Details, Details
A lot of travel-related disputes arise because the client failed to read the details of the written agreement.

Ultimately, it's up to you, the personification of the traveling public. You're the one who's guarding the Maginot Line against travel ripoffs and poor service. So use your noodle, old bean. Ask questions. Be skeptical. Never make decisions under pressure. If nothing you do helps and you feel you've been cheated, don't hesitate to take your complaint to an official agency, whether it be your local consumer affairs office or the state attorney general.

Wrapping It Up

No one admires travel agents as much as I do. But I also know that it's possible to be your own travel agent, because nobody knows your travel preferences better than you do.

Travel agents have many resources at their fingertips. Although some of that information is limited to professional travel agents, much of it is free to the public through the World Wide Web. Any traveler who takes the time to access that information, especially travel-industry and government-sponsored news, is in a much better position than the average person to be his or her own travel agent.

But face it, sometimes things go wrong. You might feel wronged by an airline or cheated by a tour operator. If so, and you're acting as your own travel agent, you must know what your rights are and how to complain effectively.

If you've been paying attention to this chapter, you now know the following:

- What a travel itinerary is and how to make one to organize your own travels.

- The kinds of resources available to travel agents, and how they can help you become your own electronic travel agent.

- How to complain about bad service or travel ripoffs so that you can stand up for yourself when making your own reservations.

Two Important Words

If I told you that by remembering two little words you could save hundreds or even thousands of dollars on your next vacation, you'd tell me I was a nutcase. But the proof is in the pudding, so when planning your next vacation, act like a real travel agent and get the discounts you'd like by telling yourself: "Just ask."

Just ask the airline agent if there are any less-expensive flights.

Just ask the hotel receptionist if it's possible to get a free room upgrade.

Just ask the rental-car clerk if there are any special deals available.

Just ask your reservationist if the price would be cheaper by changing your travel dates.

Just ask, ask, and ask again. Armed with all the information you've gleaned from your research, you'll know when you've gotten the best available price, or close to it. And then once you've committed to that cost, don't start second-guessing yourself. Don't ask others how much they paid for the same thing. This isn't a contest, fer cryin' out loud. Once you get a price that you consider fair, pay it, forget about it, and enjoy your travels.

CHAPTER 14

Making Hotel Reservations on the Web

Think back to the last time you made a hotel reservation. Chances are you'd never stayed at that hotel before, never even seen pictures of it. How did you find out about the place? Through a friend? An ad in a magazine? A one-sentence write-up in a guidebook? Be truthful—no matter how much faith you placed in the source of your hotel recommendation, weren't you at least a *little* nervous about what you'd find when you checked in?

Being in the travel business, I've heard the most pitiful war stories from travelers who hated their hotels. "The room was so small, you had to step out into the hallway just to change your mind," goes one old saw. "Hot and cold running rats," goes another. No doubt you too have ended up in a hotel that could have used a good fumigating—or atomic bombing.

Thanks to the Internet, savvy e-travelers can minimize the chances that their next hotel will be, in the words of my late father, a real stinkeroo. How? First, by accessing umpteen reviews and descriptions of a hotel under consideration and thus determining if there's a consensus regarding the hotel's quality. And second, by reviewing the hotel's Web site—not just to look at pictures of the guest rooms and public areas (although that's useful), but also to read the detailed descriptions of the property and to email the hotel management with any questions that might arise.

There are three primary ways that travelers can deal with hotels—through a private hotel reservation service, through a hotel chain, or directly with an independent hotel. All three have their benefits and drawbacks, which you'll examine in this chapter. You'll also consider the things you should look for on a hotel Web site to

What You'll Learn in this Chapter

▶ The different ways to get hotel information on the Web—directly from each hotel, through a chain, or via a commercial booking service.

▶ Points to consider when judging a hotel based on Internet information.

▶ How to make a hotel reservation on the Web.

▶ Where on the Web you can find alternatives to traditional hotels.

ensure that you're getting a full description of the property, and you'll run through some examples of what it's like to make a hotel reservation through the World Wide Web. You'll even look at hotel alternatives, like renting a private condo or apartment.

Online Hotel Reservation Services

An online reservation service—and there are scores of them—may be nothing more than a middleman that takes your reservation request and forwards it to a hotel. Or, it may be a true partner in the booking arrangements by bringing new business to the hotel on one hand, and by offering discounts that the consumer would be unable to find elsewhere on the other.

In the appendix of this book, you'll find a list of some of the major hotel booking services online. Each of them would argue that it's more than an order-taker. Indeed, each of them would swear on its Mama's old gray head that you could do no better than to make your reservations through that service.

Bottom Line

Online hotel-booking services are the best sources to find a wide choice of hotels.

Of course, the proof is in the piddling, as I always say. (Yes, it does make sense, depending on what sort of proof you're testing for.) So you should be willing to browse through numerous online booking sites before you decide on one with which you feel comfortable.

And pray tell, what qualities should make you feel comfortable? The basis for that decision isn't much different than it would be for any other consumer transaction. How long has the company been in business? Does it make an effort to provide clear, objective, and full information? Is it trying to sell you something other than the obvious (such as a hotel room booking)? Is the site easy to use? Are there clear ways to contact the firm (including phone, snail mail, and fax) if your emails fail to get through? In other words, you need to analyze each hotel-booking site the same way you would analyze any commercial enterprise with which you were thinking of doing business.

One of the oldest online hotel-booking services is Quikbook at *www.quikbook.com*, which started operating in 1988. Unusual in that it limits itself to hotels in just seven U.S. cities, Quikbook takes the position that it's better to be very good in fewer cities than it is to be moderately good in many cities. Of course, the cities it handles are no second-rate burgs. They're the major business centers in America: Boston, New York City, Washington D.C., Atlanta, Chicago, San Francisco, and Los Angeles.

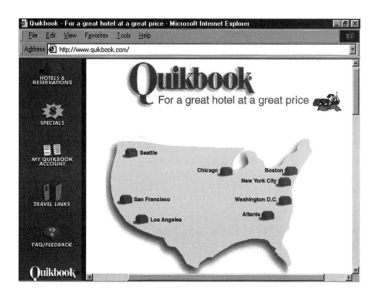

The cities available through Quikbook may be few, but the site is worth considering anyway because of the number of hotels in each city and—more importantly—the discounts you might find.

Let's take a cyber-walk through Quikbook to see how you can find a hotel in San Francisco and make a reservation.

1. From the home page, click on Hotels & Reservations in the left margin. Then, using one of the pull-down menus in the new window, do a Search by Price for a San Francisco hotel in the under $200 price range.

2. When a new screen appears with a list of hotels, choose one that looks appropriate for your needs. For this example, choose the Mark Hopkins Inter-Continental, one of the city's best-known hostelries.

3. Read over the hotel's description, including its amenities, quotes from customers, and digital pictures of the public and guest rooms. If you agree that it looks like what you want, click the Make a Reservation button near the top of the page.

4. Follow the procedures for booking, up to the point where you're asked for credit information or other personal information. Then discontinue the exercise by logging off the Web site.

▼ **Try It Yourself**

▲

Remember

Not all booking services are created equal. You have to try several of them, compare their good and bad points, and decide which one you prefer.

There are plenty of references to Quikbook's 800 telephone number, as well as its direct email address. If you run into problems, you don't have to rely solely on contact through your Web browser.

Try some of the other online hotel-booking services listed in the appendix and ask yourself the following: Are they easy to use? Do they give you pictures and other hard information on the various properties? Are the step-by-step procedures understandable? Are there other methods of contact besides the Web browser if something goes awry? Does the site feel... *right?* Before you rely on any single hotel-reservation firm, compare prices for the same hotel, on the same date, from several booking services. Then you'll know which one is right for you.

Stars in Your Eyes?

There are many different forms of hotel ratings—some awarded by government agencies, others by the editors of prominent guidebooks. Generally speaking, most ratings are based on a five-tier (or five-star) system in which five is the best and one is bottom-of-the-barrel.

★★★★★ Luxury hotel—You've died and gone to hotel heaven.

★★★★ Deluxe hotel—Upscale, fine amenities, good service.

★★★ Comfortable hotel—The sorts of amenities you'd expect at a good motel.

★★ Tourist hotel—Very basic, perhaps with a bathroom down the hall.

★ Budget hotel—One step up from a hostel. Maybe.

Hotel Chains on the Internet

I doubt you could find a more memorable honeymoon hotel in Mexico than Las Brisas, whose famous casitas are cantilevered on a hillside overlooking all Acapulco and its gorgeous bay. There are 300 casitas (freestanding suites) ranging from studios to three-bedroom units. All the casitas have private or semi-private swimming pools, which are sprinkled with hibiscus blossoms each morning by the staff. Breakfast is delivered to your room so you can laze around in bed until noon. The rooms are airy and comfortable, simply and stylishly furnished. Las Brisas resembles a Mexican village more than it does a hotel. You even stroll along cobblestone streets to get to your room.

How do I know all this? Because I'm a travel editor, you ninny! I've *been* to the place. The more germane question is, how can *you* get all that information for yourself? The trouble with Las Brisas, and other chain hotels without their own individual Web sites, is finding it on the Internet.

By the Way

If you're ever lucky enough to stay at Las Brisas, be sure you rent one of their famous pink-and-white jeeps to drive out to Acapulco's remote and beautiful Pie de la Cuesta beach.

It wouldn't be quite as hard to locate, though, if I were to tell you that Las Brisas is part of the Westin Hotels & Resorts chain, found at *www.westin.com*. With just three or four clicks of your mouse at the Westin Web site, you can learn virtually everything there is to know about Las Brisas, one of Mexico's leading resorts.

It's easy to find the romantic Las Brisas resort on the Web—easy, that is, if you know it's a Westin property.

1. Open your browser to the Westin home page. In the left margin, click on Hotel Search and Reservations.

▼ Try It Yourself

2. In the new window that appears, type in "Acapulco" and "Mexico" in the appropriate city and country forms provided. Then click on Begin Search. Before you can blink an eye, a link appears to Las Brisas. Click it.

3. At the top of the new page, which features Las Brisas, use the pull-down menu to view the resort's various attributes— accommodations, dining, services, and so on.

4. Click on Rates/Reservations at the top of the page, and then enter the requested information. Stop the exercise when you reach the page that begins You specified the following parameters. Do not enter any personal or credit information.

The Westin Internet reservation system is neatly arranged and easy to use. It's not significantly different from the many other hotel-chain Web sites out there. But perhaps you've already discovered a basic problem in choosing a hotel through a chain's Web site. No? You haven't discovered a problem? All right, how about this for a problem: You wanted to stay at Las Brisas, but you didn't know it was run by the Westin chain, and therefore you had no reason to start looking at the Westin Web site—except for the fact that I told you to. (Hey, I'm not always going to be here to hold your hand, you know.)

Where a chain-hotel Web site comes in handy is if you're a member of a chain's frequent-guest program, or if you're entitled to a discount from one chain or another, say, through your company. But if you know only a hotel's name and location, it would be a fool's errand to try to track it down through your bookmarked hotel-chain Web sites.

Contacting a Hotel Directly via the Web

There are plenty of times when you'll want to find a hotel on its own, rather than through an online booking service or through a chain. Perhaps a neighbor recommended a hotel by name and city, and you want to give it a try. Or maybe you read something about it long ago, most of which you've forgotten, but the name of the hotel stands out in your memory. Or maybe you just haven't been able to find it through any of the chain or booking-service Web sites.

Remember

When a hotel isn't affiliated with a chain and you can't find it on an online booking service, you may have to look for it using a search engine.

In such cases, you're at the mercy of our friends, the search engines. And even then, if you do find an independent hotel, you should know that you're losing a layer of consumer protection by dealing with the hotel directly. That is, if the hotel isn't part of a chain, you can't go to the chain for redress of any grievances you might have against the property. If something is fouled up with the reservation, you can't appeal to a hotel-booking service to straighten things out (or to get an alternative booking).

But oftentimes you can get discounts that might not be available elsewhere by dealing with a hotel directly, even if the hotel is part of a chain or works with an online booking service. Let's see how well you can find a hotel whose name I'll pull out of thin air—the Colony Hotel, one of the revived Art Deco properties in the South Beach area of Miami Beach. Get ready, get set... Go!

The Colony Hotel in South Beach is a cool place to hang—but to book a room there, you first have to find it on the Web.

1. Using your preferred search engine, do a search for the Colony Hotel, using whichever search phrase you think is best.

2. If you used Yahoo! and did a search for "Colony Hotel Miami Beach," you would have found the hotel's own Web site (at *colonyhotel-sobe.com*) listed as the second search result. Using AltaVista, it was listed as... well, I stopped looking for it when it didn't show up among the first 100 results. Where did it show up in the search engine *you* used?

3. Follow the link to the Colony's home page. (Cool-lookin' hotel, huh?)

4. Click the blue box at the bottom to go to the Reservations page. Review that new page, but end the exercise before filling in any information.

▼ **Try It Yourself**

▲

Hotel Alternatives—Finding Them and Using Them

Many travelers have long realized that they don't have to stay at a hotel or motel on their vacations. Instead, they stay at condos, apartments, small inns, or bed & breakfasts, all of which are valid alternatives to staying at the more usual lodging choices.

Let's say you want to rent a summer cottage on the shore north of Boston. Go to the Yahoo! Yellow Pages at *yp.yahoo.com* and click on the Real Estate section. Next you'll be asked to type in the city and state you're interested in. When you do so for Rockport, Massachusetts, you're given the names of three real estate agencies in that town. With another click, you come up with another 17 in nearby Gloucester. Any one of them can help you find a rental for the season—possibly at a price that's positively cheap compared with hotel rates.

Beware

Bed & breakfasts are wonderful places to stay, but not if you're a private person who doesn't like to meet strangers.

If you like the cozy feel of being a guest in someone's home, check out the Bed & Breakfast Channel at *www.Bedandbreakfast.com/index3.asp*. The site will lead you to B&B's across the country, as well as to special deals, recipes from some of the site's fave innkeepers, and information on destinations and activities, including the Virginia Wine country, Oktoberfests, and Shakespeare Festivals.

Cottage rentals and B&B's are certainly worth investigating as hotel alternatives, but based on questions I get from travelers, short-term condo and apartment rentals appear to be outstripping them in popularity. Sometimes these condos belong to owners who live in them part of the year and rent them out through an agency the rest of the year. In other cases, they're owned by a person or company that rents them to vacationers all year long. In either case, you can expect much more space than you'll get at a hotel (sometimes two or three bedrooms or more, plus a kitchen and perhaps two bathrooms), as well as the feeling that, for a short time at least, you're the owner of the place.

On the other hand, you may not get the same frequency of maid service you'd get at a hotel (or any at all, possibly), nor room service, nor the same sort of individual attention. The price of the condo might be equivalent to the room rate at a nearby hotel, so ultimately you have to weigh the pros and cons and see which way the scale tips.

One of the leaders in this field (especially in Hawaii, Mexico, and the Caribbean) is Creative Leisure at *www.creativeleisure.com*. This firm specializes in luxury rental homes that can accommodate six or more guests, such as Maui's Emerald Point ("Its palace-like size and amenities make it suitable for the most demanding VIP's," says the Webrochure). Your price? Just $5,650 per night. More modest condos are much less expensive, of course. Let's see what Creative Leisure might offer you in the way of a condo on the Hawaiian island of Kauai.

Focusing on the world's tropical getaways, Creative Leisure is a major source of vacation condo rentals.

1. From the icons in the left margin, choose Hawaii.

2. Access the Kauai pull-down menu at top and click Condos.

3. Read the descriptions and prices for the various available properties, decide which one appeals to you (no, you can't have them all!), and click the Tell me more about this resort button.

4. Call 1-800-413-1000 to make your reservation.

▼ **Try It Yourself**

"WHAT?! Did you say to call an 800 number?!?" Yes, folks, the sad truth is that you're among the avant-garde of the e-travel revolution, if only due to your willingness to learn about the newest innovations and trends. To think that even in these early years of the 21st century, you can find a company that has good Internet content yet still makes you use a telephone to book a reservation. It's an indication of how far yet we have to travel before we're truly an electronic civilization.

Anyway, it'd be nice to contemplate the ramifications of all this from a nice Hawaiian beach in front of my own personal condo. What was that 800 number again?

Wrapping It Up

There are many ways to access a hotel or resort on the Internet. As you've seen, you can find a hotel through online booking services, chain hotel Web sites, and Internet sites sponsored by non-affiliated hotels. You also learned that traditional hotels and resorts are just part of the accommodations spectrum. Savvy e-travelers will also consider alternatives like B&B's, summer cottages, and private condos and apartments.

Booking your accommodations online is rarely more difficult than filling in your personal information on a Web site and awaiting final confirmation of your booking. Be sure to keep an eye out for special deals and discounts that are sometimes offered only to customers who book through the Internet. And after you decide on the place you want to stay, don't be too surprised if, instead of sending your reservation request to the hotel through the miracle of cyberspace, you're asked to place your reservation via... the telephone!

Here are the key points covered in this chapter:

- What an online hotel-booking service is and how you can use it to make your hotel reservations.

- The benefits and drawbacks to using a chain hotel's Web site to find and book a hotel.

- How to track down and book a room through the Web site of a hotel that isn't part of a chain, or that you can't find through an online reservations service.

CHAPTER 15

Airline Schedules and Internet Ticketing

Air travel. No other aspect of traveling sparks as much wrath. And yet it's difficult to live a full professional or personal life without at some point taking a plane ride, whether to attend a wedding, close an important business deal, or just get away from it all on your next vacation.

My first plane ride was on a propeller-driven craft in the days when flight attendants were still called stewardesses and they all wore little hats. In those days, no traveler would even think about boarding an airplane without getting dressed up a little. ("What will you be wearing on the plane?" was a common question among women in the '50s and '60s.) Nowadays you're lucky if your fellow passengers bathe and put on shoes before boarding. Airline meals in those days were something to look forward to. Now... well, now they're not.

But were the old days any better than these days? Thirty or forty years ago, a cross-country flight might take you 15 hours with several stops en route, instead of today's six hours nonstop. Prices are high these days, but they haven't climbed at the same rate as the prices of gasoline, milk, and paperback books. And in the old days, the airlines were something of a mystery. Finding out their schedules, their seat configurations, their ticketing process, and so on required phone calls or visits to the airline or to a travel agent. Nowadays all that information is available at the touch of a button when you access an airline's Web site.

Consider some of the practicalities of air travel that you have some control over—like purchasing your ticket, getting the most affordable price, and staying informed about the best airfare deals available.

What You'll Learn in This Chapter

▶ How to know if you're getting a good price on your next airfare.

▶ How to book your ticket directly through the airlines' Web sites.

▶ How to sign up for airlines' free newsletters announcing e-discounts.

▶ How to buy through a ticket consolidator—and why you need to be careful.

Is There Really Such a Thing As the "Best" Airfare?

The last thing in the world you should ever discuss on an airplane is the price you paid for your ticket. You've probably been in the situation of finding out that the guy sitting next to you paid a hundred bucks less than you did. Unfortunately, those kinds of discrepancies are part and parcel of living in a free-market economy, where the prices of goods and services fluctuate according to supply and demand—and not, sad to say, according to your vacation schedule.

However, there are any number of tricks you can use to get the best deal available at the time you plan to travel. First of all, get a good travel agent. Interview various agents to determine their overall expertise and areas of specialization. No, this doesn't mean you should forget everything you've read in this book and just lay all your questions on a travel agent. But a good travel agent *is* one of many resources available to you.

Creative Strategies

Just as business executives enjoy the benefits of "thinking outside the box," you can use unorthodox strategies to find affordable airfares.

Surf the Internet to get an idea of the going rates for the air routes that interest you. Sign up with the airlines' email newsletters, in which they announce their special deals (mostly, but not always, for weekend travel). Check with the vacation package branches of the major airlines. They often have air/hotel deals that are no more expensive than the airfare alone would be if you went through the normal booking channels.

You can also use some creative itinerary-building that might decrease the cost of your flight. For instance, a woman once complained to me that the cheapest flight she could find from her home in Atlanta to Hawaii was $850 round-trip, including a change of planes in San Francisco. I quickly checked several different online booking services for all the available flights on that particular route on the same dates, and I found that the price she was quoted was pretty close to average.

Then I started playing around a little bit—"thinking outside the box," as they say in the business world. I checked out the price of a round-trip ticket between Atlanta and San Francisco and came up with a very good airfare of $285. Then I checked the prices of flights between San Francisco and Hawaii and found a round-trip ticket on a different airline for $500. So this woman could get a round-trip price of $785 instead of the $850 she was originally quoted. Question: Would the $65 savings be worth the hassle of buying two separate tickets, changing airlines, and having to collect her luggage from one flight to check it in for the next flight? Maybe, maybe not.

I didn't stop there. I began looking into the airlines' vacation branches (almost every airline has a department that sells vacation packages) and found one airline that was offering a package deal to Hawaii for $715. The package included five nights at a hotel, a five-day rental car, hotel taxes, and round-trip airfare from San Francisco. The end result was that this woman now had a choice of either paying $850 for airfare alone or buying the airline's vacation package, plus a separate $285 round-trip airfare between Atlanta and San Francisco, for a total of $1,000. That's a very good deal indeed. Wouldn't you be willing to pay $200 above your airfare to get five days' lodging and a rental car in Hawaii?

One poor sap once complained to me that every time he checked the price of flights to Glacier Park International Airport in Kalispell, Montana, the airfare was exorbitant. Didn't they ever offer discount fares to Glacier, he wanted to know? More the fool, he. You see, a single airline has Glacier sewn up tighter than Ivana Trump's face. A second airline flies there occasionally from Seattle, but other than that, you either fly on that one airline or you don't fly to Glacier.

A-ha! Maybe the answer is… don't fly to Glacier. I recommended that he consider flying into a somewhat larger airport within a couple hours' drive of Glacier (such as Helena, Montana, or Spokane, Washington) and picking up a rental car to complete the trip to Kalispell. Of course, he would have to factor in the additional cost of a car rental, not to mention the inconvenience of the extra drive to his destination, but it might have been worth it depending on how much cheaper his airfare was.

As you begin to investigate the Web sites for individual airlines, pay attention to their package tours. Most airlines have formed alliances with hotels, cruise lines, and car rental companies for complete vacation deals that are sometimes not much more than

the cost of airfare alone! They might be advertised on the Web
site as "vacations" or "packages" or something else. But no matter what they're called, it's worth your time to see what they have
to offer before you plan your next trip.

Straight to the Source: Airlines and Airports Online

Before we go any further, I want to give you something—a list of
airlines you should refer to every time you make travel plans. It's
at a site called All Airlines of the World (modestly enough) at
air.findhere.com. Use it wisely, Grasshopper, and only in the
name of good. The reason I recommend this site is that it will
give you immediate access to scores of foreign airlines. Why
travel with a foreign airline, you ask? Why not take a good ol'
'Merkin airline to the furrin' destination of my choice? One thing
you have to realize is that many foreign airlines are underwritten
by their national government, so turning a profit is not necessarily
always the #1 priority. A foreign airline serving your chosen destination may be having a fare sale that would cause a U.S. airline
to file Chapter 11 bankruptcy papers if it tried to sell tickets for a
similar price.

I'm going to give you another gift, a Web site called Airport
Search Engine at *www.uni-karlsruhe.de/~un9v/atm/ase.html.* At
this unique site, you can type in the name of virtually any city or
country and get links to its local airports. Let's use this site in a
practical experiment and see which airlines fly into Frankfurt
from New York, and the number of flights.

Try It Yourself ▼

1. Go to the Airport Search Engine's home page. At the top of
   the page, type in "Frankfurt" for the city and "Germany" for
   the country.

2. You're given two airports—one of which is an Air Force base
   with no link. Obviously, you want the other one. Click the
   active link—FRA Frankfurt (Rhein-Main), Germany.

3. At the Frankfurt Airport Web site, click Travel Planner and
   then click Flight Schedules.

4. On the next page, look for New York and follow the links to
   ▲   find airlines that fly between Frankfurt and New York.

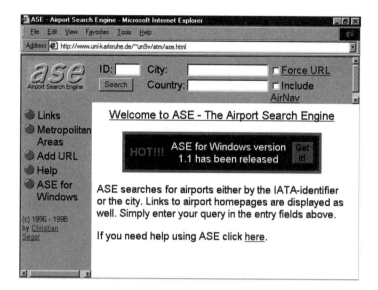

If you're not sure which airports are in or near your next destination, just type the name of the city into the Airport Search Engine.

On the day I tried this exercise, I found four daily flights operated by Delta, American, Lufthansa, and Singapore Airlines. Other, less frequent flights were operated by Lufthansa, as well as one by Kuwait Airlines. Armed with this information, I could go straight to the Web sites of each airline to find out a) what their standard airfare was, and b) if they were offering any special discounts.

Flight schedules are subject to change. Airlines add service to new cities and discontinue service to other cities. The sort of information elicited by the preceding exercise might be different from one month to the next, so be sure to check the latest status of which airline is flying to which airport.

Not every airport Web site is as functional as the Frankfurt airport's site. Don't forget that you can check flight schedules at either your departure airport or your arrival airport. If one airport doesn't have the information you want, the other one might.

Although this information can change daily as airlines rearrange their schedules, it's a fundamental way to learn which airlines fly to the destination you plan to visit. Thus, it's a useful method for figuring out which individual airline Web sites you should investigate for schedule and fare information.

Don't Forget

Airport Web sites can give you as much information about flight schedules as any individual airline Web site can. Plus, they give you schedules of all flights to and from that airport, not just flights for one particular airline.

By the way, if you have trouble with either All Airports of the World or the Airport Search Engine, you can always use Airwise—the Airport and Air Travel Guide at *www.airwise.com*. In a slightly different fashion, it leads you to much the same information as those other sites.

Booking a Ticket Through the Airline

Let's say that you've found the airline you want to fly. You've compared prices, and you're ready to book your ticket. Let's see how it's done when you deal directly with the airline.

Unusual... But Nice...

United Airlines' Web site links you to schedules and fares for all airlines that serve a destination, not just its own flights.

United Airlines is one of the major air carriers that is taking full advantage of the boom in Web bookings. As more travelers bypass traditional travel agents, United has tried to make it easier for them to buy their tickets over the Internet. In fact, the most recent figures show that the airline has Web site sales of $500 million. Of course, that's just a fraction of the company's total revenue of nearly $18 billion, but when the world's largest passenger air carrier (which flies 87 million customers a year) decides to devote significant time and resources to its Web bookings, clearly it's a trend with a solid future.

United is not just focusing on its own Web site, or even just on air travel. Lately it has become a partner in GetThere.com, an Internet venture aimed at business travel, and BuyTravel.com, another venture that sells travel on all major airlines, as well as hotel rooms, car rentals, and cruises.

As such, United's Web site is a particularly good one to use as a guinea pig. Fire up your browser, go to United's home page at *www.ual.com*, and let's have a look around.

It's immediately apparent that United's site is more concerned with doing business than looking pretty. No fancy graphics here. Just loads of information to choose from, clearly delineated between the Traveler Section, with news and services for the average traveler, and the Airline Section, with corporate-related information. Each of those categories is broken down into several subtopics. In the Travelers Section, for example, you find links to Reservations, At the Airport, In the Air, and Upon Arrival, each of which has even more specific subsections.

A no-nonsense approach to Web design gives the impression that United Airlines means business.

The beauty of this layout, which is basically an in-depth table of contents, is that you save lots of time that you might otherwise waste looking for the exact facts you need. Additionally, the site has a Shortcuts pull-down menu at the bottom of the screen that can quickly link you to the general topic you're after.

For the purposes of this section, let's concentrate on what you have to do to book a ticket. (By the way, more than half of United's tickets these days are e-tickets, so you probably won't even have to worry about how or where to pick up the actual tickets themselves.) For this exercise, keep things simple and buy a round-trip ticket on a United flight between St. Louis, Missouri, and Austin, Texas.

1. On the home page, click Reservations under the Reservations category of the Traveler Section.

▼ Try It Yourself

2. On the next page, click Guest in the box at right. On the following page, click Air Reservations.

3. Fill in the destinations and dates (make up your own travel dates). Under Preferred Airlines, check the line for No Preference. Then click Check at the bottom of the page.

4. When I tried this exercise, the least expensive flight on this itinerary was—lo and behold!—TWA and not United.

5. Choose the flight you'd prefer, and then click Price my selected itinerary at the bottom. On the next page, click the yellow Select button next to your flight information.

6. You're instructed to enter your MileagePlus membership number and password, or to sign up as a new user. Doing so will complete the transaction, other than making the final payment. Discontinue the exercise at this point.

You can see the benefits of an airline site with a reservation engine that searches for the best price available, even if it's on another airline. Try the same exercise with several other airline Web sites, using the same cities and travel dates. Compare how easy it is to use the other Web sites and see how their prices differ from your results on the United site.

Travel Partners

If it seems strange to you that United's Web site lists airfares on a competing airline, take a look at the two copyright notices at the bottom of the flight reservation screen. One is for United and the other is for United's partner, GetThere.com, an online reservation system that powers the UAL booking engine. Even if you buy a ticket on another airline from United's Web site, United still gets a cut of the action.

Weekend e-Fares and Airline Newsletters

Getting out of town for a long weekend has become the preferred way to vacation in America. And why not? In the olden days, Mr. Businessman got his two weeks off and used it up all at once— usually at the same time that everyone else was using up *their* two weeks of vacation time. Sometimes that resulted in a counterproductive attitude: "I'm on vacation and I'm going to enjoy myself, even if it kills me!"

What I find so optimistic about the trend toward taking shorter, more frequent vacations is that people are beginning to realize that travel can be a fundamental part of their lives. Not every trip has to be a Major Event.

There has been a fortunate confluence of circumstances regarding weekend travel. Business travelers, who make up the majority of passengers, usually travel on Monday through Thursday. Airlines want to encourage leisure travelers to pick up the slack on the weekends, when most business travelers are glad to be at home. Well, do I need to draw you a picture? More people are taking short weekend vacations more often. Airlines want to increase leisure travel on the weekends. So the airlines are offering... weekend fares!

Email Alert!
You can receive emails every week about the latest air-fare discounts just by signing up with an airline's email newsletter.

These weekend fares have become especially popular in the late 1990s, primarily through weekly email alerts that the airlines send to subscribing travelers. These special discount fares have a number of restrictions, though. First, the destinations aren't usually announced until the preceding Tuesday or Wednesday. Second, the flights have to be booked through the airlines' Web sites. Finally, the days on which you can travel are limited, usually allowing departures only on Friday evening or Saturday, with mandatory returns on either Monday or Tuesday. But these e-saver fares, as they've became known, have exploded in popularity. Almost all domestic airlines and many international airlines have this kind of e-saver program. And not all the airfares are strictly limited to weekends any longer.

Let's have a look at some recent examples that arrived this week in my email inbox.

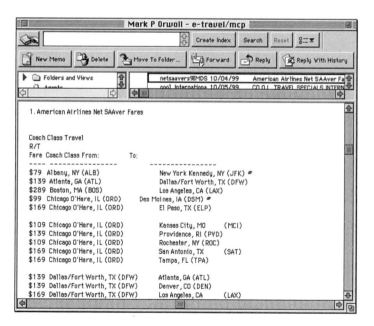

A recent email from American Airlines advertised numerous e-saver fares for weekend travel.

On the domestic front, American Airlines is offering me round-trip airfare between Boston and Los Angeles for $289 via its Net SAAver Fares newsletter. Continental Airlines calls its e-saver fares CO.O.L. Travel Specials. Its most recent newsletter includes a fare of $69 round-trip between Houston, Texas, and Jackson, Mississippi. (I imagine gasoline would cost me almost that much if I intended to drive!) TWA chimes in with its Dot Com Deals—$189 round-trip between St. Louis and Orange County, California. And if I needed to fly back and forth between Atlanta and Washington, D.C., I would have leaped at US Airways' E-Saver fare of $99.

On the international side of things, American will fly me from Chicago to Mexico City and back for just $189, and Continental will fly me round-trip from Newark to Caracas, Venezuela, for $239.

These are just a few examples of what you can receive in your email inbox every week from these and other airlines. Even if you can't get away, you've lost nothing by having a look at them. Moreover, these emails occasionally announce offers that are too good to pass up—offers that are known only to travelers who sub-scribe to the email newsletters.

How do you subscribe? The process is simple. Let's use American Airlines as an example.

Try It Yourself ▼

1. Log on to the American Airlines Web site at *www.americanair.com*. On the home page, choose Net SAAver Fares Service Center from the Specials pull-down menu.

2. On the next page, click the link to Subscribe to our Net SAAver Fares E-mail.

3. You're instructed to fill in your email address and to choose either domestic or international e-saver fares, or both.

4. Fill in the requested information and click Add. You're auto-matically added to the mailing list. If you want to take your name off the list, return to the Net SAAver Fares E-mail page, enter your email address, and click Remove.

▲

Once you begin receiving the weekly emails, you should pay attention to the other deals that are sometimes offered, including discounts on hotels and rental cars. But *always* read the fine print. In most cases, tickets have to be purchased online at the time of reservation, usually through the airline's Web site. In some cases, no changes are allowed for outbound travel. In all cases where changes are allowed, a fee of $75 or more will be charged. E-savers can't be combined with other discounts. Some additional airport fees may be charged. Nothing too surprising, perhaps, but it pays to read beyond just the discount price.

Consolidators: Steep Discounts—But at What Price?

The cost of air travel is sky-high these days, and it shows no sign of coming down to earth anytime soon. That's why smart travel consumers look beyond the airlines for good air deals. One of the places they look is consolidators.

Don't Forget

Consolidators can save you 20–30 percent or more on airline tickets—but the penalties for changing or canceling a ticket may be severe.

Consolidators are ticket brokers. They buy tickets in bulk from the airlines, at about half the full price, and sell them to consumers at a slight markup. The consolidator industry started in the mid-1980s, in little storefronts called "bucket shops." Some of these early consolidators were fly-by-night outfits, and more than one customer paid for a ticket that he never received. It has taken more than a decade for consolidators to salvage their reputations. Nowadays, the vast majority of consolidators are legitimate businessmen offering a valuable service to the consumer.

What kind of discounts might you expect? That depends greatly on the normal airline prices, the route you'll be traveling, and the time of year. Generally, you should expect to save 20 to 30 percent off the full fare.

Bear a few things in mind, though:

- Be aware that most consolidator tickets are for international travel.

- Ask the consolidator if he's a member of any travel association, like the American Society of Travel Agents.

- Find out how long he's been in business, and then call the local Better Business Bureau to find out if there are any complaints about him.

- Find out if he's approved to issue tickets directly. To do so, a consolidator has to show financial means and ticketing experience.

- Pay with a credit card, if you can. Although you may have to pay as much as five percent more than if you paid cash, you can always cancel the charge if you don't get your tickets.

- If you pay with a check or money order, call the airline directly—after booking but before paying—to ensure that you have a confirmed reservation.

- Remember that penalties for canceling a ticket can be staggeringly steep—as much as 50 percent of the ticket price.

You can find consolidators by doing a search on the Internet. But before you deal with any of them, there's a Web site you should read. At *www.travel-library.com/air-travel/consolidators.html*, author Edward Hasbrouck has a well-written treatise on the ins and outs (or should that be ups and downs?) of airline-ticket consolidators and bucket shops.

Wrapping It Up

I still find air travel to be more of a nuisance than a joy. In general, airlines treat passengers with the same courtesy that cowboys treat cattle. I find myself wishing that my flight would just hurry up and be over. But you know what? When I get a good price on airfare, I'm a little less frustrated than I might be otherwise. It's worth the effort.

Here's what you've learned in this chapter:

- How to compare airfares from different airlines' sites and decide if you're getting a good price.

- What's involved in buying a ticket through an airline's Web site.

- The benefits of receiving an airline's e-saver email newsletter, and how to sign up for the mailing list.

- What a consolidator is, and how you can save up to 30 percent or more on a consolidator ticket.

CHAPTER 16

Electronic Booking for Train Travel, Foreign and Domestic

Unlike my history with planes, my many train rides over the years are filled with pleasurable memories. I remember…

…clickety-clacking southward through Virginia toward Florida in an Amtrak sleeper car, my wife and I reading in one compartment, our children bunked down for the night in another across the hall. But then one of my daughters called to me, nervous about her new surroundings. So the kids and I all scrunched up together in one of the bunks, and I told them the train was calling the name of a long-forgotten baseball player ("Heine Manush, Heine Manush, Heine Manush, Heine Manush"). The tiny private room was dark and warm, and we watched the stars and moon outside the window, and the small towns passing by in the warm dark American night, and soon the kids were asleep in my arms. I also remember…

…as a poor student stretching his dollars during a *wanderjahre* around Europe, I bought a train ticket from Paris to Amsterdam, figuring that I could save money by sleeping in my seat and not having dinner. Into my compartment came a happy young family, two parents and three children. I made the little ones laugh by making funny faces, and they made funny faces at me. The conductor came to take our tickets and said something to me in French that I couldn't understand, and the family all laughed, and the father seemed to explain something to the conductor, who looked at me and shook his head. By the time the train was passing through Belgium, the family and I had become great friends, not understanding each other beyond a few pop culture references

What You'll Learn in This Chapter

▶ The best ways to make your reservations on Amtrak and VIA Rail for trips in the United States and Canada.

▶ The right way to plan your train travel in Europe— whether by booking through Rail Europe or directly with the individual national railways.

▶ Where to get online information about other international railroads, as well as information about railroad affinity groups on the Web.

("Ah, Archie Boon-kair, fonnee!") and yet comfortable enough
with each other in our confined quarters. Soon they had a basket
of food open before us and were thrusting sausage and bread and
cheese and wine into my hands. I also remember…

Ah, so many wonderful, happy memories of riding the rails.
There's little doubt that the quality of train travel throughout the
world has fallen off greatly. Speed and utility have taken prece-
dence over comfort and charm. And yet even today, I'd take the
Amtrak from New York to Boston before I'd buy a plane ticket.
For some of us, train travel will always be the preferred way to
go.

This chapter will have a look at Web sites devoted to various
kinds of train transportation throughout the world, how to buy
your tickets online (or at least find out online how to buy your
tickets), and how to become more familiar with the whole concept
of riding the rails, including the World Wide Web's legion of railroad fans and their fascinating sites.

American and Canadian Train Travel

What can I say about Amtrak? I can't defend its many faults, but
for better or worse, Amtrak is the national railroad of the U.S.A.
That means if you want to travel by train across This Great Land
Of Ours, you'll end up on Amtrak. Oh sure, there are a handful of
tourist railroads around, the kinds of historic trains that follow a
16-mile-long track into the countryside and then turn around and
come back. And there are the intercity commuter trains, like
Metro North in New York and BART in the San Francisco Bay
Area. But when it comes to real, honest-to-goodness train travel
across long distances, Amtrak is your one and only choice. So if
you're a good American like me, stand up, place your right hand
over your heart, and repeat after me: "Uh, conductor, there's
something sticky dripping from the ceiling."

I have to say that Amtrak's Web site often works much better than
its trains. From the moment you log on to the home page at
www.amtrak.com, all the information you'll need is well organized, highlighting the major topics of interest that any potential
train traveler might want.

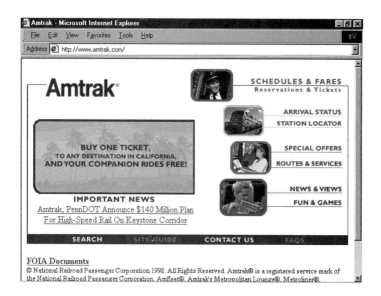

A straightforward layout for an information-filled site. Amtrak's home page is the perfect jumping-off point for America's train routes, schedules, and fares.

The main thing you probably want to know before anything else is, "Do Amtrak's trains go to my destination?" The quickest answer to that question is found by looking up Amtrak's route maps.

▼ **Try It Yourself**

1. From the Amtrak home page, click Routes & Services in the right margin.

2. Decide on a destination somewhere in the middle of the country, say, Dodge City, Kansas. Do *not* click the central part of the U.S. map or the word Central below it. Instead, scroll down to Route Maps and there click the word Central.

3. On the next page you're given a large map of the central part of the United States, with red lines for actual train routes and green lines for motor-coach connections. Follow the red line that runs from Chicago to Kansas City, and continue following it west to Dodge City. So now you know that Amtrak does indeed serve your destination.

4. Return to the home page and click Schedules & Fares. On the next page, click Schedules & Sample Fares. Choose your departure city and type it in the From form, and then type "Dodge City" into the To form. Using the pull-down menu, choose a date to travel. Then click Get Schedule at the bottom of the page.

5. On the new page is a complete schedule and routing for your proposed trip. To find out the fare, click Show Fares at the bottom of the page and read the price of the ticket. Then click the Back button. Looking again at the routing schedule, click the train number for the leg between Chicago and Dodge City. On the next page, you learn that this train is the *Southwest Chief,* running between Chicago and Los Angeles.

6. To learn more about the *Southwest Chief* and its route, return to the home page, click Routes & Services, click Trains & Routes, and click Southwest Chief.

If you decide to go ahead and book that train, follow the instructions on the page that gives you the fare. You're told to follow a link that prompts you to log on to Amtrak's booking system, which is similar to buying a plane ticket on the Internet. Or, you could call the reservation hotline number provided by the Web site and buy your tickets over the phone.

The Romance of the Rails

There may not be much comparison between the railroads of old and the slightly sterile Amtrak of today, but Amtrak does keep alive the romance of the rails in the names of its trains, including: the *California Zephyr,* the *City of New Orleans, Clockers,* the *Empire Builder,* the *Ethan Allen Express,* the *Lake Shore Limited,* the *Texas Eagle,* and the *Twilight Shoreliner.*

Our neighbors to the north have a similar train system, VIA Rail (*www.viarail.ca*). The site's home page is simple enough to understand, ringed with buttons leading to various topics from schedules and fares to photos of the trains. As with the Amtrak site, you might want to begin with a look at the route map to see just where the trains go.

Try It Yourself ▼

1. After you've clicked the word "Welcome" on the opening VIA Rail page, click the Railroad Maps button. Choose the route from Winnipeg to Churchill, in the center of the country, by placing your cursor in the middle of that route and clicking. Churchill, as you may know, is the polar bear capital of the world and directly in the path of the bears' annual migrations.

2. Next you're shown a larger version of that section of the route map. To learn more about that route, look in the frame at left and click Schedules and fares.

3. In the next window, click Schedules, fares and reservations, and then use the pull-down menus to choose Winnipeg and Churchill as your departure and arrival stations, respectively. Then click Schedules, fares & reservation form.

4. In the new window, all the appropriate information is displayed. If you want to book that trip, click Reservation at the bottom of the page. This opens a new window with the price of your ticket and forms where you fill in your booking information.

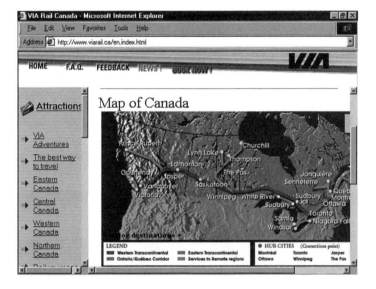

Canada is a big country, and if you want to see some big polar bears there, take the train from Winnipeg to Churchill, site of the bears' annual migration.

European Train Travel

You'll probably do most of your train travel in the United States or Canada. But if you ever have the opportunity to ride the rails in the United Kingdom or Europe, I'd urge you to do so. In most cases (although not all), you'll be able to understand why train travel holds such a powerful allure for so many world travelers.

Perhaps the main thing to understand about European train travel is that, for the most part, the trains in each individual country are operated by a governmental or quasi-governmental agency—

Fast Facts

VIA Rail has close to 3,000 employees, carries 3.8 million passengers a year, runs 430 trains per week, serves 450 Canadian cities, and has 8,680 miles of track.

Britrail, Rail-France, Hungarian State Railways, Germany's Deutsche Bahn, and dozens more. There's no single, unified European railroad system, although you can take train rides that cross the borders of many countries on a single route. Confused? You're not alone.

By the Way

The tickets and rail passes sold by the Swiss Federal Railroad are also good on more than 200 independent railways throughout Switzerland.

One of my favorite European railroad systems is the one run by the Swiss—the Schweizerische Bundesbahnen, otherwise known as the SBB or the Swiss Federal Railways. Let me make it clear that I am a neatnik. I'm orderly. I'm always on time. That's why I like the Swiss—because they're just like me. And so is their train system. You can find the SBB Web site at *www.rail.ch*, which also has a fine English version.

As you would expect, there are no worries about getting an English version of the BritRail site at *www.britrail.com*. Perhaps you want to take the train from London to Oxford. Maybe your flight landed at Manchester and you want to go by train to York. The best way to find out how easy those itineraries are—or not— is to call up the system's timetable. Let's say you got a good airfare to England by flying into the Manchester airport in the English Midlands. But because you're a party animal, you want to hightail it to London as fast as you can. Is that possible by train? Let's find out.

You'll find that a charming little country like the United Kingdom has a modern, up-to-date rail system—BritRail—with trains that seemingly go everywhere.

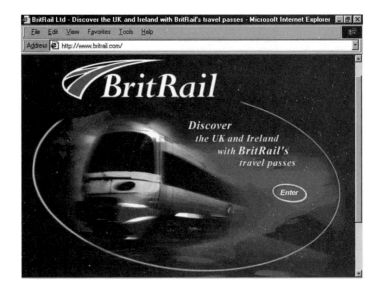

▼ **Try It Yourself**

1. From BritRail's home page, click Enter, and then click Timetable.

2. In the provided forms, type in "Manchester Airport" for the starting station and "London" for the destination station. Then click Submit at the bottom of the page.

3. On the resulting page, you're given a choice of several different trains, at various times, arriving at one of several London-area train stations. For more information, click the check box in one of the itinerary choices and then click the Details button at the bottom of the page.

Train travel in the U.K. is a piece of cake—or perhaps I should say a piece of crumpet—and a jolly good way to travel, especially if driving on the left makes you as nervous as it does me. (More than once I've written about my big idea for a mirror-like optical device that would allow you to drive on the left under the illusion of driving on the right. One of these days I'm going to make a prototype, patent it, and make millions. I'll be rich! Rich, I tell you! Richer than your wildest dreams! [Cue insane laughter])

But what if you're in England and you want to take a train to mainland Europe? There's a little problem in your way known as the English Channel. For thousands of years, it has been an overwhelming obstacle separating England and France. The idea of linking the two nations with a tunnel beneath the channel has been raised every few years since about, oh, 1066, when William the Conqueror said, "You mean we have to take a *boat*?!"

Well, imagine having a typical fried breakfast in London, going to Brussels for a lunch of beer and truffles, and then eating dinner at Joel Robuchon's newest restaurant in Paris. Sound like something only a millionaire could afford? Wrong, *charcuterie*-breath! In November 1994, the dream of linking England to the Continent became a reality with the opening of the Channel Tunnel (or Chunnel) and its premier train, the *Eurostar*.

By the Way

The *Eurostar* trains are about a quarter-mile long, seat up to 766 passengers, and reach speeds of 186 miles per hour.

A round-trip economy-class ticket between London and either Paris or Brussels currently costs about $100 U.S. Check for special deals, timetables, and other nuts-and-bolts info at *www.eurostar.com/main.html*. The *Eurostar* features attendants who speak a variety of languages, food and beverage service, and seats so comfy that you can relax and enjoy the scenery.

Passengers board the *Eurostar* at London's Waterloo Station, and in about three hours they arrive at the train terminal in either Paris or Brussels. (Yes, yes, yes, you could board in Brussels and go to Paris or London, or board in Paris and… well, you get the idea.) If you have the stamina, you can even plan a crazy trip that will take you to all three capitals in a single day. You'd be a maniac to do it—but you *could* do it. However, I'd suggest that you spend a day or two in all three cities, getting to know each of them just a bit before you hop aboard the *Eurostar* for the next leg of your hectic journey.

If Napoleon had been able to cross the English Channel by Eurostar, today's Londoners might be ordering their bangers and mash in French.

The problem with European train travel arises when you want to go back and forth between two countries. You obviously don't have the time or inclination to purchase a separate ticket from each country's railroad. Not to worry, old chum. There's a place designed just for you—Rail Europe at *www.raileurope.com/us/*. You say your next trip will take you from Italy to France to Switzerland? Or you'll be starting in Denmark and traveling through Germany and Holland? Your only logical choice (in the United States) is to choose a pass from Rail Europe. The Eurailpass, available for differing durations, covers travel through

17 countries. The Europass, which is slightly less expensive, covers train travel in up to five countries.

For travelers who plan to take the train through multiple European nations, the Rail Europe home page lists all the available options.

You might wonder if it's worth it, considering that a Eurailpass or a Europass will cost you hundreds of dollars. There's no simple answer, other than to do the math. For instance, let's say you're going to take five train trips during a vacation on the Continent—one train ride to each of the countries on your itinerary, ending up in France. Figure that each of those tickets will cost you, say, $105. So your total train ticket costs will come out to… er… hmmm… carry the five… ho ho hey! Your total will be $525. But what if you could buy a Europass, good for train travel in five countries, for $400? You'd be better off buying the pass. Just make sure that the pass is valid for all or most of the countries you plan to visit.

▼ **Try It Yourself**

1. Let's say that you've decided to buy a Europass, good for five days of travel during any two-month period. Log on to the RailEurope home page at *www.raileurope.com/us/*. In the pull-down menu at top-right, choose Europass, which automatically takes you to the next menu.

2. Scroll down the page, below the map, and click Europass. Review the options, check the prices, and scroll down to the Book Now section.

3. In the pull-down menu for "Which pass duration would you like?", choose "5 days in 2 months". In the form for "How many adult passes would you like?", enter the number 1, and then click Put into shopping basket.

4. Click No in the Pass Protection option, and then click Continue order. Note the total price (including shipping and handling), look for the Submit Order bar *but do not click it*, and then discontinue the exercise.

Other International Train Travel

The European Railway Server at *mercurio.iet.unipi.it* has links to train sites, broken down by country, as well as to sites for the TGV, *Eurostar*, ICE, AVE, and other European express/luxury trains. If you want to see lots of pictures of these trains, this is a fine site to play around with.

Faster Than a Speeding Bullet

The first Shinkansen (Japanese bullet train) ran from Tokyo to Osaka in 1964.

Few trains in the past 20 years have gotten as much exposure as Japan's so-called bullet trains, otherwise known as the Shinkansen. Find out everything under the (rising) sun about these zippity-fast trains, including route maps, details and pictures of the rolling stock, and news on the systems at *www.teleway.ne.jp/~dolittle/byunbyun/index.htm*.

The Cyberspace World Railroad at *www.mcs.net/~dsdawdy/cyberoad.html* is more or less the same idea as the European Railway Server, but it's broader in geographic scope. Check out the site's regular departments, including Oddity of the Month (which, when I checked it out, was all about Polish railroad graffiti). Cyberspace World Railroad is not your normal Web site, but it's a must-have bookmark for railroad fans.

Finally, if you have room for only one railroad bookmark, you absolutely must choose RailServe at *www.railserve.com*. Using both a hierarchy directory and a pull-down search function for more specific topics, the site can lead you to virtually every major train-related Web site in existence. Frequently updated, wonderfully maintained, and pure in its devotion to railroad information, RailServe will lead you to the answers to any questions you have about trains, whether it's history, photographs, details on rolling stock, train schedules, or links to individual railroad Web sites.

Wrapping It Up

Whether you want to travel from Peekskill to Manhattan or from Bombay to Calcutta, a train can get you there. Granted, the systems in the United States and Canada pale in comparison to their European counterparts. Nonetheless, there's a romance to riding the rails that can never be captured in the cramped quarters of a 747 or an L-1011 aircraft. And virtually every bit of information you'll ever need about rail transportation anywhere on earth is available on the Web.

If you've been paying attention to this chapter (and haven't been lulled to sleep by the "Heine Manush, Heine Manush" of the clickety-clackety rails), you should have learned the following:

- How to find out if Amtrak and VIA Rail trains go to your destinations of choice, and how to make a booking on those lines.

- Your options for getting around Europe by train, including buying a multicountry pass from Rail Europe.

- The best sources of information for other international railroads, along with additional links for the enjoyment of railroad buffs around the world.

CHAPTER 17

Rental Car Reservations by Modem

Driving is right at the top of my list of Things I Like To Do on Vacation—falling just below Drinking Guinness in Quaint Pubs, Ogling Beautiful Bods at the Beach, and Sleeping in the Shade for a Couple of Minutes Until the Spa's Chief Masseur Arrives at My Luxury Penthouse Suite to Give Me a 45-Minute Rubdown. But put me behind the leather-wrapped wheel of a cherry '66 Impala with a full tank of gas, a good road map, and the open highway before me, and you can kiss this cat adios.

Quite a bit of my recreational driving has been in the captain's seat of a rental car. And unlike many people who rent cars, I don't feel an obligation to trash the interior, grind the gears, burn rubber, or practice jackrabbit starts. I like to drive, and I like cars—and I appreciate the fact that someone else is going to be driving the car after me.

But I don't like *everything* about rental cars, that's for sure. There's nothing that makes me more upset than a car rental company that doesn't take care of its vehicles, mechanically and cosmetically. Also, I hate dealing with insurance (and I hate paying for it even more). And I get a little nervous when I have to rent a car in a foreign country.

Using the Internet to get more information about car rental companies and to reserve a car can alleviate some of these concerns (although it can't wipe the bug splatter off an uncleaned windshield). This chapter will take a look at how an e-traveler can plug into the world of car rentals on the Web.

What You'll Learn in This Chapter

- ▶ The major differences between the various domestic and international rental companies.
- ▶ How to go about booking a car in the United States through an agency's Web site.
- ▶ How to do the same thing for car rentals in foreign countries, plus what special concerns to look for when renting overseas.
- ▶ What to expect with rental car insurance and paperwork.

Aren't All Car Rental Companies the Same?

You rented a tiny little Asian-built subcompact from Hertz. I rented a tiny little Asian-built subcompact from Avis. My neighbor's Uncle Horace rented a tiny little Asian-built subcompact from Dollar… or was it National, or Alamo, or Budget, or… No matter which company rents you the car, you get a minuscule tin box with a rubber-band engine, and you end up paying somewhere between $30 and $50 a day for the privilege. What difference could it possibly make where you rented the darn thing?

It does make a difference. If you reach under the seat to find the nickel that fell out of your pocket (tightwad!) and you come away with a previous driver's discarded facial tissue, you'll understand the difference. If the tick-tick-tick from under the hood becomes a clonkety-clonkety-clonk out in the middle of nowhere just before the engine dies, you'll understand the difference. And if you're quoted a weekly rate of $175, only to be presented with a bill for $331 because of the taxes, insurance, and other hidden costs that weren't fully explained to you from the start, you'll understand the difference.

Ask the rental agency the following questions before you rent any car:

- What make and model of car will I get based on the size and price category I choose? (Also, ask yourself if you know anything about that particular type of car.)

- How new are the cars in the fleet, and how well are they maintained?

- Besides the basic rental fee, what other charges will I be assessed?

- How do I get roadside assistance if something goes wrong with the car?

- Is there a conveniently located rental agency for my needs?

- Are there any other restrictions and/or benefits of renting with this company?

Answers to most of these questions can be found at the Web sites of the major car rental companies (refer to the appendix for a list of them). Let's see how far you can get in your quest for information on the Avis Internet site at *www.avis.com*. Does Avis "try harder" when it comes to providing consumers with useful information on the Web?

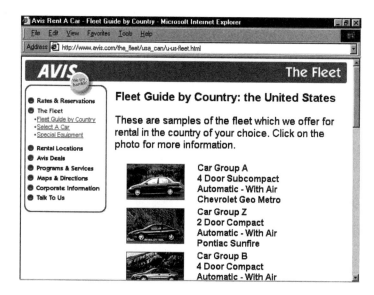

If you wonder what kind of car you might get based on such Avis terms as "Group A," "Intermediate," and "Premium," you can access pictures of the vehicles in the firm's fleet, both in the United States and abroad.

1. From the home page, follow the link for The Fleet, then Fleet Guide by Country, then United States, until you arrive at a list of autos, each with a photo and a description of its status in the Avis hierarchy. Can you find any details about the age and/or maintenance level of the fleet?

▼ **Try It Yourself**

2. To learn more about the costs, go back to the home page and click Request rate under Select function in the left margin. Follow through with your own choices until the price is given. Are you satisfied that the costs are explained adequately?

3. To find out what sort of assistance you can expect in case of an emergency, click Programs & Services at the top of the home page. Scroll down and click on Rental Services, and then choose 24-Hour Roadside Assistance from the

pull-down menu. Does this make you less worried about being stranded by a breakdown?

4. How about convenient locations? From the home page, click Rental Locations at the top of the page and follow it to the destination of your choice. Notice that once you get to your destination, you can click a button to either make a reservation at that location or view a map of that location. Did you find the city you were looking for?

5. Finally, to learn about the benefits of renting with Avis, click Avis Deals at the top of the page, as well as the various additional Programs & Services (of which Roadside Assistance is one). As for drawbacks, you should have discovered any obvious ones already in the course of carrying out this exercise.

This exercise was not designed to isolate Avis, which I've always found to be a good company. But because it is an international full-service car rental company, it was a good candidate for this experiment. Using the list of car rental company URLs in the appendix, try seeking the same information from each of the other firms to compare them with Avis and with one another.

The Domestic Market—Ladies and Gentlemen, Start Your Engines

Despite everything I've just told you, when it comes to renting a car, most people are interested in little more than the price. They assume that the car will run well, no matter which agency rents it. They assume that the car will be clean and otherwise well-maintained. They assume that if the car breaks down, the car agency will immediately send someone out to hand over the keys to a replacement car. However, as everyone knows, when you *assume*, it makes an *as* out of *sum* and *e*—or something like that.

And yet... And yet... And yet, all you want to do is to search for the best prices. So that's what you're going to do in this section, by focusing on American firms that rent cars in the United States. (For a discussion of renting in a foreign country, see "Foreign Car Rentals via the Web" later in the chapter.)

Check Your Figures

If you think you're getting a good rate on a rental car directly from the company's Web site, compare it against what's available through the major online booking sites.

As you learned earlier, most online booking agencies can arrange virtually all of your travel reservations. It's always wise to compare their rates with the ones you find when you go directly to the company involved. If you get a good deal on airfare through the United Airlines site, check it against GetThere.com and Travelocity. If you get what seems like a good price on a hotel room by booking through the Sheraton Hotels Web site, see what sort of rates are being offered at 1travel.com and American Express Travel. And if you like the price you get from a car rental company's online service, contrast it with the prices you can get from Microsoft Expedia, Trip.com, or any of the many other online reservations systems. The only way to know if you're getting a good rate on any reservation you make—hotel, airfare, cruise, rental car, or anything else—is to compare that price with the prices available elsewhere.

The same goes for the Web site interface. You'll want to find out which car rental company Web sites are easy to use, and the best way to do that is to try as many of them as you can. Let's try getting a rate quote from two different companies and compare the results. First you'll start with the Web site run by Hertz, the most popular car rental company in America.

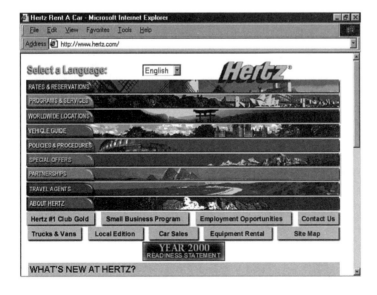

Hertz's Interactive Reservation Process is cut-and-dried. You fill in the forms for the car you want and when you want it, and you receive a straightforward price quote.

Try It Yourself ▼

1. From the Hertz home page at *www.hertz.com*, click the Rates & Reservations link at the top of the page. Then select General Rates & Reservations and click the Submit button.

2. Fill in the reservation form (without giving out your personal information) and submit it.

3. A new page details all the costs based on the information you submitted.

Who Tries Harder?

Have a look again at the Avis site in this chapter. Its motto is "We Try Harder"— that is, harder than the top dog, Hertz. Now compare it with the Hertz site and ask yourself: Who do you think tries harder to do a good job on the Web?

Don't Forget

Almost every car rental Web site has a prominently marked section devoted to limited-time discounts.

Try It Yourself ▼

Note that there were boxes where you could request "corporate rates" or other special rate codes. If you work for a corporation and are traveling on business, you may get a better rate by using your company's corporate code (available from your office manager or corporate travel office). Also, car rental companies often advertise special limited-time discounts. You have to read the fine print, which may say something like, "Ask for discount code HA-123," or something similar. If you know of such discounts and have the discount code, be sure to enter it in the appropriate box when filling out online forms. Also, be sure to indicate codes for any organizations you belong to, like the American Automobile Association (AAA) and the American Association of Retired Persons (AARP).

Now let's compare the price you were quoted with that of another major national chain, National Car Rental, which you can find on the Internet at *www.nationalcar.com*.

1. From National's home page, click Reservations, which you'll find at the bottom of the screen. On the next screen, click Rates and Reservations.

2. Fill in the reservation form in the same way you filled in the Hertz form in the previous exercise. Be sure to use the same dates, times, and locations.

3. Keep filling in forms and clicking the Continue button at the bottom of each new form until you end up with your final price. It should break down the total cost, including taxes.

Who gave you the better rate—Hertz or National? For bonus points (who am I kidding, there are no bonus points!), try the same request, using the same details, with one of the major online reservation services.

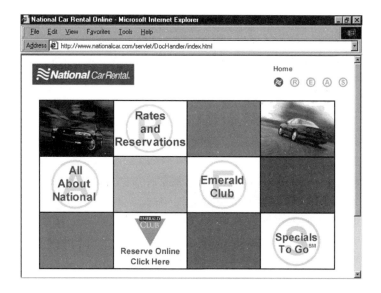

National's site has a clean and simple interface that leaves no doubt where to click for reservation information.

Consider once again the final price of your rental. The Hertz form gives the price per day or per week, as well as the mandatory taxes and/or airport concession fees, for a grand total. For comparison purposes, the grand total is more important than the daily or weekly rate. Hertz also lists the costs of supplementary insurance. All in all, it's a fairly simple reservation process with clear and understandable information. Compare how Hertz and National present these details. Do you prefer one over the other? Do you understand them both?

Foreign Car Rentals via the Web

Overseas car rental companies have glommed onto the Web in a big way. From the comfort of your own home office, it's just as easy to reserve a car in Germany as it is to reserve one in Florida. Even language differences rarely prove to be a problem because many of these sites are available in more than one language, including English. Nor are currency differences a problem because most foreign firms' Web sites calculate the total cost in whichever currency you choose.

Some of the large American companies also have locations throughout the world. So if you absolutely must use Hertz, chances are pretty good that you can find one of its offices at your foreign destination.

But the purpose of this section is to learn more about the companies that focus on foreign rentals. Some such firms, like Europe by Car and Auto Europe, are based in the United States. Let's run through a by-now-familiar exercise with Auto Europe, which you'll find on the Web at *www.autoeurope.com*.

Auto Europe gives you pictures and prices of rental cars available in 33 countries— even before requiring you to fill in reservation forms.

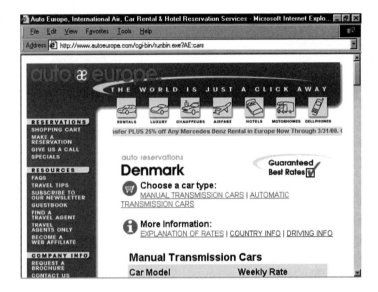

Try It Yourself ▼

1. Using the pull-down menus on the left, click Denmark under Select a Country, and click Car Rentals under Select a Service.

2. You're taken to a new screen that shows you a list of the available cars and their rates, with tiny pictures. (Be sure to read the explanation of rates at the bottom of the page.)

3. Click the Book it! shopping cart icon for the car you want to rent. Then click Make A Reservation on the next page.

4. Review, but do not complete, the reservation form on the next page, and then discontinue the exercise.

Notice that you got basic rate quotes very quickly and simply, without filling in a lot of forms. But also notice, in the explanation of rates, that in Europe there are often extremely high taxes and surcharges. In Denmark, you pay a value added tax (VAT) of 25 percent, plus a $21 surcharge if you pick up your car at an airport.

If you back up a few pages in the just-completed exercise, back to the page with the printed rates, you'll find links near the top for Country Info and Driving Info. There you'll find very useful details about Denmark and its individual driving requirements. Auto Europe provides all this information for each of the countries in which it rents cars. It includes such topics as insurance options, traffic laws, and restrictions on how and where the car can be used.

In many respects, renting a car in most foreign countries is a relatively painless procedure that doesn't differ hugely from renting a car in the United States. That holds true whether you're booking the car through an 800 telephone number or through your Internet browser. However, always beware of what may be major differences in the laws governing driving, insurance, and licensing. Fortunately, as you saw at the Auto Europe site, much of that information is available at the car rental companies' Web sites.

Documents and Insurance That You Shouldn't Screw Up

A driver's license issued in any U.S. state is valid not only throughout America, but also in Europe, Mexico, New Zealand, and most other parts of the world. But that doesn't mean you shouldn't get an International Driving Permit (IDP).

Even though technically you may not *need* an IDP, it can prove helpful. If you get pulled over for running a *luz rojo* in Spain, or for driving at night without your *feux allumés* in France, or for driving less than *eine tausend* miles an hour on the Autobahn, a cop in that country will recognize an IDP, whereas he might look askance at the license issued to you by the DMV in Tuscaloosa. I once had a Serbian patrolman give me the third degree for 15 minutes about my New York license. "And you say they gave this to you after you… *took a test*? Hmmm. And what kind of test would that be, Meester Orvolmark?" I almost expected him to add, "Just what kind of a fool do you take me for?" Imagine how much worse it might have been for me if he hadn't spoken English—another good reason to have an IDP.

An IDP can be obtained from any AAA office in the United States. (Find your local branch of the AAA online at

Remember

No matter what country you're driving in, the local police will almost always recognize an International Driving Permit.

www.aaa.com. You can even get the application form online at *www.aaa.com/vacation/idpf.html.*) You'll need a couple of passport-size photos of your beautiful kisser, and you'll have to pay a moderate fee, but the minor hassle is worth it.

Something else to concern yourself with is rental car insurance. In many instances, your own auto insurance will cover you when you rent a car. Many charge cards also provide some form of rental car insurance. Always check with your card company to find out if such coverage is primary or secondary. If it's secondary, that means your personal auto insurance must be used (or more to the point, used *up*) before the card company's insurance can take effect. When in doubt, buy the rental company's optional insurance. But it's better not to be in doubt, because that optional insurance (usually called LDW) can cost $20 or more per day.

When in Doubt

No one should spend more on rental car insurance than necessary, but if you're not sure, always err on the side of caution.

In some foreign countries, car rental companies must include basic insurance as part of the rental fee. But not in all countries. Not in Mexico, for instance. When I was a college student in San Diego, my friends and I would park our cars north of the border and walk through the international checkpoint to downtown Tijuana, specifically so that we wouldn't have to deal with car insurance. Hanging out at the Long Bar or the Blue Fox, we'd drink ourselves silly and laugh at the *turistas* who had stopped en route at the little Fotomat-style booths where insurance kingpin Oscar Padilla sold 24-hour policies that, ideally, would keep the visitors out of the hoosegow if some *campesino* with attention deficit disorder rear-ended them next to the Tia Juana Tilly's Bar on Avenida Revolución.

But we weren't as smart as we thought. Those folks who dutifully bought Mexican insurance were playing the game the right way. You see, American auto insurance isn't valid in Mexico. Several sources I've consulted use the phrase "Napoleonic Code" when referring to the Mexican system of justice, meaning that you're considered guilty until proven innocent. If you get in a car accident, you and the other party are both presumed to be liable for damages. If you cannot produce documents proving that you have authorized Mexican insurance, you'll probably go to jail until the matter can be sorted out. (You may go to jail anyway for a brief time, even if the accident isn't your fault and you do have the proper insurance.) In many instances, Mexicans involved in minor accidents mutually agree to simply drive away from the scene rather than involve the police. I wouldn't drive in Mexico without buying the full package of Mexican auto insurance from the rental agency.

It's crucial that you fully understand the local laws regarding insurance, whether you're renting a car in Seattle or Shanghai. Most of the time this information is available online from any of the various rental agencies that service your destination. You can also find it in the various online destination guides.

Wrapping It Up

Renting a car is usually a simple matter, whether it's in this country or abroad. The process is even easier now that you can do it from the comfort of your own home via the World Wide Web.

In this chapter you've learned that, although there are differences between the various companies, most people are mainly interested in getting the best price, not in which company does the best job of vacuuming their fleet's upholstery. But that's okay, because you know how to find the best rates by comparing several companies that operate at your destination. You know to check the "specials" section of each site, usually indicated on the home page. You also know that insurance and surcharges can add a lot to the total cost of your rental.

When it comes to paperwork, you've learned that it doesn't pay to mess around. An International Driving Permit (IDP) is a good thing to have if you'll be driving in a foreign country—whether the local laws require it or not. And as for insurance: When in doubt, buy more than you need. Read up on the local laws. Ask questions. See what the car rental companies' Web sites have to say on the matter. Investigate the subject more thoroughly through destination guides on the Web and online tourist bureaus for your destination. But never, absolutely *never*, be caught short-handed when it comes to insurance.

Here's what you learned in this chapter:

- Although there may be differences between the car rental companies, generally the deciding factor is price.

- The actual procedure for renting a car domestically takes little more effort than filling in forms on the Web and clicking the Submit button.

- Web sites specializing in foreign car rentals work similarly to their domestic counterparts.

- There are some not-very-interesting yet highly serious paperwork considerations—not least of which are IDPs and car insurance.

CHAPTER 18

Cruisin' the Net

I should've called this chapter "Floatin' on the Net," because it's going to discuss more than just traditional cruise ships. There are ocean cruise ships and there are river cruise ships. There are ferries that ply the seas and freighters that carry passengers between continents. Some of these ships prefer that you make your reservation through a travel agent. Others are so small or out of the way that many travel agents have never heard of them.

And even when it comes to booking through a travel agent, how do you find a good one who knows about cruises? In fact, what *is* there to know about cruises—other than that you eat 24 hours a day and from time to time Captain Stubing has to chastise Gopher the purser for having an onboard fling with some foxy widow.

If you've never been on a cruise ship, you might think it would be about as lively as a PBS documentary on lint. Wrong! After you visit a few of the online cruise sites, you'll discover that a cruise can be relaxing or active, tropical or arctic, party-till-dawn or rise-with-the-sun. A cruise can be whatever you want it to be, thanks to the unbelievable variety of ships and ports of call. In this chapter, you'll take a virtual voyage through the world of cruising and see for yourself.

CLIA—One-Stop Shopping for Cruise Information

From the moment you log on to the Cruise Line International Association's Web site at *www.cruising.org*, you know something intriguing is afoot. "You haven't lived until you've cruised." The words come floating across your screen, wafting over the image of a sleek ocean liner plowing through a deep blue sea. Without even clicking the Enter button, you're taken to the information-packed home page for CLIA, as those in the know call this well-respected industry organization.

What You'll Learn in This Chapter

▶ How to use the best all-purpose cruise site on the Web.

▶ How to access a cruise line on the Web to get details on individual ships and itineraries.

▶ Sources for other kinds of cruises—river trips, ferries, and freighters.

In previous chapters, I warned you to be fully aware of just what a Web site was trying to sell you. And just as state con/vis bureaus and national tourist offices are trying to sell you an idyllic image of their destinations, so too is CLIA attempting to sell you cruising in its idealized form. Ticker tape-like sentences run across the top of the home page to entice you further: "A resort is surrounded on four sides by land; a cruise is surrounded on four sides by forever," says one of the come-ons.

> **Caveat**
> CLIA celebrates cruising, but if you want a more objective opinion, check out the Ship Reviews section of Cruise Mates on the Web at *www.cruisemates.com*.

The lucky thing for CLIA is that cruising doesn't need too much hype to make it sound great. True, some people may get seasick. True, some people will be disappointed by the small size of their cabins. Yes, as in any kind of vacation, there are drawbacks. CLIA's site is not the place to learn about those drawbacks, however.

No matter. Whenever I research the cruise business, my first stop on the Internet is the CLIA Web site. CLIA is an association of almost all the major cruise lines, so it has a wealth of information.

On CLIA's site you'll find links to some two dozen cruise lines—not to mention FAQs, news stories, and special discounts.

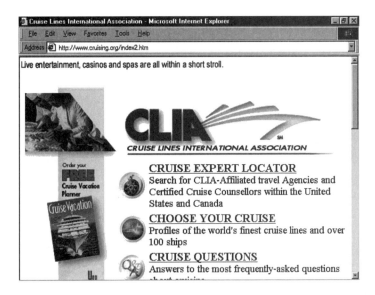

On the home page you'll find profiles of more than 100 cruise ships, frequently asked questions about cruising, cruise news and special offers, feature stories about cruise vacations, activities, and shopping, and links to the individual cruise lines' Web sites. My favorite feature is the Something for Everyone section, which allows you to investigate various cruise lines based on your interests, including selections for honeymooners, active adults, families traveling with children, and singles.

There's one especially important consideration that applies specifically to singles—most cruise lines charge a premium of 25 to 100 percent of the cruise fare for booking only one person in a cabin. The CLIA guide will tell you who has the least egregious of these "single supplement surcharges."

Open up the CLIA site on your browser and familiarize yourself with its major components. If you're new to the subject of cruising, no doubt you'll want to spend time reading the frequently asked questions. But let's sample my favorite section by creating a fictional persona. Let's see... What shall it be...? I've got it! Let's pretend that you're a honeymooner who likes to shoot skeet, and you and your new spouse want to do it on a cruise to Africa. Let's put CLIA to the test and see if they can point you toward just the right cruise line.

Beware

Singles traveling alone usually have to pay a "single supplement surcharge," which often can double the fare listed in the brochure.

1. From the main index page, click Something for Everyone and then click Cruise Guide for Honeymooners.

2. On the next page, click All Cruise Lines on the pull-down menu and then click Find. Find the cruise line with the most extras, as marked with the green balls. Looks like Costa Cruise Lines is the winner there.

3. Go back to the Something for Everyone page. This time, click on Cruise Guide for Active Adults. On the next page, using the pull-down menu, click Skeet/Trap Shooting. Scroll across the screen to see if Costa is listed... and indeed it is (on some ships).

4. Back at the Something for Everyone page, click Cruise Guide for Worldwide Destinations, and then click Africa. Notice that Costa Cruise Lines is one of the few CLIA lines with itineraries to Africa.

▼ **Try It Yourself**

▲

Granted, it took a little bit of work, but in just a few minutes you learned exactly which cruise line to consider if you're a honeymooner who enjoys skeet shooting on a cruise to Africa. The same procedures can be used no matter what your preferences—whether you're a single person who wants to scuba-dive during a cruise to the Caribbean or a family traveler who wants low-cal menus and aerobics on a cruise to Asia.

Case Study: How to Use Carnival Cruise Line's Web Site

Packing List

Pack for a cruise the way you would pack for a resort vacation—mostly casual wear during the daytime, and a bit more formal at night, including one or two "dressy" evenings.

One of the giants of the cruise industry is Carnival Cruise Line, the company that promotes its fleet as "Fun Ships." After a rocky start in 1972, when it had only a single vessel and dim prospects, the company became the 800-pound gorilla of the seas. Every year it brought out more ships, and each one was bigger, much bigger, than the ones before.

Today the cruise line sails "megaships," vessels that can hold 2,000 to 3,000 passengers, almost exclusively. In the past several years, as its enormous fleet has continued to grow, Carnival has set its sights on other cruise lines. Today the company owns Holland America Line, which is known for its old-fashioned, very classic style of cruising, the popular Windstar Cruises, which attract a jet-set crowd, and Seabourn Cruise Line, the seriously upscale boutique line whose ultra-deluxe ships virtually define the word *lavish*.

But it's the 14 Fun Ships of the Carnival fleet that most people hear about and that continue to attract thousands of first-time cruisers who expect that there will be plenty to do on these large ships aimed at youthful (not to say young) and active cruisers.

What's in a Name?

Carnival really goes in for splashy names for its ships. Can you tell which ones are real and which are the product of a warped imagination (namely, mine)?

a. *Ecstasy*	**e.** *Triumph*
b. *Elation*	**f.** *Cacophony*
c. *Scintillation*	**g.** *Destiny*
d. *Passion*	**h.** *Reprobate*

(Answer: a, b, e, and g are the real names.)

Carnival's home page at *www.carnival.com* sets the tone for the rest of the site. With the words "Just More Fun," the home page introduces you to Carny, a blue-and-red smokestack wearing sunglasses. Corny, you say? Better believe it, kiddo. If it's upscale elegance and quiet sophistication you want, you've come to the wrong place. But let's have a swing through the Web site and see what's right about it.

Clicking on Carny takes you to a simple table of contents—and in fact, you'll notice that simplicity is the hallmark of the site. Starting at the top of the index, have a look at the various sections, beginning with the Fun Ships themselves, the line's destinations, current specials, and a page devoted to the first-time cruiser.

Booking a cruise on Carnival is as simple as choosing dates and destinations from the pull-down menus.

Carnival also has a booking function. You have to be a member to use it, but signing up is an easy enough procedure.

▼ **Try It Yourself**

1. Click Book A Cruise, follow the instructions to become a member, and then log on once you've enrolled.

2. Click Create New Reservation once you've logged on. On the next page, fill in your cruise preferences using the pull-down menus.

3. As you're prompted to select destinations, dates, ships, and cabins, follow some of the hyperlinks to get more information. Continue filling in the reservation forms.

4. Confirm the reservation information you supplied on the page that begins "You have selected…" You'll soon reach a page with all your expected costs tallied, along with directions about payment.

5. Leave the Web site at that stage. Don't confirm your reservation, and don't supply credit information. As they used to say on the radio in the days when we thought the Russians were gonna bomb us, "This is only a test."

Did you notice the remarks about travel agents at the confirmation stage of the reservation process? "At Carnival Cruise Lines," it said, "we rely on the travel agent to fill our ships every year. We have found this system to be the most efficient method of doing so. While it is not necessary to have a travel agent to use our online reservations system, we suggest one be consulted."

The Other Kinds of Cruises

The world is two-thirds water. That's a lot of Perrier. So if you think that all those big ol' honkin' cruise ships have a lock on aqua transport, think again, you thilly thailor. There are still places where rickety ferries carry folks across straits, sounds, and even just itty-bitty rivers. There are sleek passenger ships that carve a wake up the great inland waterways—the Mississippi, the Amazon, the Rhine, and others. There are working-class freighters carting around widgets and gizmos from one continent to the next that may be willing to give you a berth for two weeks or more for a reasonable rate.

Do You Believe in Ferries?

To get a sense of what you might find when logging on to the site of a ferry line, many of which serve foreign destinations and are written in foreign languages, let's have a look at the site for the SNCM ferry line.

Find Out More
A great link site to learn more about ferries, freighters, river cruises, and ocean cruises is Cybercruises at *www.cybercruises.com*.

Getting to Corsica is an easy enough matter on the ferries operated by *La Societé Nationale Maritime Corse Mediterranée*, usually abbreviated as SNCM. You'll find it on the Web at *www.sncm.fr*, where you can get price information and schedules, as well as a list of European agencies that sell tickets. The company's ferries, which shuttle passengers and autos between several points in France and Corsica, range from large cruise ship-like vessels to smaller and faster hydrofoils. The ship *Ile de Beauté*, for example, which carries up to 1,554 passengers and 520 cars, leaves Nice at 9 a.m. several days a week and arrives at Corsica's capital, Ajaccio, seven hours later. That's useful information to have if you're thinking of going from France to Corsica.

Click the funny-looking Union Jack for the English version of this site.

1. Open your browser to the site's home page, and then click the Union Jack pennant for what purports to be an English version. (Note for advanced users: If that link doesn't work, click the French flag. On the next page, in the URL location

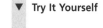

▼ **Try It Yourself**

box of your browser, delete the second "fr" and replace it with "us.")

2. If you managed to get the English version, click Schedules in the menu at left.

3. Find out the schedule for the Nice-Corsica ferry by clicking on the Marseille Toulon Nice/Corse link on the right side of the page.

4. The new page (in French; the site is not yet fully translated) asks for the dates of your travels. Fill them in (noting that "j" means day, "m" equals month, and "a" equals year) and click Continuer.

5. The new screen shows a clear and concise schedule of ferries for the requested dates. Even a non-French speaker can understand what it all means.

Language problems are bound to crop up when you're dealing with foreign ferry lines. Just keep an open mind, don't be negative about it, and use your innate intelligence to translate as best you can. But hurry up, or you may miss the boat!

Rollin' on the River

A river cruise is a terrific idea for anyone who a) doesn't like big ships, b) prefers a close-up view of the landscape, and c) is afraid of getting seasick. The pace is leisurely, there's almost always something to see as you float along, and you're usually given the opportunity to stop and walk around the more interesting cities en route. Among the most popular places for river cruises are the waterways of Europe. And the Rhine River is one of the most scenic of all, with hilltop castles and medieval villages rising from the banks for almost its entire length.

My first recommendation is KD River Cruises of Europe, if only because of the company's nearly two centuries in business and its variety of boats and itineraries. You'll find them on the Web at *www.rivercruises.com*. KD's nine ships sail the length of the Rhine and stretches of the Moselle, Elbe, Danube, Seine, and other continental waterways.

Log on and learn about the vessels. Cabins, as in most cruise ships, are small, and they include twin beds, shower, toilet, closets, radio, and telephone, along with table and chairs by the window. Cabins are made into sitting rooms during the day. You'll also learn about life on a river cruise. At the end of each day, ships stop overnight in a town, allowing you time to see some of the sights in the cities you pass. Dress onboard is mainly casual, although men are expected to wear jackets in the evening and women will want to pretty themselves up a little as well.

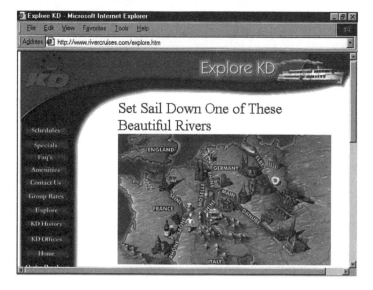

If you think all rivers are alike, visit the Explore page on the KD River Cruises site and learn more about the waterways on the company's itineraries.

KD River Cruises is one of the largest and best-known of the river cruise lines, but there are many others. If you play around with KD's Web site, you'll find the kind of information that a reputable river cruise line should offer—whether you're researching a steamboat trip on the Ohio or a lazy 1920s-style float down the Nile.

Freighter Travel—Not for Everyone

In the old days, young Americans of a romantic stripe would sign on to work on a cattle boat so they could get to Paris cheaply and have fistfights with Ernest Hemingway. Today, many people travel on freighters not to get to a destination, but rather as an experience in its own right.

You won't have the discos and casinos of the large glam ships. No floor shows in the Copacabana Lounge, no karaoke contests just before the midnight buffet. Instead, passengers on freighters spend their days quietly and contemplatively, reading, watching videotapes, relaxing on a deck chair, visiting the port of call while the freighter unloads or stocks up. Accommodations can range from very simple to very comfortable. Meals can be anything from nothing fancy to fancy indeed. But cruise rates on freighters are almost always good—around $100 per person per day on average (as compared with twice that or more on the traditional cruise ships).

One of the best sites for freighter travel is Freighter World Cruises at *www.freighterworld.com*. Freighter World is a travel agency that specializes in this kind of adventure. Whether you choose to book such a trip through the firm or not, its Web site is a good starting point to learn more. The company works with more than a dozen different freighter lines to send clients on trips to Europe, the Caribbean, Asia, Africa—virtually anywhere in the world—lasting anywhere from eight to 60 days.

Wrapping It Up

If you think a vacation on the high seas is right for you, you can refer to the various cruise links in the appendix, including Web sites for cruise-only travel agents, newsletters for cruise enthusiasts, and the cruise lines themselves.

Here are the key points covered in this chapter:

- What Cruise Line International Association (CLIA) is and how it can be a primary source for basic cruise information and cruise line links.

- How to book a cruise directly through a cruise line's Web site based on the exercise using Carnival Cruise Line's Internet booking service.

- The alternatives to traditional cruises, including river cruises, ferries, and freighters.

PART IV

Preparing on the Web for Your Departure

CHAPTER 19

Bringing a Laptop

This is an admission that will make my publisher cringe, but frankly, I would rather not travel with electronic gizmos. When it comes to communicating on the road, I confess to an utter lack of interest in anything involving the words "cellular" or "digital." Even at home I don't use a cell phone, a microwave oven, a pager, or most of the other electronic gear that has become a mainstay in most other homes and offices. I am a self-admitted Luddite. I do own a VCR, however, and have recently learned how to use the remote control. Once I get the clock to stop flashing 12:00 all day, it should really be cool.

Don't get me wrong. I do love using my computer, especially being able to sit in my office and do the research I need to do for trip-planning purposes. But there's a difference between planning and booking your trip online and actually bringing your techie tchotchkes with you on the road. I suppose there are reasons why someone might need all those devices. Perhaps you're traveling on business and your files are most easily transported by laptop. Maybe you're mountain-climbing in Switzerland, but someone back home is very ill, so you pack along a cell phone to check in every now and then. Or maybe you're just so darn hooked on hi-tech whizbangs that you go through withdrawal if you don't log on or link up at least once every 24 hours.

If you fall into any of those categories, you can probably dispense with this chapter because it's going to approach the topic from a beginner's point of view. You'll learn about using your laptop on a plane, and about hooking up to the Internet from your hotel room. You'll set up your own email account, for free, on the Internet. And you'll take a look at a few sites with the latest news on the trendy-techie goodies that go blip and beep while you're on the road.

What You'll Learn in This Chapter

▶ Taking a laptop on your next trip, including tips on security.

▶ Logging on to the Internet at your hotel through your laptop.

▶ Signing up for free email so you can send and receive messages while you're traveling.

▶ Using a cell phone on the road.

Laptop Lullaby

The type of laptop computer you buy, and the various appurte-
nances you add on, are pretty much up to you. If you use a laptop
as a second computer, or if you use it mainly for non-business
purposes while traveling, I'd suggest that you forget about all the
bells and whistles. What you want is a portable, lightweight, easy-
to-operate computer that has enough memory for your purposes
(and most laptops do), with a built-in modem that will allow you
to hook up to the Internet via a phone jack or data port.

Once you have the hardware in hand, the real fun begins—like
worrying how you're going to lug it around, whether anyone's
going to steal it, how to log on to the Internet without accruing a
$90 phone charge, and whether the hotel's phone system is digi-
tal, which may burn out your analog modem. Ahh, vacation!

Bottom Line

Don't try to save a
few bucks by cheap-
ing out on your lap-
top carrier. Why risk
your $2,000 invest-
ment just to save an
extra $20 or $30?

First things first. Your laptop may or may not have come with a
padded case, but you need to be sure you have a case that is
super-safe and durable. The one I use, made by a company called
Port in Norwalk, Connecticut, is about the size of a standard
briefcase. Not only is it well-padded throughout, but there's also a
sling in which the laptop is strapped so that it doesn't touch the
bottom of the case or absorb the shock of setting the case down.
Port calls this a "shock system." The case also provides plenty of
pockets and storage slots for modem cords and power cords,
disks, pens, notepads, and paperwork.

Not every laptop carrier has to look like an old briefcase, though.
Some manufacturers are making them to resemble daypacks, so a
would-be thief might not even realize there's a computer inside.
One such carrier, tested by Travel & Leisure, is the Laptop Transit
from JanSport. It's strong, useful, and easy to carry—plus, you
can use it as a basic shoulder bag even when you're not toting
your laptop along.

I don't care which manufacturer's carrier you use. My point is not
that you should go out and buy a laptop carrier from one specific
manufacturer or another. You're smart; you can compare various
brands. The thing to remember is that no matter which carrier you
choose, don't try to save $20 or $30 by buying one that's less
sturdy than what you need. The goal is to ensure the safety of
your $2,000 laptop.

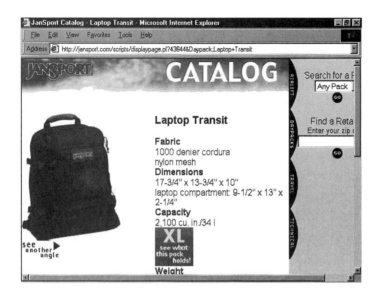

Looking as if it held nothing more valuable than used textbooks and some dirty underwear, JanSport's Laptop Transit daypack is a multipurpose bag.

So you have your hardware, and it's stored in a solid carrying case. The next thing to be concerned about is holding onto the darn thing. About 50,000 laptops a year are stolen in travel-related incidents in the United States. How do you avoid becoming one of those victims? There's no substitute for common sense. You simply have to keep your eyes wide open.

One of the most common scams happens at airports. As a laptop-carrying passenger sets down his computer to go through the X-ray machine, one of two (or more) bad guys, with lots of jangly metal in his pocket, steps in front of the victim and sets off the metal detector. As the bad guy stands there, pulling change and nail files and cigarette lighters out of his pockets, the victim's laptop has sailed through the X-ray conveyor belt. When it comes out the other side, the bad guy's partner deftly picks it up as if it were his own and walks quickly toward the nearest exit. When the hapless victim finally gets through the metal detector, his laptop is long gone.

When I'm carrying either a laptop or an expensive camera, I wait to set my things on the X-ray conveyor belt until the last possible moment so that both my belongings and I pass through the checkpoint at the same time. Plus, I try to keep my eyes on the goodies the whole time.

Hotel Security

Several manufacturers make laptop security cables that let you attach your computer to an immovable object in your hotel room.

Going Online on the Road

Take it from someone who's not a techie, going online with your
laptop in a hotel room is easier and faster than making a peanut
butter and jelly sandwich. At least, it's easy if you have everything in place before you leave. You have the laptop? Check. You
have a modem, either built-in or standalone? Check. You have
your Internet provider's local number at your destination, or its
toll-free number? What? You *don't* have a local or toll-free number? What are you planning to do, make a 60-minute long-
distance phone call from wherever the heck you are just so you
can surf the Net for a while?

Here's a Tip

Extend the charge of
your laptop batteries
by turning down the
brightness of your
screen as much as
possible (or better
yet, switching to
black-and-white
mode).

Most of the major Internet service providers (ISPs) do have such
numbers so that at most you'll pay the cost of a local phone call
to connect to the Web. You can get those numbers by calling your
ISP or looking it up on the ISP's Web site. If your provider does-
n't have local-access or toll-free numbers, and if you plan to bring
your laptop frequently on trips, consider switching to a different
ISP.

Most of the time, hooking up your computer to the Internet in a
hotel room is easy. All you have to do is connect your modem
cord from the laptop to the room's data port (which looks just like
a phone jack). Or, as I've done, simply unplug the in-room telephone and plug the modem cord into the phone jack.

Two warnings, though. Be sure to check with the hotel in advance
to find out whether its telephone system is analog or digital. (If
it's digital, you'll need a digital-compatible modem or converter.)
Also, find out in advance if the room phones use the modern
plug-in jacks or if they're hard-wired (the phone wire goes
straight into the wall, leaving you nowhere to plug in your
modem cord). If they're hard-wired, your only hope is to get an
acoustic coupler—a modem adapter that fits around the telephone
handset. You can find one, along with lots of other laptop acces-
sories, from a Web site called Laptop Travel at *www.laptop-
travel.com.*

One firm I've heard about that tries to make it easy for the jet set
to log on, whether they're in Lombok or London, is called Jet Set
(appropriately enough). It bills itself as an international roaming

service for Internet users. You can find it at *www.jetset-roam.net.*
Let's take a walk through the site to see what Jet Set is doing to
make Internet access possible when you're away from home.

Jet Set and other firms like it are going after clients like you by offering Internet access in more than 80 countries through various local ISPs.

▼ **Try It Yourself**

1. From the home page, scroll to the bottom of the screen and click What Is It? Read about Jet Set's accessibility in more than 80 countries.

2. Click Why Use It? Does the company's list of benefits sound good to you? If you had a question for Jet Set, could you find where to email it? Did you notice that this company is a based in the U.K., and that the prices are given in British currency (7.5 pence per minute)?

3. Click on How to Use It. Do the steps seem simple to you? Is the explanation clear, concise, and straightforward? Or do you find yourself scratching your mangy scalp and saying, "Huh?"

If there's only one Web site that you should check out for tips about traveling with a computer, it's a road warrior site called Roadnews at *www.roadnews.com.* It's full of laptop travel advice, articles on everything from adapters and converters to how to go online by disassembling a phone, and tech-travel links.

Email on the Road

The simplest thing I've ever done was getting a free email address to use exclusively on the road. I like to keep my private and business email separate, so I need two email addresses. But my office email system has an unconquerable firewall that can make it difficult to access office email from the road. So when I travel with a laptop, I use my personal account with Microsoft Hotmail. There are many other free email services that you can access through the Web. I chose Hotmail because of the ease with which you can sign up and the simple-to-navigate interface.

The email service is free at Hotmail and other similar sites.

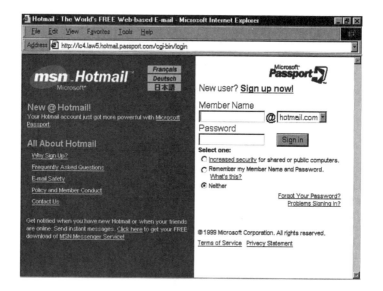

As long as you can access the Internet, you can access your Hotmail account. Let's run through the steps to see how to send and receive a message.

Try It Yourself ▼

1. Go to *www.hotmail.com* and click Sign Up Now! Fill in the requested information and return to the home page.

2. Type in your member name and password and click the Sign In button. On the new screen, click Compose. In the To box, fill in your own Hotmail email address. In the subject box, type "Test". In the body of the message box, type "You are great". Near the top of the page, click the Send button.

3. Almost instantaneously, your new message should zip through the cosmos and arrive at your email box. Under the New heading, look for a red arrow pointing to unopened messages (including the one you just sent yourself.)

4. Double-click on the name of the sender of the new email (in this exercise, you). Voilà, your new message appears.

There's a lot more. You can store mail, forward mail, reply to mail, or simply delete your mail. And as long as you can log on to the Net through your laptop's modem, you've got email at your fingertips.

Hotmail is one of scores of companies willing to give you free email, in exchange for making you scroll through all the advertising on the Web site. (Hey, they gotta pay for the service one way or another. You could get email without the ads, if you wanted... for a fee.) I have to say, however, that Hotmail is not an egregious example of that practice.

Another company that offers free email, but with a twist, is Drivernet at *www.drivernet.com*. Get this—you don't even need a laptop (although your free email account will work with your own hardware). Drivernet has outfitted 379 truck stops on major U.S. highways with its proprietary hardware. Once you have an account, you can pull into the truck stop, gulp down a greasy burger and Pepsi, and then log on to your email account at the Drivernet touch-screen information kiosk. Major caveat: Drivernet says that it may share its client list (the names and email addresses of all its clients) with others. So if you open your email to find 212 ads for Viagra and "How to Get Paid While You Surf the Net!!!", don't be surprised.

Learn the ups and downs, ins and outs, and pros and cons of any email system you sign up for, and then balance the drawbacks against the pluses. For example, there might be lots of spam, but the service is free.

Also, look for "cyber-cafes" at your destination. These are high-tech coffee shops where you can have an espresso while you check your email and surf the Net using the cafe's computers (for a modest hourly charge).

By the Way

If you need an Internet fix on the road but you don't have your laptop handy, consider visiting the nearest public library. Many libraries across the nation offer free Internet access on their computers.

E.T., Phone Home

Confession: I hate to "stay in touch." When I travel, I give a temporary phone number and address to only a few people outside my family, and I swear them to secrecy upon pain of the bastinado. Short of an emergency, I don't want you to beep me, page me, or bounce your voice off a satellite uplink to me.

By the Way

Advances in technology will soon make Internet telephones practical. They'll allow you to call long-distance for about one-tenth the cost of a normal long-distance call from a hotel.

(If I may offer a momentary aside to Modern American Youth... It wasn't all that long ago that people still wrote letters, and I continue to believe that that's a nice, sensible way of communicating with my fellow man. Sorry, Modern American Youth, I'm forgetting that you may not know the terminology. A "letter" is a charming-if-outmoded means of communication in which the sender writes words on paper to convey a message. Traditionally, the sender then delivers this message to the recipient via a third party, such as a messenger or the U.S. Postal Service.)

If you want to bring a cell phone with you on the road, particularly if you plan to travel outside your home country, you may run into problems. Because the doodads and the whatsits in U.S. cell phones differ from the thingamajigs and the whatchamacallits in their foreign counterparts, your cell phone won't necessarily work in, say, Europe. (I'll try to keep jargon like the preceding to a minimum.) Firms like Smartcoms, at *www.smartcoms.com/home.htm*, rent cell phones specifically for use in 70 overseas countries. Another company that will let you groan into their phones from Sri Lanka to Quintana Roo is Action Cellular Rent a Phone at *www.rentaphone.com*. These companies and others like them will let you rent and return phones via one of the major express-mail delivery services.

These companies may be just great. I've never rented a phone from them, and I wouldn't unless they were recommended by a knowledgeable source that I respect. As with everything else you've learned in this book, take some measure of personal responsibility, chum. Look at any of these companies as if they were offering to plan your retirement. My motto is "Be skeptical." Don't trust anyone over 30 megahertz! Power to the people, raht own!

A Laptop Diary

How can I describe the perils, pitfalls, practicalities, and joys of laptop travel? I figure the best way to give you a sense of how a laptop lightweight like myself uses a computer on the road would be to keep a journal during a business trip. I wanted to give the events some drama, some intrigue, and a soundtrack like one from an old Humphrey Bogart film. Failing that, I decided to give my diary a misleadingly gripping title. And so, without further ado, allow me to present The Mysterious Mystery of the Bizarre and Mysterious Business Trip to Galveston.

10:35 a.m., Sunday, Newark International Airport, New Jersey— I'm on the road to sit on a panel discussion at a tourism convention in Galveston, Texas. Topic: The Millennium Tourist. I arrive at the airport, paranoid that my antiquated and borrowed IBM ThinkPad laptop is going to get swiped from the security machine while I'm not looking. An hour to wait for my flight. The bars are closed (Sunday morning!), so I grab a cup of coffee at the lounge-area McDonald's and type up a few notes. That's what you've just been reading.

*1:55 p.m., Sunday, somewhere in the air over Louisiana—*The lady in front of me has her seat reclined at such an angle that I have to keep my laptop's screen half-closed. But that's okay, because the man sitting next to me has his newspaper folded open so wide that I can't see the screen anyway. Is it desirable to work on your computer in this claustrophobic situation? Is it even *possible*? Now I know why the larger seats up front are called business class—if you want to work on business, those are the only seats large enough.

*4:30 p.m., Sunday, San Luis Resort, Galveston—*Settled into the San Luis Resort overlooking the Gulf of Mexico, I plug in the laptop's power cord and hook up the modem cord to the phone jack. Just to make sure that I can log on to the Net, I dial up a toll-free number on the modem. But then I have a momentary fright. Is the hotel's phone system analog or (gulp!) digital? I forgot to ask in advance. No sound comes from my tinny little speaker to indicate the modem is dialing up. And then: "Scccqqquuuuuaaaaaccchhh! Beeble eeeble eeep.

Customs Hassle

If you take a fairly new laptop with you outside the country, carry a copy of your receipt. That way, on your return, a Customs officer won't try to charge you duty because he thinks you bought it overseas.

Kkkrrrraaaccch!" What a beautiful sound! The modem goes into operation, and I am… connected!

7:30 a.m., Monday, San Luis Resort, Galveston—Bleary-eyed from too much beer at a Moody Gardens cocktail reception last night, I nonetheless log on to the Internet and check my personal email. The only thing waiting there is mail I sent myself the previous evening before I logged off, just to make sure that my email was working. I'm such a worrywart. Then the next 90 minutes is spent reading up on the latest surveys and travel trends from the Travel Industry Association of America at *www.tia.org*. Ideally, this new information will help me sound like less of an idiot when I sit on my Millennium Tourist panel.

3:30 p.m., Monday, San Luis Resort, Galveston—The panel went just fine. I charmed the socks off the audience. (Well, they didn't boo.) Now I have the rest of the afternoon to do some sightseeing. I log on to the Internet and go to one of my favorite search engines to see if there's a Galveston tourism site. Bingo! There it is at *www.galvestontour.org*. From the pictures and descriptions, looks like my best bet is to head down to the Strand, the historic center of old Galveston. I also have a look at the restaurant listings and get some good tips on where to eat tonight.

7:30 a.m., Tuesday, San Luis Resort, Galveston—Log on to the Web to check the latest weather reports for Galveston and Houston. Occasional thunderstorms anticipated. No word of any airport delays. Check my email. Nothing of interest. Using MapQuest at *www.mapquest.com*, I have one more look at how to get from Galveston to Intercontinental Airport Houston (IAH) and then log off.

11 a.m., Tuesday, cocktail lounge, Intercontinental Airport Houston—Returned the rental car and checked in with the airline using an e-ticket. Figure I'll polish up a couple of chapters of this book. After the waitress brings me a pint of the local Shiner brew, I surreptitiously plug my laptop's power cord into an electrical outlet near my table. Half a chapter and three Shiners later, I unplug and haul ash to gate C-44 for my 1:10 p.m. return flight.

2:35 p.m., Tuesday, somewhere in the air over Tennessee—Sitting in an aisle seat with no one next to me, with plenty of room to spread out my papers and place my laptop on the tray table in front of me. The flight attendant brings me one of those little tiny bottles of Dewar's with a cup of ice, along with a bottle of Shiner, my new favorite beer. I set them on the tray table in front of the empty seat. I think about hooking up my modem cord to the in-flight phone to check my email, but at two bucks a minute I figure I can wait till I'm on the ground, cheapskate that I am. This is the life. Quiet and comfy working conditions. I could do this for hours. All I have to do now is finish that darn "Wrapping It Up" section, ask for another Shiner, and I'm done for the day.

Wrapping It Up

When I went to Europe for the first time as a muddle-headed twentysomething, I was gone for four months and carried everything I needed in a smallish backpack. Ever since then, I've vowed never to travel with more than necessary. The question I ask myself these days is whether I need to bring along a laptop computer. Business travelers often have no choice. They need information that can be accessed only through a computer. Pleasure travelers, heed my advice—don't take your laptop unless you really need it. Although you can get great information by using your computer on the road, the hassle of carting it around and keeping it safe can detract from the enjoyment of your holiday.

If I don't need a computer for anything more than checking and sending email, first I look into whether my destination has any cyber-cafes I can use. And if I feel an overwhelming urge to speak with someone on the telephone, and I'll be in places where I'm unlikely to have access to a phone, I consider renting one that can be used at my foreign destination.

Here's what you learned in this chapter:

- The pros and cons of bringing your laptop on your travels.

- How to log on to the Web in your hotel room, plus questions to ask the hotel before you arrive (analog vs. digital phone system, modular phone jacks or hard-wired phone lines, etc.).

- How to get free email that you can use on the road from any computer that has access to the Internet, like at a cyber-cafe. Also, you saw some email alternatives, like the Drivernet truck-stop kiosks.

- What to bear in mind when you take a cell phone on your next trip, for those times when you just *have* to reach out and touch someone.

CHAPTER 20

Online Info about Passports, Visas, and Customs

Bureaucracy! Who needs it? Listen, pal, you think you have it bad now? You should've been on the road in the 1700s. In those days, you never knew what to expect when crossing borders. For all intents and purposes, France, the Netherlands, and Britain were the only touristed countries with strong central governments and honest-to-goodness legal systems. Most of the other European countries were little more than loose confederations of bickering city-states and serf-filled fiefdoms. This meant problems for travelers.

There was no standard for passports. They existed, but only for society's elite. Even if you were able to obtain one, it was no guarantee that you'd be allowed to enter your foreign destination. An alternative was to get a visa. Before leaving on your trip, you would approach a foreign consul and ask for a letter authorizing such travel. This was about as easy as talking your way out of a traffic ticket. (Not that they had traffic tickets back then.) Or, you could just take your chances, go to your destination without any papers, and hope to cross the border the old-fashioned way—by bribing an immigration official. There was so much corruption along the frontiers that a few pieces of silver were at least as valid as any official documents you might be able to produce. Passports and visas were tough in the old days, boy.

And you don't even want to know about customs. Your bags were searched, and duty imposed, as soon as you crossed a national border. And then again on the turnpike through the countryside. And then again in each city you entered. And then when you left.

What You'll Learn in This Chapter

▶ Where on the Web to get passport applications and all the passport information you'll need.

▶ Which countries require a visa, and how to locate the required information on the Internet.

▶ The lowdown on customs regulations—not just for the countries you'll be visiting, but for the good ol' U.S.A.—so that you won't bring back home anything that you're not allowed to.

Your belongings could be delayed for days or even weeks in customs hell, or they could be passed through quickly… for a price.

Customs regulations began to come of age in the 19th century, but the use of modern-style passports as a commonly issued means of international identification issued by the bearer's home government didn't become prevalent until around World War I. So the next time you feel like moaning about the hassles of getting a passport, or the frustrations and cost of getting a visa, or the vagaries of customs regulations in various destinations around the world, be glad you're living in the 21st century and not the 18th. Trust me, it's better now.

Not only is it less aggravating to cross borders these days, but it's also easier to get the information you need about travel documents and customs laws—all of which is available online. In some cases, you can even download required documents from the Internet. And in the case of at least one nation, the process of obtaining a visa is almost entirely electronic. Yes, folks, the future is good, and getting better.

Passports—The Basic Form of International ID

Kids Grow Up Too Fast

U.S. passport officials used to allow children's names to be added to a parent's passport. No longer. Today, every minor who travels abroad must have his own passport.

Although I didn't apply for my first passport until I was in college, my children got their first passports before they were in elementary school. As the world grows smaller and smaller and it becomes easier and easier to travel across international borders, passports have become increasingly important. If a passport is required to enter a country, even a newborn baby has to have one issued in his or her own name.

With a passport in your hand, the entire world is open to you (except for parts of West Hollywood and the central highlands of upper Manitoba). But don't overlook the fact that there are countries that don't require a passport, specifically some countries in the Caribbean. A driver's license is sometimes all you'll need. In one or two countries, I believe, even an expired library card will do.

Mexico is one such country that will allow U.S. citizens to enter without a pesky passport. However, Mexico does require proof of citizenship (such as a notarized copy of a birth certificate) and a photo ID (such as your Official Jennifer Love Hewitt Fan Club membership card). A tourist card, which can be issued by Mexican consulates in the United States and by most airlines that fly to Mexico, is also required.

Which reminds me of a story I meant to tell you, if only to help me cough up the contractual word count commanded by my cantankerous and betimes costive editors. Once, when I was a cub reporter on a much-needed vacation, a girlfriend and I drove down to Baja California in a 1974 Chevy Vega. Some 25 miles south of Tijuana we came to a checkpoint, where a guard told us to hand over our tourist cards. To which I responded, "We ain't got no stinkin' tourist cards." The immigration official was displeased at this sort of smart-aleck response, so he waved me over to the side of the road and indicated that I had to go inside the little hut of an administrative office and see the *jefe* inside. The boss, sitting alone at his desk, looked me up and down, and then looked quickly to his right and left in an almost comical pantomime of sneakiness, before saying to me, sotto voce, "Gimme a nickel's worth of paper." I forked over a fiver real fast and vamoosed south on my way to a weekend of Latin-flavored romance.

Well, the whole point of this story is that the girlfriend waiting for me in that decrepit and soon-to-die Chevy Vega ultimately turned out to be—you guessed it!—my wife. So the moral of this story is: If you ever hope to get married and have a good life with lots of children and four weeks of vacation and a little nest egg, just head on down to Baja with your paramour and bribe the first official you see.

But where were we? Oh yes... Getting a passport is about as easy as circling the hidden words in those cheesy game booklets they sell for 79 cents by the supermarket checkout counter. Log on to the State Department Web site at *travel.state.gov/passport_services.html* and poke around. You won't have to read very far to learn that all you need to get a passport are two photos of yourself and $60 cash, along with your birth certificate and driver's license (or other current ID). Once you submit the application, it takes

Caution!

Although some countries may allow you to enter with only a copy of your birth certificate, U.S. Immigration officials require you to show proof of citizenship—like a birth certificate—*and* proof of identification—like a driver's license.

about three weeks for your passport to be mailed to you. There are even procedures for people without passports who will be going abroad soon to expedite the process and get one even sooner than that.

Unfortunately, as of yet there's no way to apply for your passport electronically. It has to be done in person—even if that person is someone you hired to do it in your place (such as a passport expediter).

As the State Department Web site says, you must apply for your passport in person—your own bad self, no one else—if it's a first-time application. If you already have a passport and you're merely renewing it, however, I can show you how you can renew that sucker without actually going down to a passport office.

First you'll need the proper form.

Try It Yourself ▼

1. From the State Department's passport page, click Print Passport Applications under Passport Services.

2. The next page explains that the passport form you require is available in PDF format, which requires Adobe Acrobat Reader. (Your Web browser may be equipped with that software already. If not, follow the directions to download it.) Click "Click here to select forms to print."

3. You're renewing your passport, so click DSP-82: Application For Passport By Mail.

4. Copy the form in the new window to your hard drive, fill in the blanks, and print it out for mailing.

5. Go to *travel.state.gov/passport_renewal.html* for details about cost and where to submit your application by mail (including a couple of pix of your lovely mug).

▲

One of these days, you'll be able to accomplish this whole procedure entirely via email, using PDF forms, JPEG photos taken with a digital camera, and an electronically notarized copy of your birth certificate. It won't be tomorrow, but when I get the okay to do an update of this soon-to-be award-winning book, I just may have some new details to add about that.

I hope so.

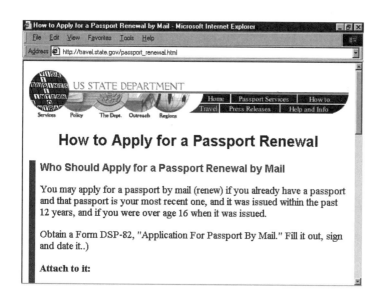

Visas—Permission to Come Abroad, Sir

One way to look at a visa is as an admission fee into a country. What other explanation can there be? If you already have a legal passport, why do some countries require that you also have a piece of paper from their U.S. consulate that says you're allowed to travel there? The only rationale I can come up with is that each country that requires a visa also requires payment. Visas are a profit center!

One of the most notoriously difficult (and expensive) visas to get is the one required to visit Russia. Got a minute? Then come along with me for a quick lesson in how a country should *not* handle its visa program.

Veni, Vidi, Visa (I Came, I Saw, I Paid)

Here are some sample visa fees: Egypt, $15; Cote d'Ivoire, $33; Tanzania, $45; Yemen, $50; Syria, $61.

Plug into the Consulate General of the Russian Federation in New York home page at *www.ruscon.com*. Click the word "English" (that is, unless you normally like to read Russian—in Cyrillic characters yet). And on the following page, choose the link for Entry visas to Russia. About the only computer-friendly aspect of the Russian visa process is that you can print out a copy of the application form in Adobe PDF format. Other than that, you'll feel as if you were back in the Stone Age (and maybe even wish you were), because each procedure has to be done manually. The visa page explains the medieval process—everything from who needs a visa (namely, anyone who isn't directly related to Boris Yeltsin), how many photos must accompany the application (three), and what sort of documentation you're required to furnish (including a voucher from an authorized tourist agency and confirmation of reservations from a Russian hotel or tour operator), to how much the dang thing is going to cost (minimum of $70 for a single-entry visa, plus a $40 penalty fee for any mistakes you make on the form). You can't submit the material by email or even fax, but only by snail mail or in person.

This is a good-looking home page, but just try following its directions for getting a visa to visit Russia!

For a brisk and refreshing change of pace, let's pay a visit to the Embassy of Australia in Washington, D.C., at *www.austemb.org/*. Simply click the Visa and Immigration link on the home page. In startling counterpoint to the rather Byzantine Russian page, you get a simple, easy-to-read block of text explaining the procedures for Australian visas. You'll quickly discover that there's a reason everyone loves Australia and wants to visit, and it's not just for a bowl of kangaroo stew. The Aussies want to make it easy for Americans to visit Down Under. As the visa page explains, the Australian government has replaced the old-fashioned visa with the Electronic Travel Authority (ETA), a sort of e-visa available for free from thousands of travel agents in North America. No forms to fill out, no rubber stamp required on the passport, no fee to pay. If Russia would follow in Australia's footsteps, not only would it get more tourists, but it would probably have a much nicer wardrobe, too.

The next obvious question is, "How do I know if my intended destination requires a visa?" Funny you should ask, because right here in my pocket... just let me get it out... hmm, yes... Right here in my pocket I have a government Web site that lists the foreign entry requirements for more than 200 nations, islands, and independent regions around the globe—the State Department site.

1. Go to one of my favorite Web sites—the State Department site at *travel.state.gov*.

2. Under the Services heading, click Passport Information.

3. Under Help and Information, click the Visa and Foreign Entry Requirements link.

4. On the next page, scroll down to review the requirements for the nations listed there.

▼ **Try It Yourself**

▲

Next time, you can go to that page directly by pointing your browser to *travel.state.gov/foreignentryreqs.html*. There you'll learn such curious facts as this: A visa to the United Arab Emirates requires a typed letter from the visitor's employer indicating the type and length of position held in the company.

And this: In Niger, you have to show proof of yellow fever vaccination when you apply for your visa.

And this: In Kazakhstan, a tourist visa requires a letter of invitation from Kazakhstan's tourist agency, with confirmation from the Ministry of Foreign Affairs.

Once you've learned whether your destination requires a visa (or a tourist card, or any other sort of pretravel paperwork), you can use any of the embassy and consulate locator Web sites you saw in Chapter 6.

I've Grown Accustomed to Your Customs

There are two main reasons that a nation has customs checkpoints. The first is to see what people are bringing into the country—especially any outlawed items that might bring harm to the land or the people (firearms, drugs, Brett Easton Ellis novels). The second is to see what people are taking out of the country— especially things that the authorities want to remain *in* the country (such as more money than you brought in, stolen goods, Heidi Klum's private phone number…).

An acquaintance of mine once flew to Darwin, Australia. Before she and the other passengers were allowed to leave, the interior of the plane, including the passengers, was fumigated. Irritated, she asked me why they did this. I explained to her that because Australia shares no borders with other countries and is completely surrounded by water, a unique ecosystem flourishes there. There are plants and animals Down Under that are found nowhere else on earth. For that reason, Australia's flora and fauna are particularly at risk from outside influences. Aussies don't mess about at the customs counter. They want to know what tourists are bringing into the country. If it's on the Bad Things list, back on the plane it goes.

Bringing Home the Bacon

Don't get caught trying to smuggle pork products into Qatar. Strict Islamic laws there also prohibit the import of alcohol, drugs, firearms, and pornography.

"There are strict laws prohibiting or restricting the entry of drugs, steroids, weapons, firearms, protected wildlife and associated products," says the Visitor's Facts section of the Australian Tourist Commission's Web site at *www.aussie.net.au*. "All animals, animal products, foodstuffs, plants and plant products are subject to quarantine control, and must be declared on arrival. The penalties for breaking these laws are severe. If you are uncertain about anything in your baggage, declare it and bring it to the attention of a customs officer."

You can find the bulk of the customs information you'll need for any destination at the State Department's site for Travel Warnings and Consular Information Sheets at *travel.state.gov/ travel_warnings.html*. Each country's write-up has at least minimal information on its customs regulations. But I would certainly encourage you to look up more information from each individual country to get the full story. Go to each country's embassy and consular Web sites. Go to its national tourist office Web site. Go to the online guidebooks and read the nuts-and-bolts sections for your destination.

When it comes to customs regulations, the Aussies don't play ostrich and stick their heads in the sand.

But knowing the customs laws in the country you visit is only part of the ballgame. You also have to concern yourself with what the U.S. Customs Service will let you bring back home with you. If you ever saw the episode of *I Love Lucy* in which Lucy tries to smuggle an Italian salami into the U.S. by dressing it up like a baby, you know what lengths people will go to. That isn't as gross as smugglers who bring in contraband by swallowing it and then later collecting it from the other end (yuck!), if they manage to get past the border guards.

You can log on to the Customs Service Web site at *www.customs.ustreas.gov/* to find out more.

1. From the Customs Service home page, click Traveler Information.

2. Next, click U.S. Customs Requirements in Brief.

3. The following page has a series of 10 topics. You can either click one of them to go straight to that section, or just scroll down the page to skim through them.

▼ **Try It Yourself**

▲

Here you'll find that you can bring back up to $400 worth of foreign goods without having to pay duty (import tax). You can also bring home 100 cigars... as long as they aren't of the Cuban variety. The list of can's and cant's, do's and don'ts, should's and shouldn'ts, makes for interesting reading. And if it also keeps you from being arrested by Customs officials at the end of your next vacation, I feel all my work has been worth it. It looks like my job here is done.

Wrapping It Up

Don't delay getting a passport. Every adult American should have one. They're affordable and easy to get, and you can even print out the form you need right from the Web. If you plan to travel outside the United States, you'll need your passport in 90% of the world's countries. So don't put it off. If you need to renew your passport, you can follow the instructions at the beginning of this chapter and get all the details you need. Unlike an application for a new passports, which requires you to submit the form in person, a renewal can be done by mail.

In addition to a passport, you also may need a visa, which is basically a permission slip from the foreign consulate allowing you to enter that country—sort of like having a hall pass in high school. You learned a shortcut for finding out which countries require visas and how to go about applying for one, with examples of how it's done by the Russians and the Australians.

Finally, you learned about customs—the kind having to do with what you bring into and out of a country, not the kind regarding your behavior there. (In Turkey, you're supposed to belch as a compliment to the chef, goes the old saying, repeated by generations of dads and schoolboys. That's dead wrong, of course. It's Switzerland, not Turkey.) And never forget that customs is a two-way street—it covers not just what is allowed into and out of your destination, but also what you can bring into and out of the United States.

And so, in the simplest form I can say it, in this chapter you
learned:

- How to get the information and forms you need to apply for a
  passport.

- What a visa is, how to find out if your destination requires
  one, and how to get one if it's required.

- The basics of international customs—which means, in a nutshell, that there are certain things you can't take across certain borders.

CHAPTER 21

Digital Photography Means Doing It with Your Fingers

Since 1997, digital cameras have outsold traditional 35mm cameras. Sure, much of their popularity has to do with the fact that more and more people have computers, which allows them to download digital images from those cameras. But if digital cameras weren't easy to use, affordable, and compact, and if they didn't take high-quality pictures, you can bet people would still "focus" their interest on the old-fashioned formats.

Most of the digital cameras on the market today are of the point-and-shoot variety (translation: made for dummies like me), and most of them cost far less than $1,000 (translation: made for guys who are always broke, like me). Just a few years ago, you would have been hard-pressed to find five or six digital cameras that fit those criteria—affordable, easy to use, and good-quality pictures. Today the market is flooded with dozens and dozens of such cameras from virtually every major and minor manufacturer in the business.

It's no surprise that a book on e-travel is talking about digital photography. Sure, most people use their cameras for family affairs—birthdays, reunions, anniversaries, and other milestones, like Grandpa finally getting a complete set of dentures so he doesn't whistle anymore whenever he says, "Sufferin' succotash." But one of the main parts of our lives when we take pictures is when we travel. Here I am "holding up" the Leaning Tower of Pisa! There's little Gigi romping in the surf. ("Gigi... Gigi, you're going out too far... help, somebody save Gigi!") Look at this one, when the police were taking that report after someone stole all our stuff from the trunk of our rental car. Cool!

What You'll Learn in this Chapter

- ▶ What a digital camera is, including its benefits and drawbacks compared with traditional cameras.

- ▶ How to use a digital camera to its best effect when traveling.

- ▶ Where to find information on the Web about buying a digital camera.

On the other hand, anyone who is serious about their photography will find that no digital camera can match the quality of a top-notch single-lens reflex film camera. If that level of quality is important to you, you'd probably do well to stick to traditional formats and buy a cheap photo scanner for your digital needs. But if you want to send picture postcards via email, or if you're tired of having 82 scrapbooks taking up all the space in your closet and would rather have a digital scrapbook instead, the new breed of cameras is worth considering.

What Is a Digital Camera, Anyway?

Digital cameras have made great advances from their earliest, almost primitive incarnations. Today, a digital camera has most of the same bells and whistles as a standard film camera. You can set the f-stops and the shutter speeds. You can get higher resolutions than ever. And although you can't always be assured of profes-sional-level photography, you can get photos that are more than good enough for Web pages, newsletters, and even printed enlargements (although you generally lose a lot of quality if you go bigger than 8 inches by 10 inches).

A digital camera doesn't look much different from a standard film camera—at first. There's a viewfinder to compose the shot, a lens through which the image is transferred, a button to activate the "shutter," and so on. Low-tech individuals like you and me don't have to worry too much about the digital camera's innards. For the most part, all you have to remember is to point the thing in the direction of the image you want to capture, push the button, and go on to the next victim.

But how does a digital camera work? Basically, instead of film, it has an image-capture chip. The beauty of this format is that, unlike a film camera, a digital camera allows you to display the photograph you just took on an LCD playback screen. If some goofball tourist walks into your shot just as you're taking a pic-ture of the Great Wall of China, you can delete that picture and take it over again.

As anyone who has ever purchased film knows, it's expensive. And so is developing. With a digital camera, you can use memory cards that allow you to take as many pictures as you want. When

Remember

In many cases, the quality of pictures taken with a digital camera is better than that of pictures taken with a tradi-tional film camera after they've been scanned for com-puter use.

you run out of memory, simply insert a new memory card into the camera. The wonder of these memory cards (most of which can hold around 36 medium-quality images) is that they can be used again and again.

The Agfa ePhoto 780, one of the new breed of digital cameras, allows you to view your pix by connecting the camera to a television.

To move the images from the memory cards to your computer, you can install an internal PC Card drive for less than $150. (It wouldn't take you long to spend $150 on film and processing with a traditional camera.) Currently, though, memory cards are still pretty expensive—as much as $25 or so per megabyte. But the prices will continue to fall even as new technology seeks to find alternatives to the memory cards. Some cameras can even link directly to a printer—although the differences between the various manufacturers have left users without a standard format. Casio cameras work only with Casio printers, Olympus cameras work only with Olympus printers, and so on.

By the Way

Virtually all digital cameras these days allow you to save your images in the JPEG format, which can be opened by most picture-viewing programs.

The User's Experience

I said that taking a picture with a digital camera is basically the same as a film camera. I forgot to mention that after you snap the shutter button on a digital camera, you'll often have a one- or even two-second delay before the image is actually captured on the chip. This was a greater problem several years ago than it is now, but you may still find it a factor in the less expensive line of cameras. Whether it's a problem for you has a lot to do with the sort of pictures you take. If you're planning to shoot pictures of a schoolyard full of 10-year-olds, it will be a bummer. If you like to take pictures of rocks, it shouldn't be an issue at all.

Kodak's DC200 Plus is a basic-level digital camera that also features megapixel technology, for images that approach the quality of film cameras.

Another thing to remember is that your ability to take pictures one after another is often limited because there's a bit of recovery time needed after each exposure. Again, this recovery period gets shorter and shorter with each new generation of digital cameras, but even today it can range from just a few seconds to a half-minute or so. For most of us, this isn't a major hurdle. But if you're planning to shoot the Grand National steeplechase in England and you want to get as many images as possible, you'd do well to find a digital camera with a minimal recovery time.

Your camera's recovery time is limited not only by its very manu-facture, but also by its batteries. If the batteries in your digital camera are low, the lag time will increase. Most cameras come with either a rechargeable Ni-Cad or nickel-hydride battery. The charge on such batteries can last from an hour (or less) up to two hours. (A smart traveler always carries extra batteries.)

Cutting-Edge Camera Technology

Let's have a look at some of the hottest new cameras out there. (By the way, this is the chapter that's guaranteed to require a new edition of this book every year or so because the technology is bound to change rapidly.)

Kodak has come out with a range of digital cameras, as you (and the company's shareholders) would expect. One of the new technologies the company is zeroing in on is called the double-megapixel. Basically, the more pixels (the little dots that make up the picture), the higher the quality. Twice the megapixels means twice the quality (well, in theory, at least). The company's newest camera in that line is the DC280. Price: $799. You can find a range of Kodak's digital cameras at *www.kodak.com/*.

Your Choice

The more complicated cameras can be a pain in the neck to operate. If you want a camera that you can use right out of the box without spending days reading directions, go for the basic models.

I remember when products from Sharp, the electronics company, were considered more or less the budget line of electronic goods, whether it was TVs, radios, or alarm clocks. To some extent that's still true, but it doesn't mean the company hasn't also been doing time on the cutting edge, producing products that any manufacturer would be proud of. The Sharp Internet ViewCam, which weighs one-third of a pound, can take video in addition to still pictures. The action is stored on a memory card that can be inserted into your computer's disk drive. Sending an electronic postcard back home is pretty cool, but sending an electronic *video* postcard is about as cool as it gets. Price: $699. You'll find details, along with details on Sharp's many other cameras and related products, at *www.sharp-usa.com/*.

Casio has long been ranked with Sharp as a budget maker of electronic goods. But man-oh-Manischewitz, is Casio doing some fun stuff when it comes to PC pictures. It's one of the growing number of manufacturers to make handheld PCs (its E-105 palm-sized PC is a case in point), and lately it has combined photographic and PC technology in a single package. It recently developed a camera that hooks into a palm PC and takes both still pictures and video. Cassiopeia E-105 PC: $599. Attachable camera: $250. Find out what else Casio is up to at *www.casio.com/*.

These are just a few examples of the sorts of cameras on the market. With just a bit of research on the other manufacturers, you'll find yourself as up to speed as it's possible to be in this realm of rapidly changing technology.

Rules to Live By

What's in Store for the Future?

In the coming years, digital cameras will have greater resolution (2-megapixel will become the industry standard), plug-and-play ports between camera and computer, and memory disks that hold even more photographs than those on the market today.

The swiftness of technological advances makes it difficult, if not impossible, to describe state-of-the-art digital photography. No sooner does one manufacturer come up with a new advance than his competitors invent a product that puts it to shame. The only way to stay plugged into the cutting edge of digital photography is to stay informed. Read the computer mags (*PC Magazine*, at *www.zdnet.com/pcmag/*, does frequent articles on digital photography). Read the e-travel articles in travel mags (*Travel & Leisure*, at *www.travelandleisure.com/*, has plenty of stories on digital cameras and other e-travel topics in its Interactive Traveler department). Stay plugged into the Web sites of the major manufacturers, including Hasselblad, at *www.hasselblad.com/*, Olympus, at *www.olympusamerica.com/*, Sanyo, at *www.sanyo-digital.com/*, Agfa, at *www.agfahome.com/*, and those manufacturers mentioned earlier, as well as virtually any other company that makes cameras.

But whatever brand of digital camera you buy, make sure you keep a few basic points in mind:

- Don't overspend. With a swiftly evolving technology like digital photography, it's easy to spend two or three times more than you need to, only to find out that prices have dropped one week later. Assess your basic needs and buy a camera that meets them. Don't go for the fanciest one you can find. A digital camera costing $300-$500 today is as good as one that cost four times that much three years ago.

- Get the greatest resolution available in your price range. The more pixels, the better the quality. Try to get megapixel resolution, which is becoming the standard.

- Removable disks rule! Who wants the hassle of hooking up cords from a camera to a computer? Not me. And not you either, if you're half as intelligent as you look. Look for a camera with removable disks that can be loaded directly into your computer (or with the aid of an add-on drive).

- Built-in flash units are de rigueur. If you don't have a built-in flash on your digital camera, your pictures will look like garbage. Is that what you want? Garbage? You don't? Okay then... get a camera that has a built-in flash. Why do you argue with me?!

Wrapping It Up

I'll confess that I've never been particularly keen on cameras in the first place. I'm a word guy from way back. Give me a pen and a notepad and I'll write you a picture better than any camera could give you. On the other hand, I look back on pictures of me 10 years ago and, man, did I look good! Even my journal entries for that period don't describe me half as well as some of those pictures.

So get a camera. Make it a digital. You don't have to be a computer geek to figure out how they work, especially if you get one with a memory disk that goes straight from the camera to your computer. And then, instead of boring all your friends with a scrapbook full of snapshots from your last vacation, you can bore them by email when you send them 231 images captured on your new digital camera!

Now you know the following:

- Exactly what the phrase *digital camera* means.
- How to use a digital camera when traveling.
- What the newest digital technology is.
- Things to look for when purchasing a digital camera.

CHAPTER 22

Packing, Handling Money, and Staying Safe

I can't believe how much we've covered in the past 21 chapters. In fact, right now I'm preparing for the inevitable moment when the apprentice surpasses the master. No, no, no. I'm not talking about you. I'm talking about *me*—surpassing the legendary Arthur Frommer.

There is so much we've covered—from virtual tourist bureaus and buying airline tickets online to traveling with a laptop and how to evaluate the validity and accuracy of a travel Web site—that it seems impossible that there's anything left for you to learn. But there are a few more things I want you to know before I send you off on your e-travels alone. So in this chapter you'll learn about packing, including what I call the "carryon conundrum"—the rules for carryons change so frequently and without any standardization between the airlines, that you may just decide never to bring a carryon aboard a plane again!

There are also plenty of things you need to know about staying healthy on the road, like what sorts of shots you need, if any. Because you'll be traveling so often by plane, I'll touch upon your rights as an airline passenger. And finally, I'm going to sit you down and explain how you can be a safe, cautious traveler, avoiding the most common scams on the unwary.

Pack Your Cares Away

There are as many ways to pack as there are people. If you ask two packing "experts" how to fold a pair of slacks, you'll have them calling each other dirty names inside of three minutes. One veteran traveler I know would never pack her clothes without

What You'll Learn in This Chapter

▶ Tips for packing. Always use this rule of thumb: Take half the luggage you think you'll need... and twice the money.

▶ The form in which you should take your traveling funds— cash, charge card, traveler's checks, or ATM card.

▶ Keeping healthy while traveling— including what you should know before you go.

▶ Scams! Rip-offs! Crime! No, not a typical night at the Orwoll household, but a primer to help you keep the bad guys at arm's length while you travel.

lining each fold with paper. Others use the "bundle" method, in which each article of clothing is laid out flat in (but overlapping the edges of) the open suitcase, and then each shirt and pair of pants is enfolded within the one beneath it. Weird.

Does It Fit Under Your Seat?

Increasingly, airlines are using carryon *templates*—metal boxes at the gate into which your carryons must fit or they won't be allowed on the plane.

And then there's the whole question of what sort of suitcase you should take along. I once saw a *New Yorker* cartoon in which an uptight business executive shopping in a luggage store says to the clerk, "But I don't *want* soft luggage. I want *hard* luggage." I agree with him, but you have to buy what's best for you, whether it's a hippie-dippy backpack, soft-sided luggage on roller wheels, or old-fashioned hardshell suitcases that can withstand mauling by a gorilla or even by Moochie, my five-year-old son.

Imagine a Web site devoted to little more than the fine art of packing, with an emphasis on carryon luggage. Freakishly, there really is such a site: the Compleat Carry-On Traveler at *www. oratory.com/travel*. Although the author, Doug Dyment, and I disagree about the spelling of "carryon," I find his single-mindedness on the topic awesome, even inspiring.

Trying to fit all your air-travel baggage into a carryon or two is the noble goal of the Compleat Carry-On Traveler.

1. Point your browser to *www.oratory.com/travel*. You can read the home page if you want, but let's start clicking buttons.

2. At the top of the page, click What to Take. Read Dyment's philosophy on what you should bring and, by extrapolation and perhaps even more importantly, what you should leave behind.

3. The list is comprehensive and practical, but it's too long to print out. Go back to near the top of the page and look for the section called The One-Page Checklist. (Note: requires Adobe Acrobat Reader.) Click Download a copy of the convenient checklist version.

4. Print out the document and use it even if you aren't limiting yourself strictly to carryon bags. Then return to the home page and browse through the other topics, including What to Take It In, How to Pack It, and Resources, the last of which includes links to carryon manufacturers' Web sites.

▼ **Try It Yourself**

▲

Remember

Many airline passengers like the bulkhead seats in coach, right behind the wall that separates coach class from business class. But remember, in the bulkhead row you can't stow your carryons under the seats in front of you... because there *are* no seats in front of you.

Few airline topics cause more confusion than the carryon rules. There's no industry standard. One airline will look away as a customer tries to cram a 150-pound footlocker into an overhead bin, but the next airline will put up a fuss if a businessman attempts to carry on his briefcase *and* a laptop computer. ("Only one carryon, sir!")

What's a poor passenger to do? My rule of thumb is to check your luggage at the check-in counter, except for the minimum you'll need for your comfort aboard the aircraft. I hear some of you whining already: "But I don't wanna wait at the baggage carousel with all those other people!" Yeah, well... tough buns.

I've traveled all over the world, and I always check in my one or two suitcases and then take one carryon bag onto the aircraft. The bag is usually stuffed with books, magazines, writing materials, some snacks, and a bottle of aspirin (for when that guy bangs me on the head with his footlocker on his way down the aisle). When I get off the jet, I boogie down to the baggage claim area and retrieve my suitcase. Rarely do I have to wait more than 10 or 15 minutes.

I don't disagree with the airlines in their crackdown on carryons. My problem with the airline execs is that they should make a set of standard rules. Perhaps all airlines should do what American Airlines does. On domestic U.S. flights, each passenger may take a total of three pieces of luggage. It might be two carryons and one checked suitcase, or two checked pieces and one carryon, or three checked bags and no carryons. (No, three carryons are not allowed.) American also has weight and size allowances. Checked bags must have total outside dimensions of no more than 62 inches long, 55 inches wide, and 45 inches high, and can weigh no more than 70 pounds. As for the carryon allowance, a brief-case or garment bag is considered one of the allowed pieces. Bags must fit into an overhead compartment or under the seat and should not exceed total dimensions of 9 inches×13 inches×23 inches. (Note: American's baggage allowance varies for interna-tional destinations.) This seems more or less logical to me. All I ask is that there be some semblance of agreement among all the airlines. For more details on American's policy, go to *www.americanair.com.*

I have my own feelings about packing. For instance, I'm often asked about the one indispensable item that I always take with me when I travel. Answer? A Swiss Army knife, that all-purpose tool that slices, dices, makes hundreds of Julienne fries in just min-utes, and even has a sharp blade that can be used as (gasp!) a knife. The one I have, made by Victorinox, has so many tools that I could just as easily uncork a bottle of Chateauneuf de Pape as skin a bear (both of which I have been called upon to do in my time). Folded into it are a fingernail file, screwdriver, carving blades, toothpick, tweezers, and scissors. It even has that can't-live-without device, a bottle opener! One of Victorinox's best-sellers, the Swiss Champ, also has a wire stripper, multipurpose hook, wood saw, hook disgorger (hook disgorger?!), magnifying glass, fish scaler, and ballpoint pen—33 implements in all. Now that's what I call a knife!

The Wenger company and Victorinox vie for the title of Most Original when it comes to the Swiss Army knife. Both seem to have a valid claim. Decide for yourself by checking out their Web sites at *genuineswissarmy.com/* and *www.victorinox.ch/home_en/ home_en.htm.*

By the Way
The three most important considera-tions when packing are 1) whether you're traveling on business or leisure, 2) what the style of dress is in your desti-nation, and 3) what the weather will be like when you travel.

When it comes to deciding what sort of clothing to pack, remember that you'll feel more comfortable if you dress more or less like the people where you're going. Take Europe, for instance. Generally speaking, the fashions in the capitals of Europe don't differ dramatically from the styles of dress in the major cities of the United States. There *are* differences, though. In France, for example, women should save the shorts for country outings. Pants on women aren't all that popular with French women either. In the city, you'll probably look and feel more in tune with the Parisians if you wear a dress or skirt. As you've learned, you can find information on specific cities and countries (including details about local dress, manners, holidays, etc.) on the Web. One of my favorite travel sites is Sky Guide. It has a terrific section on luggage and packing at *www.sky-guide.com/html/travelresources/index.html*.

But perhaps you shouldn't worry too much about all this packing stuff. After all, it's not rocket science. Talking about it so much makes me long for the days when I left home for Europe as a wayward youth, having packed nothing more than three sets of underwear and a toothbrush. And I forgot the toothbrush.

But I still had a great time.

Money Matters from ATM to Z

In my younger days I worked briefly in England as a strawberry slave, plucking the fruit from the vine for a wily and parsimonious old farmer during the sunlight hours, and sleeping in a wretched hostel at night with other berry-pickers. One of my fellow berrymen, an American, had brought over his travel savings in the form of traveler's checks in British pounds. We watched together in horror over the course of seven days as the value of the pound sterling fell from about U.S. $1.90 to U.S. $1.25. All of a sudden, his planned six months in England and Europe became four months. If only he'd had a credit card.

The major benefit of paying for your purchases with plastic is that the exchange rates for credit charges are calculated at a preferred bank rate, or the lowest rate available when the charges are processed through the bank. Although this savings is not going to make you rich, or even allow you to buy an original sofa-sized crying puppy painting from Art 'R' Us, it will shave a few shekels off your purchases. And of course, if you ever have a dispute with a merchant about your purchase, you can contest the charge through the card company.

Cash is necessary, of course. Find out from your card company or issuing bank whether you can use your credit card to withdraw money from an automatic teller machine (ATM). If possible, make sure such withdrawals are deducted from your bank account and not charged as cash advances (for which you'll be charged interest). Interest on a cash advance, usually around 18 percent, is calculated from the moment you tickle the ATM into coughing up the mazuma. A concise discussion of travel-money matters, written for the Credit Union National Association, is available at *www.hfcu.org/whatsnew/hff/sept1.htm.*

The hardest part about relying on ATMs when traveling is trying to find out exactly where they're located at your destination. Fortunately, the major card companies, including MasterCard and Visa, make that information available on the Web. For MasterCard, the URL is *www.mastercard.com/atm/.* For Visa, it's *www.visa.com/atms/.*

Wherever you go, you can find an automatic teller machine that accepts MasterCard (or Visa, or American Express, or Cirrus)—but you have to remember to find the location before you travel.

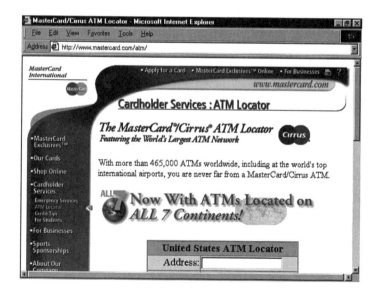

1. Log on to the MasterCard ATM site. Let's see how quickly you can find an automatic teller machine where you can use your MasterCard in London.

2. Find Worldwide ATM Locator. Next to Country, use the pull-down menu to select United Kingdom, and then click Find ATMs.

3. On the next page, use the pull-down menu to choose London, and then click Search.

4. You're given a list of 306 London ATMs where you can use your MasterCard (or Cirrus card). It may take a while to find the one closest to you, but if you're at a loss, you can always go to MapQuest (see the appendix) to get a map of an otherwise unfamiliar address.

▼ **Try It Yourself**

You understand the need for cash. You've looked at using credit cards, including at ATMs. But the backbone of my financial plans on the road is something that may sound quaint and old-fashioned: traveler's checks.

The first traveler's checks were issued by American Express, and many people continue to believe that Amex checks are the sine qua non of road money. But whether you buy your traveler's checks from American Express, Thomas Cook, Visa, or whomever, the basic principle is the same. You buy the checks in certain denominations, either in American dollars or the currency of the country you'll be visiting. You sign the checks when you buy them, and then you countersign them when you use them, thus allowing the merchant to compare your original signature and the countersignature. (You'll usually be asked for ID too.) The beauty of traveler's checks is that they'll be replaced, at no cost, if they're lost or stolen. But as you'll see later in this chapter, the goal is not to lose them in the first place!

Staying Healthy: What to Know Before You Leave and While You're on the Road

As I tell everyone when the subject of travel medicine comes up, I'm not a doctor. I just go door to door and ask beautiful young women if they'd like to have a free physical exam. Actually, I've stopped doing that, on the advice of counsel. But I continue to take an interest in health matters, especially as they pertain to travel.

When someone tells me that he's going to Africa but doesn't think he needs malaria shots, I say to him, "Haven't you ever seen Bob Hope's unforgettable classic of the cinema, *Call Me Bwana*?" Malaria is no fun, nor are cholera, sleeping sickness, dengue fever, or a whole raft of other exotic-sounding but rather nasty diseases that you're apt to get if you go gallivanting around the world without proper vaccinations. You realize, don't you, that if a food preparer doesn't properly wash his hands or your food, it doesn't matter how good the chef is or how many stars the restaurant has. You may end up with any number of yucky bugs making a condominium of your liver. It may sound terribly romantic to mop your brow, undo the bow tie of your tuxedo, and say to the ravishing beauty next to you, "Sorry, my darling, but a dash of the old dengue fever just came over me." But when you're sitting on the toilet for 20 hours straight and your fingers are too weak to grasp the teacup being handed to you, it won't seem so darn romantic then, will it, tough guy?

You'll find enough disease warnings to scare the pants off you at the Centers for Disease Control's Travel Information Web site at *www.cdc.gov/travel/travel.html*. Let's find out what you have to worry about on your next trip to, say, Papua New Guinea.

Try It Yourself ▼

1. Head over to the CDC travel home page.

2. Near the bottom of the table of contents, click Geographic Health Recommendations.

3. Under Geographic Health Recommendations, click Australia and the South Pacific. (You already knew that Papua New Guinea was in the South Pacific, of course. I know you did. I trust you.)

4. In the descriptions of diseases and suggested vaccines for this region, you read that "a high risk for malaria exists all year in Papua New Guinea, the Solomon Islands, and Vanuatu.

Travelers to these areas should take mefloquine for malaria prevention." Additionally, you're at risk for dengue, filariasis, and Ross River Virus, depending on exactly where you travel.

There, don't you feel better now?

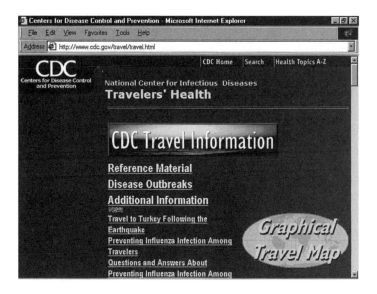

Want the skinny on malaria, dengue fever, E. coli, and other infectious diseases that you just might find on the road? Look no further than the Centers for Disease Control's Travel Information Web site.

If you're planning to travel to a part of the world where strange and frightening diseases are apt to attack the casual tourist, you might want to think twice before leaving all your vaccinations in the hands of your local intern. Sure, you've been going to him since you were a kid, but that doesn't mean he's up on the latest vaccines to combat Ross River virus and the like. Consider a travel-medicine specialist, which is a growing specialty among physicians. To find a travel-medicine clinic or doctor in your area, consult the directory at the International Society of Travel Medicine Web site at *www.istm.org*.

Lotsa Names

At last count, there were 312 names in English for traveler's diarrhea, including the Trots, the Tijuana Two-Step, Traveler's Lament, and my favorite, the Huckleberry Skitters.

I could go on about this, but I still have a touch of the globetrotter's disease—Montezuma's Revenge and all that—and I might have to leave you at any moment. Never know when it's going to strike. Sometimes, out of the clear blue sky, it—

Commonsense Precautions When You Arrive

Italy seems to be everyone's favorite country. And why shouldn't it be? After all, it's the nation that gave us Sophia Loren, Roberto Benigni, pizza, and gondolas. (Just think—what would your life be like if there were no gondolas?) But like every nation, Italy has its share of nogoodniks who are ready to pillage and plunder. Thankfully, most of the hooliganism and petty crime is not aimed specifically at tourists, but there's enough of it to rate a mention here. Theft from parked cars, particularly in the bigger cities, is a real problem (as are pickpocketing, purse-snatching, and other so-called petty crimes). Robbers in southern Italy have even taken things from cars at gas stations by breaking the windows in smash-and-grab attacks. In Naples, there have been thefts from occupied cars stopped at traffic signals.

> **Turnabout Is Fair Play**
> Just as the U.S. State Department puts out warnings on other countries when their crime affects American tourists, so too have other countries put out warnings on destinations in the United States. Consider the recent carjackings in Florida, in which several European travelers were victims.

And that's in Italy—sophisticated, modern, part-of-Europe Italy. Just think what may lie in wait for you when you go to Cote d'Ivoire, Kazakhstan, or Myanmar. The mind boggles.

You need to take some commonsense precautions whether you're going to Rome, Paris, Miami, or any number of other major metropolises around the world:

- When you make a brief stop, one person should remain with the car.

- While driving in cities and major towns, keep your doors locked, place valuables out of sight, and roll up your windows.

- Never leave valuables in an unattended car.

The chances are that if you follow these safety guidelines, you'll have a great trip without any incidents.

However, there are some places in this world where any precautions you might take won't really make a whit of difference because nasty men with guns will just block the road and threaten to shoot you if you don't give them all your valuables. In such cases, rolling up your window will do you no good. Nor will making mean faces in an attempt to scare them off.

In Mexico (and I must tell you again that it's my favorite foreign destination in the world), the U.S. State Department advises caution when traveling on all highways. State mentions numerous specific roads where crime is high, including the highway from Altamirano to Ixtapa/Zihuatanejo. Reported incidents include robbery and kidnapping. Also, the U.S. Embassy tells its employees to be extremely cautious when driving, and not to travel on Mexican highways at night.

But you could find things to complain about at so many destinations that you almost have to ask yourself, "What's the use?" Well, there is a practical purpose in knowing all this stuff, my friend—to make you alert, aware, and smart so that you don't become the next victim.

Let's say you're going to Rio de Janeiro. In the past several years, there has been a major increase in crime aimed at tourists, especially in the areas around beaches, nightclubs, hotels, discos, and other popular visitor hangouts. Incidents of robbery and other tourist-directed crimes are more apt to occur at dusk or in the evening, but they can happen at any time of day. The U.S. State Department advises Americans to avoid public buses altogether because so much crime is perpetrated on them. The increase in violence in Rio and other Brazilian cities has apparently caused a dip in the number of foreign visitors. The government has responded by creating special police patrols to concentrate on popular tourist areas.

You can learn about all these types of scams, and what the local authorities are doing about them (if anything), by looking at each country's description at the State Department's Travel Warnings Web site.

Wherever you go, you can handle the situation by being well-informed—and indeed, isn't that what this entire book has been

Did You know?

In an increasing number of countries where visitors have been robbed or attacked, the local governments are establishing "tourist police" who focus on keeping vacationers safe.

about? You'll know how to take care of yourself wherever you are and, most importantly, how to avoid getting into a dangerous situation in the first place. Short of a plague, a famine, or the next David Copperfield TV special, the smart traveler can deal with most situations and enjoy the trip without getting mugged. And don't forget, you can get robbed or pickpocketed (or worse) no matter where you go, from the villages of New Hampshire to the back alleys of New Delhi (although New Delhi might be just a little more dangerous than Dixville Notch).

Although there are measures you can take to protect yourself against traveler's diarrhea, seasickness, and other perils of traveling, there are some things you're powerless to control.

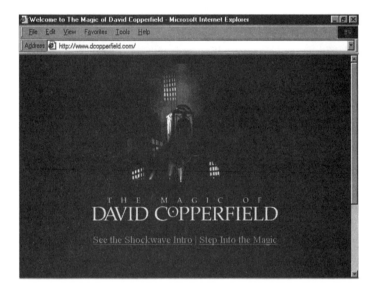

Remember the basic safety measures that all travelers should follow: Know where you're going, don't stand on busy street corners holding a map and looking dumb, stay away from unlighted streets, don't flash your cash, etc. I even heed this advice at my office!

Wrapping It Up: So Long, It's Been Good to Know You...

It's difficult to believe that we're at the end this book. You've come a long way in your knowledge of e-travel. When you first picked up this book, way back in Chapter 1, you were a babe in arms. Sure, maybe you could have figured out how to make an airline reservation on Travelocity or how to rent a car through the

Avis Web site, but you didn't know much more than that. And you were so tiny. Just an itsy-bitsy thing. I could have fit you into my pocket. And then next thing you know, you're borrowing my car to go to the prom, graduating from college after three years of academic probation, getting fired from your first "real" job… Oh, wait a minute. Somehow the closing remarks from *Sams Teach Yourself e-Parenting Today* accidentally got into this book.

And so we say… not good-bye, but farewell. But what's the difference between "good-bye" and "farewell" anyway? Don't they pretty much mean the same thing? The answer, of course, is anybody's guess.

Here's what you learned in this (sniff, sniff), our last (snort, snurkle, mffft) chapter (grunt, !@#$%*, ahoooo, ahoooo) together:

- The different approaches to packing (such as using only carryons or traveling with multiple bags), with suggested Web sites to visit for more details.

- How to use money when traveling, whether it's cash, credit cards, ATM cards, or traveler's checks.

- Some things to bear in mind if I come to your house offering a free physical exam, plus ways to figure out if you're going to get really, really sick on your next vacation. And if so, how to figure out which vaccines you might want to take first.

- How to keep up with the increasing number of travel-related street scams out there, and how to avoid them by being a smart traveler.

- Why you should buy at least 10 copies of this book and give them out as presents to your friends. Heck, give them out to complete strangers on the street, for all I care. And then buy more copies. And more copies! You'll make me rich… rich, I tell you! Richer than my wildest dreams!

PART V

Appendix

APPENDIX A

Web Sites

The Web sites in this appendix reflect my own eclectic choices based on years of Internet travel research and, in a few cases, my own personal preferences. This appendix is not meant to be comprehensive, but it is meant to be wide-ranging. Many of these sites will provide you with links to other sites not listed here. My hope is that you will use the sites in this appendix to build an even larger roster of bookmarks that will suit your own travel and research needs.

Air Travel

Domestic Airlines

Alaska Airlines: *www.alaskaair.com*

Aloha Airlines: *www.alohaair.com*

America West Airlines: *www.americawest.com*

American Airlines: *www.aa.com*

ATA/American Trans Air (charter): *www.ata.com*

Continental Airlines: *www.flycontinental.com*

Delta: *www.delta-air.com*

Frontier Airlines: *www.frontierairlines.com*

Hawaiian Airlines: *www.hawaiianair.com*

Midway Airlines: *www.midwayair.com*

Midwest Express: *www.midwestexpress.com*

National Airlines: *www.nationalairlines.com*

Northwest Airlines: *www.nwa.com*

Southwest Airlines: *www.southwest.com*

Tower Air: *www.towerair.com*

Trans World Airlines: *www.twa.com*

United Airlines: *www.ual.com*

US Airways: *www.usairways.com*

Vanguard Airlines: *www.flyvanguard.com*

Foreign Airlines

Aer Lingus: *www.aerlingus.ie/usa/*

Aeroflot: *www.aeroflot.org/index.htm*

AeroMexico: *www.aeromexico.com*

Air Canada: *www.aircanada.ca*

Air France: *www.airfrance.com*

Air India: *www.airindia.com*

Air New Zealand: *www.airnz.com/home.htm*

Alitalia: *www.alitalia.it/eng/index.html*

All Airlines Of The World: *air.findhere.com*

British Airways: *www.british-airways.com*

Cathay Pacific Airways: *www.cathay-usa.com*

El Al Israel Airlines: *www.elal.co.il*

Finnair: *www.us.finnair.com*

Garuda Indonesia: *www.aerowisata.com/garuda/*

Iberia Airlines: *www.iberia.com*

Japan Airlines: *www.jal.co.jp/english/index_e.html*

KLM: *www.klm.com*

Korean Air: *www.koreanair.com*

Lufthansa: *www.lufthansa.com/ehome.htm*

Qantas: *www.qantas.com.au*

Sabena Airlines: *www.sabena-usa.com*

Scandinavian Airlines/SAS: *www.flysas.com*

Singapore Airlines: *www.singaporeair.com*

Swissair: *www.swissair.com*

TAP-Air Portugal: *www.TAP-AirPortugal.pt*

Virgin Atlantic: *www.virgin-atlantic.com*

Air Travel General Resources

Airlines of the Web City Codes: *flyaow.com/citycode.htm*

Airport Search Engine: *www.uni-karlsruhe.de/~un9v/atm/ase.html*

Worldwide Airport and City Code Database:
www.cowtown.net/users/rcr/aaa/ccmain.htm

Air Travel: Laws, Advice

Air Traveler's Handbook:
www.cs.cmu.edu/afs/cs/user/mkant/Public/Travel/airfare.html

AirSafe.com: *airsafe.com*

Airwise—The Airport and Air Travel Guide: *www.airwise.com*

Aviation Consumer Protection—Department of Transportation
(DOT): *www.dot.gov/airconsumer/*

Consolidators (info sheet):
www.travel-library.com/air-travel/consolidators.html

Office of Airline Information/DOT On-Time Stats:
www.bts.gov/oai/

Round-The-World Travel Guide—Airlines:
www.travel-library.com/rtw/html/rtwairlines.html

Rules of the Air: *www.onetravel.com/rules/rules.cfm*

SkyGuide Air-Travel Resources: *www.sky-guide.com*

WebFlyer—The Web's Frequent Flyer Authority:
www.insideflyer.com

Air Travel Organizations

Air Line Pilots Association (ALPA): *208.217.189.50*

Air Transport Association: *www.air-transport.org*

AirportNet: *www.airportnet.org*

Aviation Associations: *www.robinsfyi.com/aviationgroups.htm*

Federal Aviation Administration (FAA): *www.faa.gov*

International Air Transport Association (IATA): *www.iata.org*

International Civil Aviation Organization (ICAO): *www.icao.int*

Consumer Rights—Air Travel

Air Travel Complaints: *www.airtravelcomplaints.com*

Airline Complaints Registry: *www.airlinecomplaints.com*

Aviation Consumer Action Project (ACAP): *www.acap1971.org*

DOT's Air Consumer Fly Rights:
www.dot.gov/airconsumer/flyrights.htm

Passengerrights.com: *www.passengerrights.com*

Rules of the Air: *www.rulesoftheair.com*

General Travel

100hot Travel: *www.100hot.com/travel/*

Fam Trips: A Travel Agent Resource Site:
www.redshift.com/~talisman/FamConnection.html

Kasbah Travel Search Engine: *www.kasbah.com*

TAgent.com: *www.tagent.com*

Travel Library: *www.travellibrary.com*

Yahoo! Travel: *travel.yahoo.com*

Zagat.com: *www.zagat.com*

Associations (Travel-Related)

American Automobile Association (AAA): *www.aaa.com*

American Society of Travel Agents (ASTA): *www.astanet.com*

Travel Industry Association of America (TIA): *www.tia.org*

U.S. Tour Operators Association (USTOA): *www.ustoa.com*

Business Travel

Biztravel.com: *www.biztravel.com*

Business Travel from About.com: *businesstravel.about.com*

Business Travel from The Mining Co.:
businesstravel.miningco.com

SkyGuide: *www.sky-guide.com*

Car Rental

Alamo: *www.goalamo.com*

Auto Europe: *www.autoeurope.com*

Avis: *www.avis.com*

Budget: *www.budgetrentacar.com*

Dollar: *www.dollarcar.com*

Europe By Car: *www.europebycar.com*

Hertz: *www.hertz.com*

Kemwel: *www.kemwel.com*

National: *www.nationalcar.com*

Practical (U.K.): *www.practical.co.uk*

Cruises

Cruise Lines International Association (CLIA): *www.cruising.org*

Cruise News Daily: *www.reply.net/clients/cruise/cnd.html*

Cruise Observer Online: *www.traveletterz.com*

CruiseMates: *www.cruisemates.com*

National Association of Cruise Oriented Agencies (NACOA): *www.nacoa.com*

SNCM (Mediterranean Ferries): *www.sncm.fr*

Tutto Crociere—the Cyberspace Cruise Magazine: *www.cybercruises.com*

Destinations

Automobile Association (UK): *www.theaa.co.uk/hotels/*

Bonjour Paris: *www.bparis.com*

BTA's Visit Britain: *www.usagateway.visitbritain.com/BTA-USA.htm*

Caribbean Hotel and Resort Guide: *www.where2stay.com/islands/*

Caribbean Travel Planner: *www.caribbeantravel.com*

European Country Codes: *easytour.dr-staedtler.de/nat_kz.asp*

Hawaii Visitors & Convention Bureau: *www.gohawaii.com*

LondonTown.com: *www.londontown.com/index.phtml*

Mexico OnLine: *www.mexonline.com*

Embassies and Consulates

Electronic Embassy: *www.embassy.org/embassies/*

Embassy World: *www.embassyworld.com*

EmbassyWeb: *www.embpage.org*

Family Travel

Family.com: Travel: *family.go.com/Categories/Travel/*

Family Travel Files: *www.thefamilytravelfiles.com*

GORP—Great Outdoor Recreation Pages: Family: *www.gorp.com/gorp/eclectic/family.htm*

Travel & Leisure Family: *www.pathfinder.com/travel/TL/family/index.html*

Travel With Kids: *travelwithkids.about.com*

Government Travel Facts

CIA World Factbook: *www.odci.gov/cia/publications/factbook/index.html*

Federal Aviation Administration (FAA): *www.faa.gov*

State Department Travel Advisories: *travel.state.gov/travel_warnings.html*

U.S. Customs Service: *www.customs.ustreas.gov*

U.S. Department of Transportation (DOT): *www.dot.gov*

Guidebooks Online

Arthur Frommer's Budget Travel Online: *www.frommers.com*

Fielding Worldwide: *www.fieldingtravel.com*

Fodor's Travel Online: *www.fodors.com*

Lonely Planet Online: *www.lonelyplanet.com*

Michelin Travel: *www.michelin-travel.com*

Rick Steves' Europe Through the Back Door: *www.ricksteves.com*

Health (Travel)

Centers for Disease Control (CDC) Travel Information Page: *www.cdc.gov/travel/travel.html*

HealthLink Travel Medicine: *healthlink.mcw.edu/travel-medicine*

International Society of Travel Medicine: *www.istm.org*

Travel Health Online: *www.tripprep.com/index.html*

High-Tech Travel

Laptop Travel: *www.laptoptravel.com*

Drivernet: *www.drivernet.com*

JetSet: *www.jetset-roam.net*

Magellan's Travel Supplies: *www.magellans.com*

Hotel Reservations

123france—Hotels in Paris: *www.123france.com*

1-800-USA-Hotels: *www.1800usahotels.com*

Accommodations Express: *www.accommodationsexpress.com*

All-Hotels: *www.all-hotels.com*

Asia Travel: *www.asiatravel.com*

Bed & Breakfast Channel: *www.Bedandbreakfast.com/index3.asp*

British Hotel Reservation Centre: *www.bhrc.co.uk*

Central Reservation Service: *www.reservation-services.com*

Hotel Discount Reservations: *www.hoteldiscounts.com*

Hotel Reservations in Australia and Asia: *www.cia.com.au/hotels/index.htm/*

In Italy Online: *www.initaly.com*

Mexico Hotels: *www.mexicohotels.com*

Quikbook: *www.quikbook.com*

Money Matters

American Express ATM Locations: *maps.americanexpress.com/expresscash/mqinterconnect?link=home*

Credit Union National Association: *www.hfcu.org/whatsnew/hff/sept1.htm*

MasterCard ATM Locations: *www.mastercard.com/atm/*

Visa ATM Locations: *www.visa.com/atms/*

Online Magazines—Travel

ABCNEWS.com Travel Index: *abcnews.go.com/sections/travel/*

Best Fares Discount Travel Magazine: *www.bestfares.com*

Cahners Travel Group: *www.reedtravelgroup.com/cahners.html*

Leisure Travel News: *www.ttgweb.com*

MSNBC Travel: *www.msnbc.com/news/*

The Ticked-Off Traveler: *www.ticked.com*

Travel & Leisure: *www.travelandleisure.com*

Travel Weekly Crossroads: *www.twcrossroads.com*

USA TODAY: Travel Guide: *www.twcrossroads.com*

Online Reservations

1travel.com: *www.1travel.com*

American Express: *www.americanexpress.com*

Biztravel.com: *newhome.biztravel.com*

Carlson Wagonlit Travel: *www.carlsontravel.com*

Cheap Tickets: *www.cheaptickets.com*

Economy Travel: *www.economytravel.com*

Internet Travel Network (ITN): *www.itn.net*

LowestFare.com: *www.lowestfare.com*

Microsoft Expedia: *expedia.msn.com*

Priceline.com: *www.priceline.com*

SkyAuction.com: *www.skyauction.com*

Trip.com: *www.thetrip.com*

Travelocity: *www.travelocity.com*

Tourist Bureaus—Domestic

ConventionBureaus.com: *www.conventionbureaus.com*

USA CityLink: *usacitylink.com*

Tourist Bureaus—Foreign

International Tourist Bureaus:
www.armchair.com/bureau/inttb.html

International Tourist Offices: *www.tvlon.com/International.html*

Special-Interest Travel

Disabled Travel

Access-Able Travel Source: *www.access-able.com*

Disabled travel (car rentals): *www.actcom.co.il/~swfm/*

Global Access: *www.geocities.com/Paris/1502/*

Mobility International USA: *www.miusa.org/index.htm*

Moss Rehab Resource Net: *www.mossresourcenet.org/travel.htm*

Society for the Advancement of Travelers with Handicaps (SATH): *www.sath.org*

Pets

DogFriendly.com: *www.dogfriendly.com*

Traveling With Your Pet: *www.avma.org/care4pets/safetrav.htm*

U.S. State and Territory Animal Import Regulations: *www.aphis.usda.gov:80/vs/sregs/*

Women's/Religious/Gay Travel

Christian Travellers International: *www.christiantraveller.org*

Jewish Travel: Your World Wide Guide: *www.jewishtravel.com*

Journeywoman: *www.journeywoman.com*

PlanetOut: *www.planetout.com*

The Women's Travel Club: *www.womenstravelclub.com/index.html*

Tools and Resources for Travelers

Currency Calculators

CNNfn Currency Converter: *cnnfn.com/markets/currencies/*

Interactive Currency Table: *www.xe.net/ict/*

OANDA Currency Converter: *www.oanda.com/converter/classic*

Distance Calculator

How far is it?: *www.indo.com/distance*

Foreign Language Study

Travlang: *www.travlang.com*

Maps

Excite Maps: *maps.excite.com*

MapBlast: *www.mapblast.com*

MapQuest!: *www.mapquest.com*

Maps On Us: *www.mapsonus.com*

National Atlas of the United States: *www-atlas.usgs.gov*

PCL Map Collection: *www.lib.utexas.edu/Libs/PCL/
Map_collection/Map_collection.html*

World City Maps: *www.lib.utexas.edu/Libs/PCL/
Map_collection/world_cities.html*

World Factbook Reference Maps:
www.odci.gov/cia/publications/factbook/ref.html

Xerox PARC Map Viewer: *pubweb.parc.xerox.com/map*

Xpeditions: *www.nationalgeographic.com/xpeditions/main.html*

Route Planners—Europe

CW Lease Routeplanner: *www.cwlease.com/cwlint/selection.html*

Easy Tour Route Planner:
easytour.dr-staedtler.de/routenplanung_engl.asp

Reise Route Planner: *www.reiseroute.de/route_uk.htm*

Shell Route Planner: *shell.route66.nl/shell/route.html*

Sommaire: *www.iti.fr*

Route Planners—USA

See also "Maps" under "Tools and Resources for Travelers".

AutoPilot: *www.freetrip.com*

Microsoft Expedia Maps—Driving Directions:
www.expediamaps.com/DrivingDirections.asp

Yahoo! Maps and Driving Directions:
maps.yahoo.com/py/maps.py

Time Converters, Time Zones

Time Zone Converter: *www.timezoneconverter.com*

World Time Locations:
www.isbister.com/worldtime/wt-location.html

Weather

Intellicast: *www.intellicast.com*

USA Today Weather Page:
www.usatoday.com/weather/wfront.htm

Weather Channel: *www.weather.com/homepage.html*

World Climate: *www.worldclimate.com*

Tour Operators

Abercrombie & Kent: *www.abercrombiekent.com*

Backroads: *www.backroads.com*

Butterfield & Robinson: *www.butterfieldandrobinson.com*

Geographic Expeditions: *www.GeoEx.com*

INTRAV: *www.INTRAV.com*

Ker & Downey Safaris: *www.kerdowney.com*

Lindblad Special Expeditions:
www.expeditions.com/docs/index2.htm

Maupintour: *www.maupintour.com*

Micato Safaris: *www.africansafari.org/micato/*

Mountain Travel-Sobek: *www.mtsobek.com*

Rascals in Paradise: *www.rascalsinparadise.com*

Tauck Tours: *www.tauck.com*

Travcoa: *www.travcoa.com*

Vermong Bicycle Touring: *www.vbt.com*

Trains

Amtrak: *www.amtrak.com*

CTU Railway Page: *www.cvut.cz/home/railway.htm*

Cyberspace World Railroads:
www.mcs.net/~dsdawdy/cyberoad.html

Eurostar: *www.railpass.com/eurostar/*

European Railway Server: *mercurio.iet.unipi.it*

Great Little Trains of the Harz:
mercurio.iet.unipi.it/tog-ch/dngharz.dir/harze0.htm

Harzer Schmalspurbahnen: *www.hsb-wr.de*

Japanese Bullet Trains:
www.teleway.ne.jp/~dolittle/byunbyun/index.htm

Orient-Express: *www.orient-expresstrains.com/index.html*

Rail Europe: *www.raileurope.com/us/*

RailServe: *www.railserve.com*

Swiss Rail: *www.rail.info.ch*

VIA Rail Canada: *www.viarail.ca*

Vacation Activities

Active/Outdoor

GORP—Great Outdoor Recreation Pages: *www.gorp.com*

National Park Service at *www.nps.gov*

Offbeat/Miscellaneous

Hidden America: *www.hiddenamerica.com*

Roadside America: *www.roadsideamerica.com*

Spa Vacations

Spa Vacations from Spa-Finders: *www.spafinders.com*

Summer Sun, Surf, and Sand

Best Beaches from Dr. Beach: *www.petrix.com/beaches/*

Sandcastle Central: *www.unlitter.com/sandcastle/*

Snap: Beaches & Islands:
home.snap.com/directory/category/0,16,-47100,00.html

Surfline: *www.surfline.com*

World Surf Cameras: *goan.com/menus.html*

Winter Sports

Ski-Guide Resorts Guide: *www.ski-guide.com*

Villa Rentals

Barclay International: *www.barclayweb.com*

Hideaways International: *www.hideaways.com*

New York Habitat: *www.nyhabitat.com*

World Wide Travel Exchange: *www.wwte.com*

World Calendars of Events

CultureFinder: *culturefinder.com*

EventsWorldWide: *www.eventsworldwide.com*

Festivals.com: *www.festivals.com*

INDEX

Symbols

100hot Web site, 87-88

A

AAA (American Automobile
  Association) Web site, 213
About.com Web site, 103
accuracy of Web sites, testing, 34-35
Action Cellular Rent a Phone Web
  site, 236
adventurers (traveler types), 90-91
Agfa ePhoto 780 digital camera, 255
Agfa Web site, 258
Ahwahnee Lodge, 124-126
airfares, 182-183. *See also* airlines;
  airports
    consolidators, 191-192
    vacation packages, 183
    weekend fares, 188-190
Airline Complaints Web site, 166-167
Airline-Ticket Consolidators and
  Bucket Shops Web site, 192
airlines, 184-186. *See also* airfares;
  airports
    Airline Complaints Web site,
      166-167
    Airport and Air Travel Guide
      Web site, 186
    Airport Search Engine Web site,
      184
    All Airlines of the World Web
      site, 184
    American Airlines Web site,
      190, 264
    Aviation Consumer Action
      Project Web site, 166
    booking tickets, 186-188

carryons
    Compleat Carry-On
      Traveler Web site,
      262-263
    rules, 263-264
foreign airlines, 184
newsletters, 190
PassengerRights.com Web site,
  166
United Airlines Web site,
  186-188
Airport and Air Travel Guide Web
  site, 186
Airport Search Engine Web site,
  15, 184
airports, 184-186. *See also* airfares;
  airlines
    Airport and Air Travel Guide
      Web site, 186
    airport codes, 15
    Airport Search Engine Web site,
      184
All Airlines of the World Web site,
  184
American Airlines Web site, 190, 264
American Automobile Association
  (AAA) Web site, 213
American Express Web site, 149
American Veterinary Medical
  Association (AVMA) Web site, 97
Amtrak Web site, 194-196
apartment rentals, 178-180
Arizona Guide Web site, 32
Arizona Republic newspaper, 32
Armchair World Web site, 73
Arthur Frommer's Budget Travel
  Online Web site, 44-45
ASTA (American Society of Travel
  Agents), 154-156
    Web site, 153-154, 162

Athens, 132
ATMs (automatic teller machines), 266-267
Australia
    Australian Tourist Commission Web site, 248
    Embassy of Australia Web site, 246
Auto Europe Web site, 212-213
AutoPilot route planner (Free Trip Web site), 16-17, 127
Aviation Consumer Action Project Web site, 166
Avis Web site, 207-208

B

Bali Online Web site, 14
Bed & Breakfast Channel Web site, 178
beginners (traveler types), 86-88
Biztravel Web site, 93-94
Black Mountain Travel Web site, 86
Bombay, 132-133
booking airline tickets, 186-188
booking engines, 149-150
bookmarks, 22-25
    creating
        in Internet Explorer, 23-24
        in Netscape Navigator, 22-23
    organizing in folders, 25-26
    renaming
        in Internet Explorer, 25
        in Netscape Navigator, 24
Borneo Bulletin, 56-57
British Tourist Authority Web site, 74-76
BritRail Web site, 198-199
browsers
    Internet Explorer bookmarks
        creating, 23-24
        renaming, 25
    Netscape Navigator bookmarks
        creating, 22-23
        renaming, 24

bucket shops, 191
bullet trains, 202
business travelers (traveler types), 93-94
Bwana Zulia's Kenya Travel Guide Web site, 116-117

C

cameras (digital cameras), 254-259
    Agfa ePhoto 780, 255
    buying tips, 259
    Casio Web site, 257
    information resources, 258
    Kodak DC200 Plus digital camera, 256
    Kodak Web site, 257
    limitations, 255-256
    memory cards, 254-255
    new technology, 257-258
    Sharp Web site, 257
Canada, VIA Rail Web site, 196-197
car rental companies, 206-213
    Auto Europe Web site, 212-213
    Avis Web site, 207-208
    comparing, 206-208
    domestic companies, 208-211
    foreign companies, 211-213
    Hertz Web site, 209-210
    insurance, 214-215
    National Car Rental Web site, 210
    questions to ask, 206-207
Carhenge, 126
Carlson Wagonlit Travel Web site, 150-152
    booking trips, 153
    privacy statement, 151-152
Carnival Cruise Line, 220-222
    Web site, 221-222
carrying cases (laptop computers), 230
carryons
    Compleat Carry-On Traveler Web site, 262-263
    rules, 263-264
    templates, 262

Casio Web site, 257
Cassiopeia E-105 PC, 257
cell phones, 236
Centers for Disease Control's Travel Information Web site, 268
Channel Tunnel (Chunnel), 199
chat sites, 115
CIA World Factbook Web site, 111-113
CLIA (Cruise Line International Association) Web site, 217-220
clothing, packing, 265
Colony Hotel in South Beach Web site, 177
commercial Web sites, 31
Compleat Carry-On Traveler Web site, 262-263
computers (laptop computers), 230-238
    author's laptop diary, 237-238
    carrying cases, 230
    email accounts, 234-235
    Internet connections, 232-233
    Jet Set Web site, 232-233
    Laptop Travel Web site, 232
    Roadnews Web site, 233
    theft-prevention, 231
Concord Times, 59-60
condo rentals, 178-180
consolidators (airfares), 191-192
consul, 65
Consular Information Sheets (State Department Web site), 110-111
consulates, 65-67
    Consulate General of Italy Web site, 65-67
    Electronic Embassy Web site, 67-69
    Embassy Web Web site, 70-71
    Embassy World Web site, 71-72
convention and visitor's bureaus, 76-79
    I Love New York Web site, 78
    Pennsylvania Visitors Guide Web site, 77
    terminology, 79
Corsica, 113
Costa Rica, 114

cottage rentals, 178
countries, researching
    CIA World Factbook Web site, 111-113
    private Web sites, 113-114
    State Department Travel Warnings & Consular Information Sheets Web site, 110-111, 164-165, 248
Creative Leisure Web site, 179
credit cards, 265
crime (safety precautions), 270-272
Cruise Line International Association (CLIA) Web site, 217-220
Cruise Mates Web site, 218
cruises, 217-226
    Carnival Cruise Line, 220-222
    Web site, 221-222
    Cruise Line International Association (CLIA) Web site, 217-220
    Cruise Mates Web site, 218
    Cybercruises Web site, 223
    ferry lines, 222-224
    freighter travel, 225-226
    river cruises, 224-225
    SNCM (La Societé Nationale Maritime Corse Mediterranée) Web site, 223-224
customs, 247-249
Customs Service Web site, 249
CW Lease Routeplanner Web site, 18
cyber-cafes, 235
Cybercruises Web site, 223
Cyberspace World Railroad Web site, 202

D

Dangerfinder section (Fielding Travel Guides Web site), 43
Daytona Beach ConVis Bureau's Spring Break Web site, 123
digital cameras, 254-259
    Agfa ePhoto 780, 255
    buying tips, 259
    Casio Web site, 257
    information resources, 258

Kodak DC200 Plus digital
  camera, 256
Kodak Web site, 257
limitations, 255-256
memory cards, 254-255
new technology, 257-258
Sharp Web site, 257
directories (Internet directories), 10
disabled travelers, 94-96
diseases, 267-269
distance calculators, 14-16
double-megapixel technology (Kodak
  digital cameras), 257
Drivernet Web site, 235

E

e-saver fares (airfares), 189-190
Easy Tour Online Route Planner
  Web site, 18
Electronic Embassy Web site, 67-69
email accounts, 234-235
email newsletters (airline
  newsletters), 190
embassies, 65-72
  Electronic Embassy Web site,
    67-69
  Embassy of Australia Web site,
    246
  Embassy of Italy Web site,
    65-67
  Embassy Web Web site, 70-71
  Embassy World Web site, 71-72
England, train travel, 198-199
ETA (Electronic Travel Authority),
  246
Eurailpass, 200-201
Europass, 200-201
European Railway Server Web site,
  202
European route planners, 18
European train travel, 197-202
  BritRail Web site, 198-199
  Eurailpass, 200-201
  Europass, 200-201
  European Railway Server Web
    site, 202

Eurostar Web site, 199
Rail Europe Web site, 200-202
Swiss Federal Railways (SBB)
  Web site, 198
Eurostar Web site, 199
events, planning around, 137-139
EventsWorldWide Web site, 138

F

fall vacation activities, 126-128
  Free Trip Web site, 127
  Roadside America Web site,
    126-127
family-vacation travelers (traveler
  types), 100-101
fast-paced (traveler types), 88-90
favorites. See bookmarks
ferry lines, 222-224
Fielding Travel Guides Web site,
  42-43
Fodor's Travel Online Web site, 41-42
folders, organizing bookmarks (Web
  browsers), 25-26
foreign airlines, 184
foreign consulates, 65-67
foreign newspapers, 56-58
foreign rental car companies, 211-213
free email accounts, 234-235
Free Trip Web site, 16, 127
freighter travel, 225-226
Freighter World Cruises Web site, 226

G

Galveston tourism Web site, 238
Global Access: A Network for
  Disabled Travelers Web site, 95-96
GORP Web site, 90
government statistics (travel informa-
  tion), 163-165
government Web sites, 64
Great Britain, train travel, 198-199
guidebooks, 39-49
  Arthur Frommer's Budget Travel
    Online Web site, 44-45
  Fielding Travel Guides Web site,
    42-43

Fodor's Travel Online Web site, 41-42
Lonely Planet Online Web site, 45-47
Rick Steves' Europe Through the Back Door Web site, 47-48

H

Hanscom Federal Credit Union Web site, 266
Hasselblad Web site, 258
health issues, 267-269
Hertz Web site, 209-210
high season, 135-136
HotBot Web site, 105
    Personal Travelogues, 114
hotels, 172-180
    alternatives, 178-180
    Colony Hotel in South Beach Web site, 177
    contacting directly via the Web, 176-177
    Fodor's Travel Online Hotel Index, 41
    Las Brisas, 174-176
    online reservation services, 172-174
    Quickbook Web site, 172-173
    ratings, 174
    Westin Web site, 175-176
Hotmail Web site, 234-235

I

I Love New York Web site, 78
IDPs (International Driving Permits), 213
insurance, rental car insurance, 214-215
Intellicast Web site, 134-135
Interactive Currency Table Web site, 18
International Society of Travel Medicine Web site, 269
Internet connections (laptop computers), 232-233

Internet directories, 10, 103-104
Internet Explorer bookmarks
    creating, 23-24
    renaming, 25
Internet Public Library Web site, 54-55
Istanbul, 132
Italy, consulate/embassy Web sites, 65-67
itineraries, 160-162

J-K

JanSport Laptop Transit daypack, 230
Japanese bullet trains (Shinkansen), 202
Jet Set Web site, 232-233
Journeywoman Web site, 99-100

KD River Cruises of Europe Web site, 224-225
Ker & Downey Web site, 90-91
Kodak DC200 Plus digital camera, 256
Kodak Web site, 257

L

La Societé Nationale Maritime Corse Mediterranée (SNCM) Web site, 223-224
laptop computers, 230-238
    author's laptop diary, 237-238
    carrying cases, 230
    email accounts, 234-235
    Internet connections, 232-233
    Jet Set Web site, 232-233
    Laptop Travel Web site, 232
    Roadnews Web site, 233
    theft-prevention, 231
Largest Newspaper Index on the Web Web site, 55
Las Brisas, 174-176
length of trip, planning, 139-140
Lonely Planet Online Web site, 45-47
low season, 136-137

luggage, 261-265
   carryons
      Compleat Carry-On
      Traveler Web site,
      262-263
      rules, 263-264
      templates, 262
   clothing, packing, 265
   Sky Guide Web site, 265

M

major events, planning around,
   137-139
map sites, 12-14
MapBlast Web site, 13
MapQuest Web site, 13, 17, 238
Maps On Us Web site, 17
MasterCard Web site, 266-267
media directories, 52-56
   Internet Public Library, 54-55
   Largest Newspaper Index on
      the Web, 55
   NewsDirectory.com, 53-54, 56
   Newspapers Online, 56
memory cards (digital cameras),
   254-255
message boards, 116-117
Mexico
   car rental insurance, 214-215
   Mexico Online Web site, 35
Microsoft Expedia Maps Web site, 17
Mile-High Club, 104
money issues, 265-267
   automatic teller machines
      (ATMs), 266-267
   credit cards, 265
   Hanscom Federal Credit Union
      Web site, 266
   traveler's checks, 267
Mumbai, 133

N

naming bookmarks, 24-25
National Car Rental Web site, 210
National Geographic Society
   Xpeditions Web site, 13

National Park Service ParkNet Web
   site, 124-126
national tourist offices, 72-76
   British Tourist Authority Web
      site, 74-76
   search terms, 74
   Tourism Offices Worldwide
      Directory Web site, 73
   Travel & Leisure Web site, 73
   Travel-On Web site, 73
Netscape Navigator bookmarks
   creating, 22-23
   renaming, 24
New South Polar Times, 54-55
NewsDirectory.com Web site,
   53-54, 56
newsletters (airline newsletters), 190
newspapers, 51-61
   Borneo Bulletin, 56-57
   Concord Times, 59-60
   foreign newspapers, 56-58
   New South Polar Times, 54-55
   online media directories, 52-56
      Internet Public Library,
         54-55
      Largest Newspaper Index
         on the Web, 55
      NewsDirectory.com,
         53-54, 56
      Newspapers Online, 56
   safety information, 58-61
North American route planners, 16-17

O

OANDA Currency Converter Web
   site, 19
off season, 136
official Web sites, comparing to unofficial sites, 30-33
Olympus Web site, 258
online hotel reservation services,
   172-174
   Quickbook Web site, 172-173
online media directories, 52-56
   Internet Public Library, 54-55
   Largest Newspaper Index on the
      Web, 55

NewsDirectory.com, 53-54, 56
Newspapers Online, 56
online reservations sites, 106-107
online travel agencies, 146-156
    booking engines, 149-150
    Carlson Wagonlit Travel Web
        site, 150-152
        booking trips, 153
        privacy statement,
            151-152
    determining legitimacy of,
        155-156
    privacy issues, 151-152
    questions to ask online agents,
        146
    searching, 147-149
        WebCrawler Web site,
            148
        with trade organizations,
            153-154
        Yahoo! Travel Agents
            listings, 147-148
    tour operators, 147
ownership information (Web sites),
    35-36

P

packing, 261-265
    carryon rules, 263-264
    clothing, 265
    Compleat Carry-On Traveler
        Web site, 262-263
    Sky Guide Web site, 265
    Swiss Army knives, 264
pampered (traveler types), 91-93
PassengerRights.com Web site, 166
passports, 242-244
PC Magazine Web site, 258
Pennsylvania Visitors Guide Web
    site, 77
Perry-Castaneda Library Map
    Collection Web site, 12
Personal Travelogues (HotBot), 114
pet people (traveler types), 96-97
phones (cell phones), 236

Phuket.com Web site, 105
planners (traveler types), 85-86
privacy, online travel agencies,
    151-152

Q-R

Quickbook Web site, 172-173

Rail Europe Web site, 200-202
RailServer Web site, 202
ratings, hotel ratings, 174
renaming bookmarks, 24-25
rental car companies, 206-213
    Auto Europe Web site, 212-213
    Avis Web site, 207-208
    comparing, 206-208
    domestic companies, 208-211
    foreign companies, 211-213
    Hertz Web site, 209-210
    insurance, 214-215
    National Car Rental Web site,
        210
    questions to ask, 206-207
rental car insurance, 214-215
rental cottages, 178
rental homes, 178-180
reservations Web sites, 106-107,
    149-150
    Travelocity Web site, 106, 149
restaurants, Fodor's Travel Online
    Restaurant Index, 41-42
Rick Steves' Europe Through the
    Back Door Web site, 47-48
river cruises, 224-225
Roadnews Web site, 233
Roadside America Web site, 126-127
Rome, 132
Round-the-World Travel Guide Web
    site, 89-90
route planners, 16-18
    European route planners, 18
    North American route planners,
        16-17
Russian Consulate of New York Web
    site, 245

S

safaris, 90-91
safety
    newspaper information, 58-61
    precautions against crime,
        270-272
    State Department Travel
        Warnings & Consular
        Information Sheets Web site,
        110-111, 164-165, 248
Sanyo Web site, 258
SBB (Swiss Federal Railways) Web
    site, 198
search engines, 10-12, 104-105
    HotBot Web site, 105
    Yahoo!, 10-11
searching
    online travel agents, 147-149
        WebCrawler Web site,
            148
        with trade organizations,
            153-154
        Yahoo! Travel Agents
            listings, 147-148
    tourist offices, 74
seasonal vacation activities, 119-128
    fall, 126-128
    spring break, 122-124
    summer, 124-126
    winter, 119-122
security, laptop computers, 231
Sharp Internet ViewCam, 257
Sharp Web site, 257
Shell Route Planner Web site, 18
Shinkansen Web site, 202
shoulder season, 136-137
Sierra Leone Web site, 60
Ski Guide Web site, 120-121
Ski Utah Web site, 120
SkiResorts.com Web site, 121
Sky Guide Web site, 265
Smartcoms Web site, 236
SNCM (La Societé Nationale
    Maritime Corse Mediterranée) Web
    site, 223-224
SpaFinders Web site, 92-93

spring break, 122-124
State Department Travel Warnings &
    Consular Information Sheets Web
    site, 110-111, 164-165, 248
State Department Web site,
    243-244, 247
suitcases, 261-265
    carryons
        Compleat Carry-On
            Traveler Web site,
            262-263
        rules, 263-264
        templates, 262
    clothing, packing, 265
    Sky Guide Web site, 265
summer cottages, 178
summer vacation activities, 124-126
Surf and Sun Beach Vacation Guide
    Web site, 105
Swiss Army knives, 264
Swiss Federal Railways (SBB) Web
    site, 198

T

Taking Your Pet Along Web site, 97
Tangier, 132
theft-prevention, laptop computers,
    231
time converters, 19-20
Time Zone Converter Web site, 19-20
timing vacations, 135-140
    high season, 135-136
    low season, 136-137
    major events, planning around,
        137-139
    off season, 136
    shoulder season, 136-137
    trip length, planning, 139-140
tour operators, 147
Tourism Offices Worldwide Directory
    Web site, 73
Tourist in Europe, The, 40
tourist offices, 72-76
    British Tourist Authority Web
        site, 74-76
    search terms, 74

Tourism Offices Worldwide
Directory Web site, 73
Travel & Leisure Web site, 73
Travel-On Web site, 73
train travel, 194-202
Amtrak Web site, 194-196
bullet trains, 202
Cyberspace World Railroad Web
site, 202
European train travel, 197-202
BritRail Web site,
198-199
Eurailpass, 200-201
Europass, 200-201
European Railway Server
Web site, 202
Eurostar Web site, 199
Rail Europe Web site,
200-202
Swiss Federal Railways
(SBB) Web site, 198
RailServe Web site, 202
Shinkansen Web site, 202
VIA Rail Web site, 196-197
Travel & Leisure Web site, 73, 258
online chats, 115
Travel & Leisure Family Web site,
100-101
travel agencies, 146-156
booking engines, 149-150
Carlson Wagonlit Travel Web
site, 150-152
booking trips, 153
privacy statement,
151-152
determining legitimacy of,
155-156
learning to be your own travel
agent, 162-165
government statistics,
163-165
travel industry news,
162-163
travel rights, 165-168
privacy issues, 151-152
questions to ask online agents,
146

searching, 147-149
WebCrawler Web site,
148
with trade organizations,
153-154
Yahoo! Travel Agents
listings, 147-148
tour operators, 147
Travel Agents listings (Yahoo!),
147-148
Travel Industry Association of
America Web site, 238
travel industry news, 162-163
travel rights, 165-168
Travel Warnings & Consular
Information Sheets Web site,
110-111, 164-165, 248
Travel Weekly Crossroads Web site,
162-163
travel-medicine specialists, 269
Travel-On Web site, 73
traveler types, 84-101
adventurers, 90-91
beginners, 86-88
business travelers, 93-94
disabled travelers, 94-96
family-vacation travelers,
100-101
fast-paced, 88-90
pampered, 91-93
pet people, 96-97
planners, 85-86
women traveling alone, 98-100
traveler's checks, 267
Travelocity Web site, 106, 149
Travelogues, 114
trip length, planning, 139-140
TripTik, 16

U

Ultimate Arizona Vacation Guide
Web site, 30-31
United Airlines Web site, 186-188
unofficial Web sites, comparing to
official Web sites, 30-33
USA CityLink Web site, 123

USTOA (United States Tour Operators Association), 155-156
  Web site, 154
Utah Ski & Snowboard Association, 120

V

VIA Rail Web site, 196-197
Victorinox Web site, 264
Visa Web site, 266
visas, 65, 245-247
  Electronic Travel Authority (ETA), 246
  Embassy of Australia Web site, 246
  Russian Consulate of New York Web site, 245
  State Department Web site, 247

W

weather information, 132-135
  Intellicast Web site, 134-135
  WorldClimate Web site, 133
Web browsers
  Internet Explorer bookmarks
    creating, 23-24
    renaming, 25
  Netscape Navigator bookmarks
    creating, 22-23
    renaming, 24
Web sites
  100hot, 87-88
  About.com, 103
  accuracy, testing, 34-35
  Action Cellular Rent a Phone, 236
  Agfa, 258
  Airline Complaints, 166-167
  Airline-Ticket Consolidators and Bucket Shops, 192
  Airport and Air Travel Guide, 186
  Airport Search Engine, 15, 184
  All Airlines of the World, 184
  American Airlines, 190, 264

American Automobile Association (AAA), 213
American Express, 149
American Society of Travel Agents (ASTA), 153-154, 162
American Veterinary Medical Association (AVMA), 97
Amtrak, 194-196
Arizona Guide, 32
Armchair World, 73
Arthur Frommer's Budget Travel Online, 44-45
Australian Tourist Commission, 248
Auto Europe, 212-213
Aviation Consumer Action Project, 166
Avis, 207-208
Bali Online, 14
Bed & Breakfast Channel, 178
Biztravel, 93-94
Black Mountain Travel, 86
Borneo Bulletin, 56-57
British Tourist Authority, 74-76
BritRail, 198-199
Bwana Zulia's Kenya Travel Guide, 116-117
Carlson Wagonlit Travel, 150-152
  booking trips, 153
  privacy statement, 151-152
Carnival Cruise Line, 221-222
Casio, 257
Centers for Disease Control's Travel Information, 268
CIA World Factbook, 111-113
Colony Hotel in South Beach, 177
commercial Web sites, 31
Compleat Carry-On Traveler, 262-263
Concord Times, 59-60
Consulate General of Italy, 65-67
Creative Leisure, 179
Cruise Line International Association (CLIA), 217-220

Cruise Mates, 218
Customs Service, 249
CW Lease Routeplanner, 18
Cybercruises, 223
Cyberspace World Railroad, 202
Daytona Beach ConVis Bureau's
 Spring Break site, 123
Drivernet, 235
Easy Tour Online Route
 Planner, 18
Electronic Embassy, 67-69
Embassy of Australia, 246
Embassy of Italy, 65-67
Embassy Web, 70-71
Embassy World, 71-72
European Railway Server, 202
Eurostar, 199
EventsWorldWide, 138
Fielding Travel Guides, 42-43
Fodor's Travel Online, 41-42
Free Trip, 16, 127
Freighter World Cruises, 226
Galveston tourism, 238
Global Access: A Network for
 Disabled Travelers, 95-96
GORP, 90
government Web sites, 64
Hanscom Federal Credit Union,
 266
Hasselblad, 258
Hertz, 209-210
HotBot, 105
 Travelogues, 114
Hotmail, 234-235
I Love New York, 78
Intellicast, 134-135
Interactive Currency Table, 18
International Society of Travel
 Medicine, 269
Internet Public Library, 54-55
Jet Set, 232-233
Journeywoman, 99-100
KD River Cruises of Europe,
 224-225
Ker & Downey, 90-91
Kodak, 257
Laptop Travel, 232

Largest Newspaper Index
 on the Web, 55
Lonely Planet Online, 45-47
MapBlast, 13
MapQuest, 13, 17, 238
Maps On Us, 17
MasterCard, 266-267
Mexico Online, 35
Microsoft Expedia Maps, 17
National Car Rental, 210
National Geographic Society
 Xpeditions, 13
National Park Service ParkNet,
 124-126
New South Polar Times, 54-55
NewsDirectory.com, 53-54, 56
Newspapers Online, 56
OANDA Currency Converter, 19
official sites vs. unofficial sites,
 30-33
Olympus, 258
ownership information, 35-36
PassengerRights.com, 166
PC Magazine, 258
Pennsylvania Visitors Guide, 77
Perry-Castaneda Library Map
 Collection, 12
Phuket.com, 105
Quickbook, 172-173
Rail Europe, 200-202
RailServe, 202
reservations Web sites, 149-150
Rick Steves' Europe Through the
 Back Door, 47-48
Roadnews, 233
Roadside America, 126-127
Round-the-World Travel Guide,
 89-90
Russian Consulate of New York,
 245
Sanyo, 258
Sharp, 257
Shell Route Planner, 18
Shinkansen, 202
Sierra Leone on the Web, 60
Ski Guide, 120-121
Ski Utah, 120

SkiResorts.com, 121
Sky Guide, 265
Smartcoms, 236
SpaFinders, 92-93
State Department, 243-244, 247
State Department Travel
  Warnings & Consular
  Information Sheets,
  110-111, 164-165, 248
Surf and Sun Beach Vacation
  Guide, 105
Swiss Federal Railways (SBB),
  198
Taking Your Pet Along, 97
Time Zone Converter, 19-20
Tourism Offices Worldwide
  Directory, 73
Travel & Leisure, 73, 258
  online chats, 115
Travel & Leisure Family,
  100-101
Travel Industry Association of
  America, 238
Travel Warnings & Consular
  Information Sheets, 110-111,
  164-165, 248
Travel Weekly Crossroads,
  162-163
Travel-On, 73
Travelocity, 106, 149
Ultimate Arizona Vacation
  Guide, 30-31
United Airlines, 186-188
United States Tour Operators
  Association (USTOA), 154
USA CityLink, 123
VIA Rail, 196-197
Victorinox, 264

Visa, 266
WebCrawler, 148
Wegner, 264
Westin, 175-176
World Time Locations, 20
World Wide Airport and City
  Code Database, 15
WorldClimate, 133
Xerox PARC Map Viewer, 14
Yahoo!, 10-11
  Real Estate section, 178
  route planner, 16
  Travel Agents listings,
  147-148
  Travelogues, 114
WebCrawler Web site, 148
weekend fares (airfares), 188-190
Wegner Web site, 264
Westin Web site, 175-176
Where the Boys Are, 123
winter vacation activities, 119-122
women traveling alone (traveler
  types), 98-100
World Time Locations Web site, 20
World Wide Airport and City Code
  Database Web site, 15
WorldClimate Web site, 133

X-Y-Z

Xerox PARC Map Viewer
  Web site, 14

Yahoo!, 10-11
  Real Estate section, 178
  route planner, 16
  Travel Agents listings, 147-148
  Travelogues, 114

Tell Us What You Think!

As the reader of this book, *you* are our most important critic and commentator. We value your opinion and want to know what we're doing right, what we could do better, what areas you'd like to see us publish in, and any other words of wisdom you're willing to pass our way.

You can email or write me directly to let me know what you did or didn't like about this book—as well as what we can do to make our books stronger.

Please note that I cannot help you with technical problems related to the topic of this book, and that due to the high volume of mail I receive, I might not be able to reply to every message.

When you write, please be sure to include this book's title and author as well as your name and phone number. I will carefully review your comments and share them with the author and editors who worked on the book.

Email: *internet_sams@mcp.com*

Mail: Mark Taber
Associate Publisher
Sams Publishing
201 West 103rd Street
Indianapolis, IN 46290 USA

SAMS Teach Yourself Today

e-Auctions

Bidding, Buying and Selling at eBay and other Online Auction Sites

Preston Gralla
ISBN: 0-672-31819-9
17.99 US/ 26.95 CAN

Other Sams Teach Yourself Today Titles

e-Personal Finance
Ken and Daria Dolan
ISBN: 0-672-31879-2
17.99 US/ 26.95 CAN
Available Feb. 2000

e-Music
Brandon Barber
ISBN: 0-672-31855-5
17.99 US/ 26.95 CAN
Available Jan. 2000

e-Real Estate
Jack Segner
ISBN: 0-672-31815-6
17.99 US/ 26.95 CAN
Available Dec. 1999

e-Job Hunting
Eric Schlesinger and Susan Musich
ISBN: 0-672-31817-2
17.99 US/ 26.95 CAN
Available Feb. 2000

e-Banking
Brian Nixon and Mary Dixon
ISBN: 0-672-31882-2
17.99 US/ 26.95 CAN
Available Feb. 2000

e-Trading
Tiernan Ray
ISBN: 0-672-31821-0
17.99 US/ 26.95 CAN
Available Feb. 2000

All prices are subject to change.

SAMS

www.samspublishing.com